Beyond Requirements

Beyond Requirements

Analysis with an Agile Mindset

Kent J. McDonald

Illustrations by Jeff Rains

✦ Addison-Wesley

New York • Boston • Indianapolis • San Francisco
Toronto • Montreal • London • Munich • Paris • Madrid
Capetown • Sydney • Tokyo • Singapore • Mexico City

For information about buying this title in bulk quantities, or for special sales opportunities (which may include electronic versions; custom cover designs; and content particular to your business, training goals, marketing focus, or branding interests), please contact our corporate sales department at corpsales@pearsoned.com or (800) 382-3419.

For government sales inquiries, please contact governmentsales@pearsoned.com.

For questions about sales outside the U.S., please contact international@pearsoned.com.

Visit us on the Web: informit.com/aw

Library of Congress Cataloging-in-Publication Data
McDonald, Kent J.
 Beyond requirements : analysis with an agile mindset / Kent J. McDonald ; illustrations by Jeff Rains.
     pages   cm
 Includes bibliographical references and index.
 ISBN 978-0-321-83455-3 (pbk. : alk. paper)—ISBN 0-321-83455-0
 1. Decision making. 2. Requirements engineering. 3. Business requirements analysis. I. Title.
 T57.95.M384 2016
 658.4'0354—dc23
                                                        2015022866

ISBN-13: 978-0-321-83455-3
ISBN-10: 0-321-83455-0
Text printed in the United States on recycled paper at RR Donnelley in Crawfordsville, Indiana.
First printing, September 2015

To all of those who asked, "Is the book done yet?"
Yes, yes it is.

Contents

Preface xv
Acknowledgments xxv
About the Author xxvii

Part I: Ideas 1

Chapter 1: Guiding Principles 3
    Introduction 3
    Deliver Value 4
    Collaborate 5
    Iterate 7
    Simplify 8
    Consider Context 9
    Decide Wisely 10
    Reflect and Adapt 11
    Conclusion 12
    If You Remember Nothing Else 12

Chapter 2: Helpful Concepts 15
    Introduction 15
    Needs and Solutions 15
    Outcome and Output 19
    Discovery and Delivery 20
    If You Remember Nothing Else 23

Chapter 3: Influence of Lean Startup 25
    Introduction 25
    Customer Development 25
    Build-Measure-Learn 29
    Metrics 31
        Good Metrics 32

Things to Consider with Metrics 34
Creating Your Metrics 36
If You Remember Nothing Else 38

Chapter 4: Decision Making 39
Introduction 39
A Structure for Decision Making 39
Determine the Decision Maker 39
Select a Decision Mechanism 41
Determine What Information Is Needed 42
Make a Timely Decision 43
Build Support with Peers/Stakeholders 45
Communicate the Decision 45
Enact the Decision 46
Real Options 46
Cognitive Biases 48
Elicitation 49
Analysis 51
Decision Making 52
If You Remember Nothing Else 53

Chapter 5: Deliver Value 55
Introduction 55
Feature Injection 55
Identify the Value 56
Inject the Features 59
Spot the Examples 61
Minimum Viable Product 63
Minimum Marketable Features 65
If You Remember Nothing Else 67

Chapter 6: Analysis with an Agile Mindset 69
Introduction 69
What Is the Need? 71
What Are Some Possible Solutions? 71
What Should We Do Next? 72
What Are the Details of This Part (i.e., Telling the Story)? 73
If You Remember Nothing Else 73

Part II: Case Studies 75

Chapter 7: Case Study: Conference Submission System 77

    Introduction 77

    The Need 77

    The Possible Solution(s) 78

    The Deliveries of Value 79

        Define-Build-Test 81

        The Incident of the Themes 84

        Agile2014 90

    Lessons Learned 92

Chapter 8: Case Study: Commission System 95

    Introduction 95

    The Need 96

    The Possible Solution(s) 96

    The Deliveries of Value 97

    Lessons Learned 98

Chapter 9: Case Study: Data Warehouse 101

    Introduction 101

    The Need 101

    The Possible Solution(s) 102

    The Deliveries of Value 103

    Lessons Learned 110

Chapter 10: Case Study: Student Information System 111

    Introduction 111

    The Need 111

    The Possible Solution(s) 114

    Lessons Learned 118

Part III: Techniques 121

Chapter 11: Understanding Stakeholders 123

    Introduction 123

        Stakeholder Analysis 123

        User Analysis 124

    Stakeholder Map 124

        What It Is 124

An Example 125
When to Use It 126
Why Use It 126
How to Use It 126
Caveats and Considerations 129
Additional Resources 129
Commitment Scale 129
What It Is 129
An Example 129
When to Use It 130
Why Use It 130
How to Use It 131
Caveats and Considerations 132
Additional Resource 132
User Modeling 133
What It Is 133
An Example 133
When to Use It 135
Why Use It 135
How to Use It 136
Caveats and Considerations 137
Additional Resources 137
Persona 138
What It Is 138
An Example 138
When to Use It 139
Why Use It 139
How to Use It 139
Caveats and Considerations 140
Additional Resources 140

Chapter 12: Understanding Context **141**
Introduction 141
Purpose-Based Alignment Model 142
What It Is 142
The Quadrants Explained 143
An Example 144
When to Use It 145
Why Use It 145

How to Use It 145

Caveats and Considerations 146

Additional Resource 147

Six Questions 147

What It Is 147

An Example 148

When to Use It 148

Why Use It 148

How to Use It 149

Caveats and Considerations 149

Additional Resource 150

Context Leadership Model 150

What It Is 150

An Example 154

When to Use It 154

Why Use It 155

How to Use It 155

Caveats and Considerations 156

Additional Resource 157

Chapter 13: Understanding the Need 159

Introduction 159

Decision Filters 160

What It Is 160

An Example 160

When to Use It 161

Why Use It 161

How to Use It 161

Caveats and Considerations 163

Additional Resources 163

Project Opportunity Assessment 163

What It Is 163

An Example 164

When to Use It 165

Why Use It 166

How to Use It 166

Caveats and Considerations 166

Additional Resource 167

Problem Statement 167
    What It Is 167
    An Example 167
    When to Use It 168
    Why Use It 168
    How to Use It 168
    Caveats and Considerations 169
    Additional Resource 169

Chapter 14: Understanding the Solution(s) 171
    Introduction 171
    Impact Mapping 173
        What It Is 173
        An Example 173
        When to Use It 174
        Why Use It 176
        How to Use It 176
        Caveats and Considerations 177
        Additional Resources 177
    Story Mapping 177
        What It Is 177
        An Example 178
        When to Use It 178
        Why Use It 178
        How to Use It 180
        Caveats and Considerations 182
        Additional Resources 182
    Collaborative Modeling 182
        What It Is 182
        An Example 183
        When to Use It 184
        Why Use It 186
        How to Use It 186
        Caveats and Considerations 188
        Additional Resources 188
    Acceptance Criteria 188
        What It Is 188
        An Example 189
        When to Use It 190

Why Use It 190

How to Use It 190

Caveats and Considerations 191

Additional Resources 192

Examples 192

What It Is 192

An Example 193

When to Use It 194

Why Use It 195

How to Use It 195

Caveats and Considerations 196

Additional Resources 196

Chapter 15: Organizing and Persisting Solution Information 199

Introduction 199

Discovery Board 200

What It Is 200

An Example 200

When to Use It 201

Why Use It 201

How to Use It 202

Caveats and Considerations 203

Additional Resources 204

Definition of Ready 204

What It Is 204

An Example 204

When to Use It 205

Why Use It 205

How to Use It 205

Caveats and Considerations 206

Additional Resources 206

Delivery Board 206

What It Is 206

An Example 207

When to Use It 208

Why Use It 208

How to Use It 209

Caveats and Considerations 210

Additional Resources 210

Definition of Done 211
    What It Is 211
    An Example 211
    When to Use It 211
    Why Use It 211
    How to Use It 212
    Caveats and Considerations 212
    Additional Resources 213
System Documentation 213
    What It Is 213
    An Example 214
    When to Use It 214
    Why Use It 214
    How to Use It 215
    Caveats and Considerations 215
    Additional Resources 217

Part IV: Resources **219**

Glossary 221

References 245

Index 249

Preface

What This Book Is About

I wrote *Beyond Requirements* to paint a picture of analysis in **IT** projects and how it can be applied with an agile mindset to make those projects more effective. For the purposes of this book I think of analysis as the activities involved with

- Understanding **stakeholders**
- Understanding **context**
- Understanding the **need**
- Understanding the **solution**(s)
- Organizing and persisting solution information

Performing these activities with an agile mindset, which I explain in Chapter 1, best positions teams to satisfy stakeholder needs. As a result, I assume that people are approaching work with an agile mindset (which is up to each individual to adopt) and that they are using agile techniques. Most of the techniques I describe can also be used in other environments, of course, but they're most effective when combined with agile approaches.

Who Is This Book For?

If you find yourself performing analysis on a project in order to make sure the project is delivering the right thing, this book is for you. You may identify yourself as a **business analyst** (or derivation of that title), product owner, product manager, project manager, tester, or developer.

I chose to target those performing analysis activities or possessing analysis skills rather than analysts as a role, or even analysts as a profession. While it is true that the people who are most endowed with the analysis skill set are those who generally fill an analyst role, I didn't want the advice in this book to get hung up on discussions such as, "The analyst does this, the developer does that, the tester does this other thing." I'd much rather focus on describing why and when techniques are most appropriate and leave it up to you and your team to determine who is the best person to do various activities. In many cases, multiple people on your team will end up doing analysis in order to take advantage of strong technical and business knowledge.

The business analyst role exists primarily because in the past several organizations used a prescriptive, phase-based approach to software development. In this approach, there was a time period in the project when the main work was eliciting and documenting **requirements**. Since it made sense to structure the software development organization according to how project work was done, all the people doing work in the analysis phase were lumped together and called business analysts. But gathering and documenting requirements didn't generate much respect for the people doing it. Members of the analysis community longingly eyed the success project managers had enjoyed by proclaiming project management a profession, and they chose to do the same.

A lot of good things have come from the "professionalization" of **business analysis**, including more consideration of, training on, and attention to analysis skills. However, the benefits are somewhat diluted by the effort required to justify a separate profession for people who elicit, document, and manage requirements, and the overspecialization that may result. That effort would be better spent figuring out how analysis can be used to make projects more successful.

That doesn't change the fact that you have a business analyst title and you have spent a considerable amount of your career honing your business analysis skills. Where does that leave you? Looking at analysis as an activity more than a role, title, or profession means that you can use your in-depth knowledge of analysis techniques to help your teams solve the right problems in the right way and help out with other activities on the project whenever possible.

To What Context Does This Book Apply?

This book focuses on the analysis that occurs on **IT projects**. An IT project is any project that results in solutions, often involving software, that support internal business processes, automate manual processes, or streamline current processes. Examples include building a system to support the session submission process for a conference, implementing a system to calculate and deliver commissions, reporting and data warehousing solutions, or implementing a solution to track student information at a nonprofit school.

I chose this focus for a few reasons. First, activities labeled as business analysis and the role of business analyst seem to be more prevalent in IT projects than in activities focused on **product** development. Second, most of the existing literature in the analysis space seems to assume a product development context, and the context of the IT departments of an organization strikes me as under-served. Third, and probably most important, it's where most of my experience lies, so focusing on that topic gives me the opportunity to write from actual experience.

As I describe how analysis with an agile mindset works on IT projects, I won't delve too much into how to do tried-and-true analysis techniques. There are already enough resources that do a fantastic job of explaining those techniques, and it dilutes the focus of this book. Instead, I'll focus on why those techniques are helpful and when they are best used. I do introduce a few techniques from other skill sets not commonly known in analysis circles, and in those cases I provide a more detailed description of how to perform that technique. In all cases, I provide my favorite references for more information about those techniques.

The word project has acquired a certain stigma in the agile community. Those who apply that stigma feel as though the use of the word project implies some of the downsides of the way that projects are managed in a waterfall setting.

The term project often suggests the following:

- The temporary nature of projects is applied to the teams that work on them. People are brought to the work instead of the work being brought to the team.

- It takes a while to get an effort going due to the extensive chartering and planning that come with trying to predict the future 6 to 12 months out.

- Even though projects are intended to be temporary (or maybe because of that), they are rarely stopped once they get started. Sponsors and teams get enamored with projects and become more reluctant to end a project the longer it goes on.

- The project funding approach may encourage grouping multiple small **changes** together in order to justify expenditure, increasing the time before the changes are delivered to waiting stakeholders.

While these problems certainly exist, merely using the word project does not ensure that they will happen. I reasoned that most people are familiar with the idea of the project, and it would be more useful to explain that these patterns are antipatterns and it's possible for projects to work differently than to use a new term for an existing concept and deal with all of the confusion that could cause. As Deanna, one of my editors, suggested, I should just "own it" when it comes to using the word project.

What Problem Is This Book Trying to Solve?

Analysis is often portrayed as eliciting and documenting requirements, frequently in terms that sound a lot like asking people what they want and writing it down. Deep philosophical discussions about analysis often center on the best way to capture requirements: "Should I use a use case, or should I use a **user story**?" Requirements are important, but they are a means to an end, not the end in and of themselves. As I described previously, analysis is about understanding your stakeholders and their needs, identifying the best solution for satisfying those needs in your particular context, and then building a shared understanding of that solution. Requirements play a part in that work, especially around describing the need, but they are certainly not the end product.

One fundamental problem this book is trying to solve is how to determine whether your IT project is doing the right thing and how analysis can help you do that. It's about changing the purpose of analysis from requirements gathering and capture to problem solving and building shared understanding. Along with that comes a substantial change in how your team views requirements and **designs**. They are no longer deliverables that get tossed over the wall to the people performing the next step in the process. Now both requirements and designs are tools that teams can use to build a shared understanding of the solution they seek to deliver in order to reach a desired **outcome**.

A second fundamental problem this book attempts to solve is to demonstrate how to do analysis in an agile setting. As many teams first adopt agile approaches, they struggle with finding the right balance between identifying a viable solution and describing that solution in too much detail too early. This book aims to show you how to perform analysis in an iterative fashion so that you can take advantage of the learning that occurs during development, testing, and deployment. While doing so, it also demonstrates that many analysis techniques are applicable in an agile setting with changes to when and to what extent you perform those techniques. I sought to solve this problem because many teams that adopt agile think analysis is no longer necessary, and as a result they end up creating solutions that don't solve the identified problem, or don't solve any problem at all.

How the Book Is Organized

This book is organized into three main parts to make it a bit easier to consume. The first part, "Ideas," covers the agile mindset and some key principles that underlie the agile mindset and effective analysis. The second part, "Case Studies," features four case studies that show how to practically apply the ideas in a variety of situations. The third part, "Techniques," takes a deeper view of some techniques that are very helpful for using analysis in an agile setting.

Part I: Ideas

The first section takes a look at some key ideas that I consider essential for effectively performing analysis in an agile setting. These include the concepts that describe an agile mindset, and some helpful concepts from outside traditional analysis thinking that supplement typical analysis techniques. Finally, I build on those ideas to place analysis techniques in context.

Chapter 1: Guiding Principles

As I help teams adopt agile and tighten up their analysis approach, I find that adopting the appropriate mindset is more important than mastering a specific set of techniques. With the proper mindset and a great deal of self-discipline a team can be successful with minimal process. Without the proper mindset, teams find that they must continuously add process to aid the **collaboration** that comes naturally to those who have the right mindset.

What is the proper mindset? There are a variety of perspectives on that. The original definition of the agile mindset is encapsulated by the "Manifesto for Agile Software Development" and the corresponding principles. Others have expanded on those original ideas to describe the agile mindset, and I have done the same, placing emphasis on aspects that encourage building the right thing. I describe my perspective on the agile mindset through seven guiding principles:

- Deliver **value**
- Collaborate
- Iterate
- Simplify
- Consider context
- Decide wisely
- Reflect and adapt

Chapter 2: Helpful Concepts

I use this chapter to introduce some ideas that form the conceptual basis for the following chapters. The ideas discussed include

- Needs and solutions
- Outcome and **output**
- **Discovery** and **delivery**

Chapter 3: Influence of Lean Startup

This chapter explores some concepts of Lean Startup and describes how these concepts can be applied effectively to the context of IT projects. Those concepts include

- **Customer** development
- **Build-Measure-Learn**
- **Metrics**

Chapter 4: Decision Making

This chapter discusses decision making in more detail, specifically a structure for decision making, the idea of **Real Options,** and the cognitive biases I find can get in the way of effective decision making.

Chapter 5: Deliver Value

In this chapter I discuss some key concepts surrounding value delivery, including **Feature Injection, minimum viable product,** and **minimum marketable feature.**

Chapter 6: Analysis with an Agile Mindset

While I'm not necessarily advocating a new "analysis process," I wanted to provide a general description of how analysis flows alongside the lifecycle of a project. This chapter positions the techniques from Chapters 11 through 15 in their usual location in the project lifecycle.

I don't spend a great deal of time talking about this flow specifically because it is not the same on every project, but going through the whole flow once helps put the techniques into the proper perspective and helps to explain why certain techniques make more sense in some contexts than in others.

Part II: Case Studies

In this part of the book, I share four stories intended to describe analysis in a real-world setting. These stories illustrate the ways a variety of IT projects used the ideas described in Chapters 1 through 6 and the techniques described in later chapters. While I cannot cover every possible situation, I hope this mix of case studies provides fairly broad coverage of the various environments in which you may find yourself. In addition, they should furnish ideas for using the same techniques in different situations and adjusting your approach based on your current context.

Chapter 7: Case Study: Conference Submission System

This is the story of developing and maintaining the submission system for the Agile2013 and Agile2014 conferences. This was a fairly straightforward project, but it provides the opportunity to position several analysis techniques in their proper context.

Chapter 8: Case Study: Commission System

This case describes what happened when a health insurance company undertook a project to replace multiple commission systems. The case explores some good techniques for projects involving off-the-shelf software and the tendency to gold plate.

Chapter 9: Case Study: Data Warehouse

This case tells the story of a project to incorporate a new source of data into an existing data warehouse. This story explores analysis in a business intelligence project, another environment that can benefit from an agile mindset.

Chapter 10: Case Study: Student Information System

This case explores analysis in a nonprofit setting and focuses on the decisions that need to be made when a project is initially being considered.

Part III: Techniques

In this section I describe a series of techniques that can be helpful in many different settings using my technique brief format. That format covers the following aspects of a technique:

- What it is
- An example
- When to use it
- Why use it
- How to use it
- Caveats and considerations
- Additional resources

Chapter 11: Understanding Stakeholders

This chapter describes some techniques that are helpful for understanding the people you work with. The first two techniques are useful for understanding the people whose needs you are trying to satisfy—better known as **stakeholder analysis**. The other two techniques in this chapter will help you better understand the people who are actually going to use the solution you deliver; let's call this **user analysis**. The techniques I cover include

- Stakeholder map
- Commitment scale
- User modeling
- Persona

Chapter 12: Understanding Context

Understanding context means familiarizing yourself with the nature of the business and sharing that information with the rest of the team. You want to put the project in the perspective of the overall organization and determine what the project is intended to do. If the project does not support something explicitly related to the organization's **strategy** or ongoing operations, don't do it.

This chapter introduces several techniques for understanding the organization as a whole and using that information to guide decisions about your projects. The techniques described in this chapter are often called **strategy analysis** (formerly enterprise analysis) in the analyst community.

- **The Purpose-Based Alignment Model**
- **Six questions**
- **The Context Leadership Model**

Chapter 13: Understanding the Need

A key and often overlooked aspect of IT projects is figuring out the real need that must be satisfied, determining if it is worth satisfying, and sharing that understanding with the entire team. If those activities were done more frequently, the story told about IT projects would undoubtedly be much brighter.

In this chapter, I introduce a set of techniques that I have found very helpful for performing those activities:

- **Decision filters**
- **Project opportunity assessment**
- **Problem statement**

Chapter 14: Understanding the Solution(s)

Once we understand the need we're trying to satisfy and we've determined that it's worth satisfying, we should investigate possible solutions. The plural form is intentional. Project teams often limit themselves by focusing on one possible solution too soon instead of leaving their options open. In many cases there are multiple options.

In this chapter I identify a variety of techniques for exploring multiple solutions and describing the solutions that seem best, all in a way that is meaningful for everyone working on the project:

- Impact mapping
- Story mapping
- Collaborative modeling
- Acceptance criteria
- Examples

Chapter 15: Organizing and Persisting Solution Information

This chapter describes techniques that help teams visualize progress and the aspect of the solution they are working on, as well as a way to persist key information about the solution for future reference. The techniques described in this chapter include

- Discovery board
- Definition of ready
- Delivery board
- Definition of done
- System documentation

Part IV: Resources

In this final part of the book, I provide a couple of resource sections that summarize key definitions and reference sources collected from the rest of the book.

Glossary

It's always a good practice to establish a common language for your projects. Since I am trying to be very specific about how I refer to certain concepts, and in the interest of eating my own dog food, I decided to establish a glossary for *Beyond Requirements*. This should help me be consistent in my use of certain words, or at least give you a chance to catch me if I am inconsistent. Words in the glossary appear in bold the first time they are mentioned in the text.

References

Throughout the book I reference several great sources of additional information about the topics I discuss. This section compiles all the references into a single list. Take some time to check out the references listed here; there's some great stuff.

In addition to the resources included in the book, beyondrequirements.com features additional thoughts on analysis with an agile mindset, new technique briefs, and updates to the material in the book.

Acknowledgments

This is not the first book I have written, but it is the first I took on by myself, or at least that's what I thought the case was when I started. It turns out that while I'll be listed as the only author, this book would not have been possible without the help of several people.

There are two people who played the biggest part in how the book looks and reads. Jeff Rains created all the hand-drawn graphics in the book. It was important that the graphics reinforce the idea of having a conversation at a whiteboard. Jeff's great work allowed me to get that message across while allowing you to be able to read the graphics. Deanna Burghart provided the first line of defense that prevented me from doing horrendous things to the English language. I have worked with Deanna for several years as she edited my pieces for ProjectConnections.com. I knew when I started working on this book a . . . um . . . couple of years ago that I wanted her editorial help. She, as always, did a great job helping me sound like me.

I have been fortunate in my professional life to work and interact with brilliant people who look at things in a slightly different way and who do not hesitate to share their perspective with me. Several of those people played a part in this book, but it's important that I thank three especially. It is truly an honor and a privilege to be able to fall back on these three to discuss ideas and ways to describe them. Gojko Adzic's extensive review notes were an immense help during the editing stage and helped me see things from a different and better perspective. Todd Little reviewed most of the book during the final editing stages and, as always, provided practical and insightful advice to help me crystallize my revisions. Chris Matts, long a primary source of cutting-edge, yet eminently practical thought in the space of analysis, generously discussed several ideas for this book and was a key source of many of the more important ones. My understanding of the nuances of analysis and IT project work is due largely to being fortunate enough to know these three practitioners.

I was fortunate to receive feedback from a wide range of professionals. Special thanks go to Robert Bogetti, Sarah Edrie, James Kovacs, Chris Sterling, and Heather Hassebroek for reading and commenting on the entire draft. Their comments were very helpful in shaping and refining my initial thoughts into something that I hope is a bit more coherent. Thanks also to Diane Zajac-Woodie, Deb McCormick, Brandon Carlson, Mary Gorman, Julie Urban,

Pollyanna Pixton, Matt Heusser, Tina Joseph, and Ellen Gottesdiener, who all gave feedback on aspects of the draft.

Finally, thanks to Chris Guzikowski, acquisitions editor at Addison-Wesley, who had the patience to stick with me through the drawn-out writing process, and Jeffrey Davidson, who didn't let an opportunity go by without nagging me about finishing the book. Jeffrey, I'm not sure if Chris put you up to that or not, but I suspect he's glad you did, regardless.

About the Author

Kent J. McDonald uncovers better ways of delivering value by doing it and helping others do it. His years of experience include work in business analysis, strategic planning, project management, and product development in a variety of industries, including financial services, health insurance, performance marketing, human services, nonprofit, and automotive. He is active in the business analysis and agile software development communities helping people share stories about what does and does not work.

Kent has a Bachelor of Science degree in industrial engineering from Iowa State University and an MBA from Kent State University.

Kent is also a coauthor of *Stand Back and Deliver: Accelerating Business Agility.*

Part I

Ideas

Chapter 1

Guiding Principles

Introduction

Perhaps the biggest influence agile approaches have had on me is the idea that teams' approaches should be based on values and principles rather than a set of practices. Practices tend to be very sensitive to context—the set of practices you use for a Web application are different from those used for a commission system, which are different from those used in a mainframe payroll system. Using the same practices in all three cases is a recipe for trouble. Values and principles meanwhile tend to be more widely applicable. The "Manifesto for Agile Software Development" and the "Principles behind the Agile Manifesto" are generally considered to be representative of agile values. This chapter discusses the philosophy central to my approach to knowledge work.

The following list of guiding principles, based on agile principles, describes desirable characteristics for any **initiative**:

- Deliver value
- Collaborate
- Iterate
- Simplify
- Consider context
- Decide wisely
- Reflect and adapt

Deliver Value

Value is very difficult to define. In many ways it's like beauty, quality, and obscenity: "I'll know it when I see it." What is worthwhile and important to one person may be of little importance to someone else. Like many other things, delivering value is very context specific. To me, assessing value is like trying to understand whether "it" is worthwhile, where "it" may be undertaking or continuing an initiative or delivering a specific feature.

Your team is delivering value when what you deliver (output) satisfies your stakeholders' needs (provides the desired outcome). Delivering value also suggests a different basis for making decisions and measuring success in **projects**. You still pay attention to the **triple constraints** of cost, time, and **scope**, but scope is defined based on whether you achieve the desired outcome, not based on the number of outputs your team delivered. You'll find that your team takes actions that seek to maximize outcome with the minimum outputs, while staying within identified cost and time constraints.

Changing the definition of scope from output to outcome can make quantifying whether you have delivered the agreed-upon scope more difficult. That's where **goals, objectives,** and **decision filters** (a technique I describe further in Chapter 13) can come in handy. Goals, objectives, and decision filters provide both a clear way to describe the outcome you seek and a way to determine when you have achieved that outcome. Defining the scope you intend to meet in those terms also provides your team with more flexibility in how you meet that scope and also can prevent your team from producing output that is not needed, thereby increasing the chances that you are able to live inside the project's cost and time constraints.

Projects can accumulate many potential features that seemed like good ideas at the time but end up being nonessential to the ultimate goal of the project. One of the easiest ways to deliver value is to cut out all outputs that do not directly contribute to achieving the desired outcome. Those outputs include **functionality** that while cool and desired by a vocal stakeholder does nothing to solve the problem the project set out to address. Limiting features to those with truly discernible value returns to the premise that we want to focus on those few features that users actually use—the features users perceive as valuable, based on their behavior.

As Gojko Adzic reminded me when reviewing early drafts of this book, it's a good idea to focus on things that drive toward the desired outcome, rather than getting distracted by functionality that users may use or requirements that stakeholders represent as valuable but do not have any relation to the desired outcome.

The conference submission system (described in Chapter 7) is an example where we focused on outcome over output. The primary goal for the project was to support the session submission process for the Agile2013 conference. We did establish a backlog of features that the system needed to contain (the outputs of the project), but the backlog was more a starting point for estimating and planning than a hard-and-fast definition of scope. Throughout the project we added features to the backlog based on things we discovered, and we also deferred several features because they were not absolutely essential to meeting the business goal within our firm time guideline.

One important caveat to remember is that outputs such as system documentation and paperwork to satisfy regulatory or security requirements may still contribute to the desired outcome if for no other reason than that the **organization** may not be allowed to deliver the solution, or the organization could incur penalties, if those outputs are not completed.

I discuss some additional ideas about delivering value in Chapter 5.

Collaborate

Collaboration has two aspects. One is the ability of the team members to work together as effectively as possible. This is probably the one aspect of all projects—really all group endeavors—that can always be improved. In practical terms, this means that barriers prohibiting effective communication are removed from the team environment, and there are team members who can effectively **facilitate** the group interactions.

The more subtle but equally important aspect of collaboration is that the team members who are actually doing the core work of the project are the ones doing the planning and status reporting. This is a shift from the traditional view of projects, where the project leader is responsible for those types of tasks. Team members are the people who are most familiar with the work and are best positioned to determine what really needs to be done. As a result, team members should volunteer to work on various items, as opposed to getting assignments from someone else.

This guiding principle should be used on every project, regardless of **methodology** and approach. Yet this is probably the one principle with which teams have the most difficulty. Some project managers have deeply ingrained command-and-control habits. Teams have a tendency to look to someone else to tell them what to do, even when they don't appreciate being handed assignments. Changing course on this often goes against human nature.

Collaboration, like everything else, is best done in moderation. Some collaboration is certainly necessary to make sure the team is aware of key information.

But when keeping everyone up to speed on everything slows down the team's ability to deliver value on a regular basis, it goes from collaboration to churning, and it may be a symptom of the team's inability to work well together.

Collaboration also does not necessarily mean **consensus**. There will be times when conflict is appropriate and healthy. Unfortunately, too much conflict can cause much more harm than good, especially if it's not channeled in the right direction.

I once worked with a team that, for whatever reason, was never able to work together appropriately. I can't put my finger on exactly why, but I think there were several factors.

Some members of the team came from a toxic environment. They had switched to a team that used agile approaches in order to get out of their previous situation. Unfortunately, I'm not sure they ever bought into the principles and values of agile. These team members used "We're being agile" as an excuse for various dysfunctional behaviors. For instance, their lack of focus was supposedly due to frequent interaction with their teammates.

The team had identified "leads" who tended to be more experienced in analysis, development, and testing skills, as well as knowledge of the agile approach. These leads unfortunately slipped into command-and-control behavior styles, at one point even telling team members they needed to stop talking to each other about a problem. One team member said he felt like he went from having one boss to having four.

The team was unable to discuss their concerns openly, and on the rare occasions they tried to do so, they wrapped the discussion up in so much process that nothing was accomplished.

The team was finally disbanded, partly due to lack of work, but mostly because it was dysfunctional. Interestingly enough, the team never failed to meet commitments. Some may say that they deserve a second chance because they were able to deliver.

Contrast that with another team I was on. This team was not working in an agile environment but decided to try an agile approach. As in the previous case, the developer did not fully buy in. Echoing the concerns on that other team, the reluctant developer initially said that he thought he had two or three bosses instead of one. We were able to work through the issues, talk through each other's concerns, and use those disagreements to identify opportunities to improve. We established some working agreements, and the command-and-control approach never surfaced on this team. This was primarily because we respected each other and were able to talk through issues without drenching them in process.

At its most basic, collaboration means that the people working on the project form a real **team**, not a **work group**. This allows them to be able to work through just about any difficulty without sulking or rushing off to find the nearest decision maker.

Collaboration also means, perhaps more importantly, that the team members commit to meeting a joint goal, and they are not afraid to step outside their area of specialization to help others on the team. Everyone on the team has a specialty, such as development, testing, or analysis, that they spend a considerable part of their time doing, but when the need arises, they are able to jump in and work on something else to help the team meet its overall goals. For a business analyst, this might look like facilitating whole team collaboration, using team member and stakeholder insights to aid in analysis, and helping out with testing and documentation when others on the team get stuck. This also means that analysts no longer hoard all of the analysis work for themselves, nor can they only do analysis. They are dedicated full time to a team as a team member, not in the more limiting role of the business analyst. Roles get blurred as a result of this type of collaboration, but the team is better positioned to deliver frequent increments from which they can receive meaningful feedback.

Iterate

One little-known synonym for *iterate* is *rehearse*. If you think about it, that is a characteristic of **iterations**. You may be building a software application feature by feature or building several preproduction models of vehicles to try out the assembly process and produce vehicles for the test track. Either way, you are rehearsing your approach and your design decisions. Iteration gives your team an opportunity to propose an approach and try it out without building so much that you waste a lot of work if you made a suboptimal decision.

The key to an iterative approach is getting some actionable feedback on the output of the iteration so that you know if you are on the right course toward the desired outcome. In order to get useful, actionable feedback, you need a portion of your working solution that your stakeholders can look at and react to. An ongoing series of iterations that result in actionable feedback leads to continuous learning.

Unlike operational work, IT projects and other types of knowledge work never use directly repeatable processes. When you are engaged in operational work, such as assembling a vehicle or processing a claim, many of the steps can be directly copied from one unit to the next. It becomes easy to identify improvements, because there is often very little time between cycles of a particular set of work tasks. Operational work is repetitive and fairly predictable. If you want to, you can repeatedly learn how to do it better.

Knowledge work, on the other hand, is a bit different. Projects are like snowflakes: no two are alike. You may get the opportunity to experience a couple of different projects, and chances are the lessons learned from one project aren't all applicable to a different project. A focus on continuous learning, with iterations being a key component of that, reminds your team that they need to stop every so often and figure out what they can revise. This also helps to identify meaningful milestones, with progress shown as actual working output rather than intermediate artifacts.

In the conference submission system, we used iteration to our benefit in a couple of different ways. First, the team would produce a regular flow of features that I would look at as product owner and provide feedback, either on the look and feel of the system or its functionality. The team used my feedback to influence later features they produced. We also released the submission system to the users in multiple **releases** and used the feedback from people who used the first release of the submission system to influence how features were designed moving forward, in addition to providing an input into our decision about which features we released next and which we deferred.

Simplify

One of the principles behind the Agile Manifesto is to "maximize the amount of work not done." This means you want to deliver the minimum output that will maximize outcome (as described in the "Deliver Value" section) and do it using only processes that are absolutely necessary. I talked about delivering the right things in the "Deliver Value" section. Here I want to discuss simplifying the way you deliver the right thing.

Simplify means your team should start with a **barely sufficient** approach. When your team starts a new project, you should first determine the activities that are absolutely essential for the success of the project and then do only those activities. Over the course of the project, after some reflection, you may realize that a few additional activities are needed to overcome challenges you experienced. This is fine as long as your team is also willing to let go of activities you no longer need. You want to start with a barely sufficient approach because teams tend to find it much more difficult to stop doing activities than to add new ones. By starting with a small set of activities, you're giving your team a fighting chance of maintaining a streamlined process.

Simplify means taking the most straightforward path to your destination and ruthlessly questioning why someone wants to take a different path.

Simplify means not letting the perfect be the enemy of the good. I'm mostly talking about the arcane semantics of modeling, use case format, business rule language, and the like. I've seen far too much time wasted on pedantic arguments about whether the model is 100% correct, when the model was needed only as an aid to a communication about the final product. There are cases when precision is warranted and necessary: for example, when putting together a **glossary** for use by the team and stakeholders and when recording business rules for future reference. But if the model or work is for intermediate communication purposes, don't sweat the details. You can always have a conversation to clarify.

Simplify means letting simple rules guide complex behavior. Don't count on prescriptive processes to dictate how your team works. Provide your team with some straightforward guidance, and let them take things from there. Some of the most elegant solutions are the simplest. Don't fall into the trap of developing a needlessly complex solution.

And finally, simplify means that if a model is not easily memorable, the chances of its being used are slim to none. That is why I prefer two-by-two matrices, such as the **Context Leadership Model** and **Purpose-Based Alignment Model** (both discussed in Chapter 12). The limited idea of two dimensions may be a dreadful oversimplification, but it increases the likelihood of the model being used for some good purpose. In addition, because these models are quite simple, there is a good likelihood that they contain several nuances, which makes them extremely powerful and applicable in several different situations.

When we started working on the conference submission system, we started with a very minimal process, which after a few tweaks we found worked well for us (due to our small size and familiarity with the **domain**). We found that sprint planning meetings, standups, and demos were too much process overhead for us because we had a shared understanding about the sequence of the user stories we wanted to work with for a given release, and we communicated via our repository when user stories were ready for me as the product owner to look at and provide feedback. As we progressed through the project, we added a couple of additional activities when they seemed warranted, but on the whole we were able to keep our overall approach very effective.

Consider Context

The term *best practice* is frequently used to describe techniques or processes that have been successful for one project or organization and are being copied by others. Unfortunately, what works great in one project may not work as well in other situations. Many environmental factors can play a role in how effective a practice is on a given project. Because of this, I usually prefer to use the term **appropriate practices** or *good practices* to emphasize the fact that there really are no best practices across all projects.

Teams need to consider context when choosing which processes, practices, and techniques they use so they can be sure they are doing the things that will make them successful and are not doing the things that don't need to be done. When it comes down to it, perhaps considering context is the only real best practice around.

A key point that may not be immediately obvious is that project teams need to determine what practices, processes, and techniques they are going to employ during a project and be willing to change those practices as they learn more throughout the life of the project. Project teams often work within an organizationally defined process they believe they must follow to the letter, many times to the detriment of the project. Usually if those project teams examine reality a little, they will find they have more latitude than they thought.

Decide Wisely

Success in many types of organizations—whether they are for-profit, not-for-profit, or governmental organizations—depends on well-informed, timely decisions. I've worked on successful projects in successful organizations, and one characteristic that always seemed to be present was clear decision making. Conversely, in those cases where I had the opportunity to learn from less-than-desirable situations, one of the factors that always seemed to be present was poor or nonexistent decision making.

Don't get me wrong; you won't hear me say, "It's all about decision making." Otherwise this would be my only guiding principle. But decision making plays a big part in IT projects. This revelation has crystallized for me during the past few years, and the thing that really helped pull it into focus was my work on *Stand Back and Deliver*. Chapter 5 of that book, "Decisions," focuses on the use of a **business value model** to help structure conversations in order to make informed decisions. At about the same time I was writing that chapter, the profound implications of Real Options as described by my friend Chris Matts were slapping me upside the head. The timing of decisions is as important as the decisions themselves.

An equally important aspect of decision making is who is actually making the decisions. You want the person making decisions to be as informed as possible and also to be in a position to make the decisions stick. The interesting thing in many organizations is that the people who are expected to make most of the decisions—senior leadership—are not the best informed to make many of those decisions. This is because the decisions require in-depth, detailed knowledge that the leaders do not have, either because they are just not capable of having that much information over the broad scope of their responsibilities or they are not provided the necessary information because of the filtering that occurs as information moves from individual contributors, to supervisors, to managers, to executives. One very effective way to resolve these issues is to spread decision making out into the organization. This helps to ensure that the people with the relevant information are the ones who make certain decisions. A prime example of this is teams deciding the best way to approach a project given that they have the proper understanding of the desired outcome for that project and the constraints in which they must work.

Another set of important concepts for decision making is the various **cognitive biases** that keep humans from being anywhere close to the rational beings that economists and others would like to believe they are. Daniel Kahneman, Dan Ariely, and others have done a lot of work on cognitive bias over the past several years. (See the cognitive bias resources in the References list at the end of the book.) These ideas can have a big impact on decisions made in IT projects, and I think it's worth exploring them a little further.

Decision making is not given the coverage it is due in business analysis circles, perhaps because people who fill the role of business analyst may not be the ultimate decision makers. That doesn't change the fact that they often facilitate decision making, which in many ways can be much more difficult. Understanding the challenges involved in making sure decisions are made, communicated, and enacted can be very helpful for the success of IT efforts, and those challenges are a recurring theme throughout this book.

I take a closer look at decision making in Chapter 4.

Reflect and Adapt

Your team should continuously learn from its experiences to improve your approach and the outcome of the project. Projects often last longer than a couple of months. During that time, business conditions, team member understanding of the purpose of the project, and the environment surrounding the project will all grow and change. Your team should seek to use that change to its advantage in order to make sure the project's outcome meets the needs of your stakeholders when the result is delivered, not just the perceived needs of the stakeholders when the project started.

Project teams have long done postmortems or lessons-learned sessions where team members gather together at the end of the project to talk about what happened—usually the negative aspects—in hopes that they can remember to do better next time. If that approach is considered a good practice, wouldn't it make sense to do the same thing during a project, when the team still has time to make changes and impact the outcome? This is the idea behind **retrospectives**, which provide teams with a mechanism to discuss what has transpired on the project to date—both things the team did well and opportunities for improvement—and decide what course corrections need to be made.

Retrospectives are a handy technique that is useful regardless of what approach you are using. As an example of where retrospectives can be very helpful, a few years ago I was involved in a very large project to revise the load decision process for a large financial institution. I was a part of the team tasked with eliciting business rules from a new combined credit policy. We found that in addition to referring to the policy itself, we also needed to engage with a set of **subject matter experts** (SMEs) from across the company. The most effective way we could make this happen was to gather the SMEs together on a weekly basis for business rule working sessions. At the end of each week we held a retrospective to discuss how the sessions were going and to identify improvements. Over the course of the several weeks when we held the sessions, we found that each session ran a bit more smoothly than the one before it, and we often found that items identified as needing improvement one week were described as going well just a couple of weeks later.

Conclusion

I did not come up with these guiding principles overnight. They came about during the course of many years of experience and trial and error. The event that initially caused me to think about creating a list was one of the founding meetings for what was then known as the Agile Project Leadership Network (APLN). As a way of introducing ourselves, Alistair Cockburn suggested we share our views of the world and, in effect, why we were there. At the time I struggled to articulate my perspective, but after returning home and thinking about it a bit, the first version of this list sprang to mind. I've revised it a couple of times since, but the ideas have stayed pretty consistent, and they tend to be the first principles I fall back on when trying to figure out how to address situations I have not encountered before. I encourage you to keep them in mind as you read the rest of this book.

If You Remember Nothing Else

- You are delivering value when you maximize outcome with minimal output.
- Your team should constantly look for ways to work together to deliver value.

- Shorten the feedback cycle to encourage continuous learning.
- Don't do anything you don't absolutely need to do to deliver value.
- It depends.
- Be intentional about your decision making.
- Learn from the past to improve your future.

Chapter 2

Helpful Concepts

Introduction

This chapter describes some concepts that underlie the approach and techniques I describe in the rest of the book. These concepts relate to ways of categorizing how we think about analysis:

- Needs and solutions
- Outcome and output
- Discovery and delivery

By introducing these concepts I hope to create a common language used in the rest of the book. The terms used in these concepts are also included in the glossary.

Needs and Solutions

In the Preface, I described analysis as the activities involved with

- Understanding stakeholders
- Understanding context
- Understanding the need
- Understanding the solution(s)
- Organizing and persisting solution information

It occurs to me that some key definitions are in order. For that purpose I'd like to refer to the Business Analysis Core Concept Model (**BACCM**) from the *Guide to the Business Analysis Body of Knowledge Version 3* (**BABOK v3**), which defines six core concepts as outlined in Table 2.1.

Table 2.1 *Core Concepts in the BACCM*

Core Concept	Description
Change	The act of transformation in response to a need.
	Change works to improve the performance of an **enterprise**.
Need	A problem or opportunity to be addressed.
	Needs can cause changes by motivating stakeholders to act. Changes can also cause needs by eroding or enhancing the value delivered by existing solutions.
Solution	A specific way of satisfying one or more needs in a context.
	A solution satisfies a need by resolving a problem faced by stakeholders or enabling stakeholders to take advantage of an opportunity.
Stakeholder	A group or individual with a relationship to the change, the need, or the solution.
	Stakeholders are often defined in terms of interest in, impact on, and influence over the change. Stakeholders are grouped based on their relationship to the needs, changes, and solutions.
Value	The worth, importance, or usefulness of something to a stakeholder within a context.
	Value can be seen as potential or realized returns, gains, and improvements. It is also possible to have a decrease in value in the form of losses, **risks**, and costs.
	Value can be tangible or intangible. Tangible value is directly measurable. Tangible value often has a significant monetary component. Intangible value is measured indirectly. Intangible value often has a significant motivational component, such as a company's reputation or employee morale.
	In some cases, value can be assessed in absolute terms, but in many cases it is assessed in relative terms: one solution option is more valuable than another from the perspective of a given set of stakeholders.
Context	The circumstances that influence, are influenced by, and provide understanding of the change.
	Changes occur within a context. The context is everything relevant to the change that is within the environment. Context may include attitudes, behaviors, beliefs, competitors, culture, demographics, goals, governments, infrastructure, languages, losses, processes, products, projects, sales, seasons, terminology, technology, weather, and any other element meeting the definition.

The **core concepts** that are most relevant here are need and solution as they describe the subject of analysis. It is important to understand the difference between the two concepts, because many IT projects suffer from not having determined the need before charging forward with a solution.

You probably already know that before starting an IT project you should understand why you are doing it—in other words, what problem you are trying to solve. If you understand the problem you are trying to solve, or the opportunity you're trying to exploit—the need—you have a better chance of picking the most effective solution and avoiding needless time and effort creating a solution that is not needed. Yet I suspect you can also name several IT projects you were on where your team skipped understanding the problem and dove into delivering the solution you were handed. I know I have been involved in my fair share of those projects.

Why do teams repeatedly skip understanding the need, even though they generally know it's good practice? Sometimes it can be pressure from sponsors who have fixated on a particular solution and are suffering from some of the cognitive biases described in Chapter 4. More likely, teams don't know how to describe needs in a way that helps them determine the appropriate solutions. Fortunately, such techniques exist, and they have been under our noses the whole time: goals and objectives.

The BABOK v3 provides the definitions of *business goal* and *business objective* (which for the purpose of this book I've shortened to *goal* and *objective*) as shown in Table 2.2. The nice thing about these definitions is that they provide a way to differentiate these two concepts that are easily confused.

To put it more concretely, a goal is what we want to accomplish (the need we want to satisfy); an objective is how we measure how successful we are in accomplishing a goal. In this book, I am very intentional about when and where I have used each term.

Since objectives are intended to be measurable, it's helpful to keep a set of characteristics in mind when you establish them with your team. They are commonly referred to as SMART and are described in Table 2.3. Note that there are different variations of what the acronym stands for, and I chose to use the formulation

Table 2.2 *Goals and Objectives*

Term	Definition	Health Insurance Example
Goal	A state or condition that an organization is seeking to establish and maintain, usually expressed qualitatively rather than quantitatively	Increase the ability to handle an expected increase in claims.
Objective	A measurable result to indicate that a goal has been achieved	Reduce paper claims from 1,000 per week to 500 per week by 12/31.

Table 2.3 *Characteristics of Good Objectives*

Attribute	Description
Specific	You know exactly what you're trying to achieve and you have clear expectations.
Measurable	You need to be able to tell when you are making progress toward your objective.
Agreed upon	Everyone involved in meeting the objective needs to agree on what the objective actually is, that it is worth meeting, and how you will know when you have met it. This concept reinforces the idea of shared understanding. It's no good having an objective that's attainable if the entire team of people trying to reach it don't understand it, or don't think it's the right objective.
Realistic	You don't want to frustrate your team by giving them an objective that is impossible to reach. You may have to stretch a little bit, but you're not doing yourself any favors by setting an objective that has absolutely no chance of being met given the constraints under which the team is working.
Time framed	You have to know when you expect to be done. Otherwise you can keep going on forever and end up never really accomplishing anything.

where *A* stands for "agreed upon" to reinforce the idea that when your team agrees on what the objectives are and what they mean, there is a better chance they will have a shared understanding of what you're trying to accomplish.

To help reinforce the characteristics of good objectives, Tom Gilb in *Competitive Engineering* suggests the set of attributes shown in Table 2.4, which you can identify for each objective.

Note in this example that the constraint is the same as the baseline. What this indicates is that if this were an objective for your project, and you were not

Table 2.4 *Attributes for Objectives*

Attribute	Description	Example
Name	Unique name for the objective	Reduce paper claims received per week.
Units	What to measure (Gilb refers to this as scale)	The number of paper claims received per week
Method	How to measure (Gilb refers to this as meter)	Count the number of claims received per calendar week with a submission type of paper.
Target	Success level you're aiming to achieve	500 claims/week
Constraint	Failure level you're aiming to avoid	1,000 claims/week
Baseline	Current performance level	1,000 claims/week

able to make any change to the number of paper claims you receive in a week, the project is considered a failure, but any improvement is at least a step in the right direction. In other cases, you may find the constraint set as an intermediate value between the baseline and the target, meaning the project would be a failure if you don't accomplish at least some improvement. An important aspect of value that comes out of setting these attributes is the discussion that occurs in order to decide what the target and constraint should be, as it allows the team to get a clearer understanding of what success looks like.

Understanding the need first and being able to describe it via goals and objectives gives you the opportunity to build a shared understanding with your team surrounding why you are considering starting (or continuing) a particular project. It also gives you a basis for asking the question "Is this need worth satisfying?" So in the paper claims example in Table 2.4, the team can ask:

- Is it worth it to increase our ability to handle paper claims right now?

- Why do we think there is going to be an increase in claims received?

- Are paper claims the biggest hurdle to our ability to handle claims?

- What are we forgoing by increasing our ability to handle paper claims?

Separating consideration of need from solution allows your team to identify multiple potential solutions and have options to pick from when it's time to determine the specific solution that you will deliver. Having those options increases the chance that your team will effectively deliver a solution that meets the needs of your stakeholders while keeping within constraints such as time and budget.

Separating consideration of need from solution also helps to clarify responsibilities between stakeholders and teams. Needs come from your stakeholders, specifically **sponsors**, while solutions come from your team. Reality is not that clear-cut. Your team certainly helps your stakeholders describe the need in a useful fashion, and your team certainly needs to collaborate closely with your stakeholders to identify potential solutions.

Finally, separating need from solution also ties in nicely with a change in mindset that comes along with a focus on delivering value—the move from being concerned about output to being concerned with outcome, which is discussed more in the next section.

Outcome and Output

When your team builds a shared understanding of the need your IT project intends to satisfy, you effectively understand the intended outcome of the project. Outcome is the change in the organization and changes in the behavior of stakeholders as a result of an IT project. You don't know what the outcome of your IT project is until you deliver something—the output—and observe how that output impacts the organization and your stakeholders. Output is anything that your team delivers as part of your IT project. This includes software, documentation, processes, and other things that tend to be measured in order to gauge how the project is going.

The problem is, the goal of IT projects, or any efforts for that matter, is not to produce output; it's to reach a specific outcome. In fact, as mentioned in the section on "Deliver Value" in Chapter 1, a successful IT project seeks to maximize outcome with minimal output. Why do you want to do that? Well, you want to maximize outcome because that represents the change you want to see in your organization and your stakeholders' behavior (or as Jeff Patton says, in his book *User Story Mapping*, the change you want to see in the world). At the same time you want to minimize output, because that means less work to produce the output, and less work to maintain the output, freeing you up to deliver other outcomes. It ties into the agile principle "Simplicity—the art of maximizing the amount of work not done—is essential."

As mentioned in the section on "Deliver Value" in Chapter 1, you want to change the way you define and measure progress and ultimate success. You no longer want to measure progress based on how much output you've produced (i.e., features delivered, velocity, and the like). Rather you want to measure how you are doing on reaching the desired outcome. This can be more difficult because outcome is not always as easily measured. Goals and objectives certainly help, as do **leading indicators**, discussed in the "Metrics" section in Chapter 3.

To look at it another way, satisfying the needs of your stakeholders is the outcome you seek, and the solution you deliver to satisfy those needs is the output you use to reach your desired outcome.

Discovery and Delivery

The third way of categorizing analysis is along the lines of when we do it. It is often helpful to compartmentalize activities. This is probably one of the reasons that people latched onto the various phases described in plan-based approaches (analysis, design, development, testing). There are certainly some advantages to splitting up the activities that go into knowledge work. No single person is really good at every aspect of knowledge work, so organizing the activities into groups can certainly help break things down into manageable chunks and apply focus to the various aspects.

But what is the best way to organize those chunks? When people reference the Winston Royce paper that is cited as the source of waterfall planning (www.serena.com/docs/agile/papers/Managing-The-Development-of-Large-Software-Systems.pdf), they usually zero in on the diagram showing several different phases that occur when building a large system. But on the first page, there is an interesting and often overlooked picture of two boxes, "Analysis" and "Coding," along with the following comment:

> There are two essential steps common to all computer program developments, regardless of size or complexity. There is first an analysis step, followed second by a coding step as depicted in Figure 1. This sort of very simple implementation concept is in fact all that is required if the effort is sufficiently small and if the final product is to be operated by those who built it—as is typically done with computer programs for internal use. It is also the kind of development effort for which most customers are happy to pay, since both steps involve genuinely creative work which directly contributes to the usefulness of the final product.

Royce goes on to say that this approach is woefully inadequate for larger software development projects and reveals a bit of his philosophy about how to treat software development teams:

> An implementation plan to manufacture larger software systems, and keyed only to these steps, however, is doomed to failure. Many additional development steps are required, none contribute as directly to the final product as analysis and coding, and all drive up the development costs. Customer personnel typically would rather not pay for them, and development personnel would rather not implement them. The prime function of management is to sell these concepts to both groups and then enforce compliance on the part of development personnel.

While I don't agree with everything in that passage, I find it interesting that Royce focuses on analysis and coding as the two activities customers value. I had been searching for some straightforward way to describe the key activities in IT efforts which, based on my own experience, tend to break down into "figuring out the right things to build" and "building the things right."

Ellen Gottesdiener and Mary Gorman identify the right words to put around those ideas in their 2012 book *Discover to Deliver*. There it is: discovery and delivery. It has alliteration and everything. They further cement the concept by wrapping the two words in an infinity symbol to represent how both activities interact and influence each other. Royce would be proud that someone finally listened.

Here's how Gottesdiener and Gorman define *discovery* and *delivery*. I'll assume these definitions going forward in this book.

> Discovery: work that explores, evaluates, and confirms product options for potential delivery
>
> Delivery: work that transforms one or more allocated candidate solutions into a releasable portion or version of the product

The most helpful aspect of this concept is having a label to associate with different types of activities. Traditionally teams have tracked what was going on from a delivery perspective but have frequently not visualized discovery activities. Tracking their efforts to figure out the right thing to build can be just as helpful as tracking how they are building the solution, so I often use separate discovery and delivery boards. I'll talk more about those in Chapter 15.

All aspects of knowledge work involve some aspect of discovery. We're still "discovering" things about the need and solution when we're in the process of building it, testing it, and deploying it. It's useful to differentiate the two activities to reinforce the focus of each activity. Discovery increases your understanding of the need and solution to set up delivery. Delivery is primarily about building, testing, and deploying output, but those activities help your team build further understanding of the need and solution, which in turn influences your discovery. Sure, discovery still happens in delivery, but the majority of work done there is building stuff to help increase understanding.

So where is design, and why is it not called out as a separate activity? Some design occurs in discovery, and some design occurs in delivery. Design occurs in discovery through the use of **design thinking** techniques to gain a better understanding of users, and through describing the solution using models, examples, and acceptance criteria (as described in Chapter 14). BABOK v3 distinguishes between requirements and design as shown in Table 2.5, then goes on to say: "The distinction between requirements and designs is not always clear. The same techniques are used to elicit, model, and analyze both. A requirement leads to a design, which in turn may drive the discovery and analysis of more requirements. The shift in focus is often subtle."

Table 2.5 *Requirements and Design*

	Definition	Example
Requirement	A requirement is a usable representation of a need. Requirements focus on understanding what kind of value could be delivered if a requirement is fulfilled. The nature of the representation may be a document (or set of documents) but can vary widely depending on the circumstances.	View the number of paper claims received in a week per provider.
Design	A design is a usable representation of a solution. Design focuses on understanding how value might be realized by a solution if it is built. The nature of the representation may be a document (or set of documents) and can vary widely depending on the circumstances.	A report mockup

Design occurs during delivery as your team figures out how to technically satisfy the user stories given your chosen technology and architectural constraints. That activity is interwoven with development and testing as your team will have some initial discussions about design but then revise that understanding as they learn through experience.

As a result, calling design out as a separate activity doesn't add any value to the process and leads to pointless arguments about whether a particular item is in discovery, design, or delivery, whereas having an explicit split between discovery (getting ready for an iteration) and delivery (delivering it) is a much clearer delineation.

If You Remember Nothing Else

- Build a shared understanding of the need you are trying to satisfy before trying to deliver a solution.
- Your team delivers output in order to achieve some outcome. It's the outcome that's more important.
- You discover the right thing to build to put you in the best position to deliver the thing right.

Chapter 3

Influence of Lean Startup

Introduction

In 2011, Eric Ries wrote a book called *The Lean Startup*. In the book he explains a process influenced by the scientific method that a **startup** (defined as an organization dedicated to creating something new under conditions of extreme uncertainty) uses to build new companies and launch new products. On the surface, the startup context does not seem appropriate for IT projects. In reality, with a few small adjustments, ideas from Lean Startup can be very helpful for IT projects. In this chapter I want to discuss three of these ideas that are particularly useful in effective analysis of IT projects:

- **Customer development**
- Build-Measure-Learn
- Metrics

You can read more about another idea from Lean Startup, the minimum viable product (MVP), in Chapter 5 where I discuss it in the context of other concepts surrounding delivering value.

Customer Development

Abby Fichtner (www.slideshare.net/HackerChick/lean-startup-how-development-looks-different-when-youre-changing-the-world-agile-2011) describes the two parts of Lean Startup as customer development—originally described by Steve Blank in his book *The Four Steps to the Epiphany*—and agile development. She positions the two aspects in this way:

> Customer Development is helpful when we don't know the problem.
>
> Agile Development is helpful when we don't know the solution.

"Don't know the problem." That's something you most likely face quite often in IT projects, usually in the guise of having a solution thrust upon you without identifying the core problem you're meant to solve. You usually aren't trying to satisfy market needs (directly at least) with an IT project, but customer development might still provide some insight into how you can approach IT projects in a way that clarifies the need you are meant to satisfy.

In *The Entrepreneur's Guide to Customer Development* (I suggest reading this before trying to tackle *The Four Steps*) Brant Cooper and Patrick Vlaskovits define customer development as "a four-step framework to discover and validate that you have identified the market for your product, built the right product features that solve customers' needs, tested the correct methods for acquiring and converting customers, and deployed the right resources to scale the business" (p. 9).

Table 3.1 shows the four steps as summarized by Cooper and Vlaskovits, along with their relevance for IT projects.

Customer discovery provides a helpful framework for validating assumptions. This framework helps you determine whether you understand the need you are trying to satisfy and are satisfying the right need. Cooper and Vlaskovits suggest the eight steps in Table 3.2 in a startup setting.

Table 3.1 *Steps of Customer Development in Relation to IT Projects*

Customer Development Step	Definition	Applicability to IT Projects
Customer discovery	A product solves a problem for an identifiable group of users.	Understanding the stakeholders and their needs
Customer validation	The market is scalable and large enough that a viable business might be built.	Understanding whether any of the proposed solutions are worthwhile
Company creation	The business is scalable through a repeatable sales and marketing roadmap.	Is the solution scalable enough to satisfy all of the relevant stakeholder needs?
Company building	Company departments and operational processes are created to support scale.	What additional support needs to be in place as the use of the solution grows?

Table 3.2 *Customer Discovery Steps*

Customer Discovery Step	Description
1. Document **customer-problem-solution hypothesis**	Make sure you know who your customers are, what needs they have, and what solution you think is best to satisfy those needs. Make this information explicit so that you know what hypothesis you are trying to test.
2. Brainstorm business model hypothesis	Record all of the assumptions that you want to validate. Note any assumptions you have about the current environment and the changes you want to make.
3. Find prospects to talk to	Identify customers who you believe have the need that you are trying to satisfy so you can figure out whether your solution will satisfy that need. The prospects you identify help you validate your assumptions and test your hypothesis about the solution.
4. Reach out to prospects	Contact the potential stakeholders you identified in step 3 and ask if they would be willing to provide feedback.
5. Engage prospects	Engage with prospects willing to provide feedback to discover whether your proposed solution will solve their particular problem. These conversations allow you to validate your assumptions to some extent and to test your hypothesis.
6. Phase Gate I: Compile | Measure | Test	Determine if the information you have acquired from your interactions with potential customers has verified your assumption and your hypothesis passes the first test, or if you have to iterate back to step 1 and start with a revised or completely new hypothesis (**pivot**). This step provides a checkpoint: Do we have a viable solution based on what we know right now, or do we need to revisit it?
7. **Problem-solution fit/MVP** testing	Begin developing your product and frequently testing it with your users, not necessarily from a usability standpoint but from a suitability standpoint: Does the product solve the customers' problems? Frequent interactions with customers provide you with feedback on things you are actually building. You can also determine whether changes in the environment or new insights prompted by seeing iterations of your solution change your customers' understanding of and perspective on the need. Often, seeing a little bit of functionality sparks insights or thoughts that result in a different approach to satisfying the need.
8. Phase Gate II: Compile | Measure | Test	Deploy something to your customers that generates some sort of value for them. This step provides you with another opportunity to determine whether to continue with the solution you have suggested, revise course, or stop trying to satisfy the need. You'll want to make that decision based on data from several sources.

Table 3.3 is a summary of the customer discovery process, as applied to IT projects.

This customer discovery process influenced my approach to analysis with an agile mindset as I describe it in Chapter 6.

The most important thing to remember about validating assumptions is the admonition to **"get out of the building."** (For IT projects, this may be better phrased as "Get out of your cubicle.") In other words, talk to your stakeholders to validate your assumptions, or better yet, observe them in the environment in which they work to truly understand their needs.

Table 3.3 *Customer Discovery Applied to IT Projects*

Step	Description
1. Identify the need.	When starting an IT project, you may not always immediately know the actual need you are trying to satisfy. In some cases you are handed a solution, at which point you need to work backward to figure out the need you are really trying to satisfy.
2. Hypothesize potential solutions.	Once you have an understanding of the true need, hypothesize a potential solution. If you were initially handed a solution to deliver, you can include that as a candidate, but you may find that the need you're satisfying requires a completely different solution.
3. Identify assumptions.	Identify assumptions that are central to your hypothesized solution, including assumptions about • Business environment • Project dependencies • Minimum requirements for a solution • Change management required A helpful way to identify assumptions is to ask, "What must be true for this solution to be effective?"
4. Validate assumptions.	Talk to stakeholders and gather data to validate your assumptions and test your solution. There are many different ways you can go about validating assumptions. I describe a few inspired by the Lean Startup community later in this chapter.
5. Start delivering.	Once you feel you have validated a sufficient number of assumptions, start delivering a minimal, yet viable, solution and get frequent feedback from your stakeholders on whether the solution meets their needs.
6. Constantly reevaluate your solution.	Constantly reevaluate your solution to make sure it is still worthwhile based on new information that comes to light. Regularly ask whether you should **commit to, transform, or kill** the solution.

Several techniques have sprung from the Lean Startup community that provide helpful ways to go about validating assumptions (and improve **elicitation** in general). I describe a couple of those techniques in what follows.

Cooper and Vlaskovits describe a technique suggested by Steve Blank for conducting these discussions. It involves creating a piece of paper or slide with three columns:

- The problem
- Stakeholder current solution (work-around)
- Your solution

As you talk with your stakeholders, start with only the problem column visible. Once the stakeholders are confident that you understand their problem, reveal the current solution column and discuss that. Finally, uncover the column with your solution. Facilitating the discussion this way can often reveal a great deal of information about the stakeholders' perspective on their needs.

Another technique, or rather a collection of good practices for stakeholder interviews, is what Rob Fitzpatrick calls "**The Mom Test**":

1. Talk about their (stakeholders') lives instead of your idea.
2. Ask about specifics in the past instead of generics or opinions about the future.
3. Talk less and listen more.

Fitzpatrick describes The Mom Test and many other good practices for interviewing customers and stakeholders in his book *The Mom Test*.

Both of these techniques are intended to help you talk with your stakeholders and reduce the impact of cognitive biases (Chapter 4) on those discussions. Even if you use these techniques, you can't always rely completely on what your stakeholders say. Therefore, it can be very helpful to gather other information about those problems to see what your stakeholders actually do. That investigation should also be a part of validating assumptions and testing your hypothesis. This is where a working knowledge of cognitive biases is helpful, so you will know when the stakeholder feedback you're hearing is real and when it is . . . bunk.

Build-Measure-Learn

The **Build-Measure-Learn loop** (Figure 3.1) is a concept coined by Eric Ries in *The Lean Startup* to capture the feedback loop startups use to convert ideas into products.

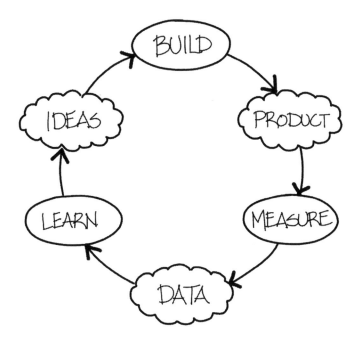

Figure 3.1 *Build-Measure-Learn loop*

The Build-Measure-Learn loop is an application of the **Plan-Do-Study-Act** (PDSA) cycle, originally created by Walter Shewhart and advocated by W. Edwards Deming. The PDSA cycle has been used by organizations for several decades to enable continuous improvement efforts. The main thing that the Build-Measure-Learn loop adds to the PDSA is an emphasis on getting through the cycle as quickly as possible in order to validate assumptions and test hypotheses about solutions, reinforcing the tie between the activities of a startup and experiments.

As mentioned in the section about customer development, it's important to validate assumptions early on in your project so that you can determine if you have identified the right solution to the right problem. Asking your stakeholders for feedback is helpful, but due to the influence of cognitive biases, they can sometimes give you misleading information. That's where the Build-Measure-Learn loop comes in. It provides a way to validate assumptions in conjunction with talking to your stakeholders. It also encapsulates the overall approach to building and getting feedback, which is a key aspect of the guiding principle to reflect and adapt.

Quick cycles through the Build-Measure-Learn loop also help your team reduce the uncertainty that often comes along with IT projects. Rapid trips through the Build-Measure-Learn loop to validate assumptions reduce the uncertainty bit by bit. You want to start by tackling the biggest or riskiest

Table 3.4 *The Build-Measure-Learn Loop Explained*

Step in the Loop	Description
Idea	Your stakeholders have a need. You understand that need and you think you've identified a solution that may satisfy that need. In other words, a desired outcome is based on a bunch of assumptions that you should validate in some way. You need to identify some form of metric based on your overall goal that you can use later on as a measuring stick to tell whether you are successful.
Build	You pick a specific solution (or piece of the solution) to deliver. This is an output. Impact mapping (Chapter 14) can help you pick the right output. Your goal in delivering this output is not necessarily the be-all and end-all; it is to understand the impact this output has on satisfying the need (reaching the desired outcome).
Product	The output of the project
Measure	You've delivered this output in isolation so you can see its impact on the outcome free from any other influences (as much as possible at least).
Data	Observe the impact on the metric you identified.
Learn	Examine the data and decide whether the change you delivered made the impact you wanted. If it did, great! You may be done. If not, you have to try something else. And you start the whole cycle all over again by looking at your remaining options and picking the next one.

assumptions first. Eric Ries calls those the "leap-of-faith assumptions," but it may be easier to think of them as the assumptions that, if proved wrong, can really hose the chances of the project being successful.

Table 3.4 gives a closer look at each step in the Build-Measure-Learn loop.

In some IT projects you know what needs to be accomplished, and there is a clearly defined set of things to be done. This is often the case when the project was created to implement part of an organizational strategy. In those cases, the Build-Measure-Learn loop gets bigger, and there may be other ideas that are more helpful in the short run—specifically whether everything originally included in the scope of the project is necessary.

Metrics

Because measurement is such an important aspect of the Build-Measure-Learn loop, it's helpful to have a good understanding of how you can use measurements effectively. If your team measures anything, it probably reflects the output the team is producing using such metrics as committed versus actual story points, or the cumulative story points delivered. When used properly, those metrics can identify trends that may indicate that some assumptions about your team's capacity may not be valid. In order to gauge the success of your project, your team should also look at metrics that indicate whether you are achieving the desired outcome. These types of metrics are not as prevalent because they are more difficult to measure. Douglas Hubbard points out in his book *How to Measure Anything* that people tend to factor in the cost of collecting a metric but not the value of the metric when deciding which metrics to use. As a result, measures of output are common whereas measures of outcome are rare.

Good Metrics

So what does a good metric look like? Alistair Croll and Benjamin Yoskovitz in their book *Lean Analytics* suggest some characteristics of good metrics that apply equally to IT projects and startups. These are listed in Table 3.5.

Table 3.5 *Characteristics of Good Metrics*

Characteristic	Description
Comparative	If you can compare a metric between two time periods, groups of users, or competitors, it's easier for you to identify trends and the direction of those trends.
	For example, it's more meaningful to know that you received 650 paper claims last week and 500 paper claims this week than just to know how many paper claims you received this week.
Understandable	You want people to be able to remember, discuss, and interpret your metrics so that they are more likely to change their behavior. If people can't remember it and discuss it, it's much harder to turn a change in the data into a change in the culture.
	For example, if your team is working on a project to increase **inventory turns**, it's helpful to know that inventory turn is calculated as cost of goods sold/average inventory, so your team has an idea of what factors can bring the desired outcome.
Is a ratio or rate	Ratios make good metrics because they • Are easier to act on • Inherently compare different factors • Are good for comparing factors that have some tension between them
	For example, in the conference submission system (Chapter 7) looking at reviews per session is more informative about the general trend of session reviews than a mere count of reviews.

Table 3.5 *Characteristics of Good Metrics (Continued)*

Characteristic	Description
Changes behavior	This is the most important characteristic of a metric. The main reason you track metrics is to change behavior. If the metric does not do that, it's a waste of time to track it. This is a key point to remember when identifying metrics to track outcomes. For example, a health insurance company is concerned about being able to handle an anticipated increase in claims. They do not want to hire additional staff, and they have identified that entering claims received on paper takes a considerable amount of processing time. The company therefore establishes a metric of paper claims received per week as a way of measuring how their actions change the behavior of providers to start submitting their claims electronically.

Table 3.6 *Examples of Good Metrics*

Goal	Objective	Metric
Improve stock-buying practices and reduce inventory.	Increase inventory turns from 5/year to 10/year by the fourth quarter.	Inventory turnover
Improve the ability to handle an anticipated increase in claims volume.	Reduce paper claims received per week from 1,000/week to 500/week by the fourth quarter.	Paper claims received/week
Increase the feedback that submitters receive on their sessions.	90% of sessions should have one review within one week of submission and three reviews within two weeks of submission.	Reviews/session

Keeping those characteristics in mind, Table 3.6 gives some examples of good metrics that focus on outcome rather than output. I have shown how these metrics are derived from goals and objectives.

Let's take a closer look at the last metric in Table 3.6, which is for the conference submission system described in Chapter 7. The objective implies a change in behavior of the reviewers to provide more feedback to submitters and is an important reference for assessing what type of functionality the team should develop in order to drive behavior change in the reviewers. Among the functionality implied by that metric:

- The ability to post a session (assuming that it's not there)
- The ability to post reviews

- Notification when new session proposals are posted to a given track
- Knowledge of when the session proposals were submitted
- Knowledge of how many reviews were submitted to a session proposal

In this case the metric speaks to the outcome the team wanted to achieve and therefore provides information that can be useful for deciding what output to deliver.

Things to Consider with Metrics

Croll and Yoskovitz also describe five things to consider when you're identifying metrics for your IT projects. These considerations will play a big part in how effectively your metrics provide usable information when you are trying to make decisions.

Qualitative versus Quantitative

Qualitative data is unstructured, anecdotal, and hard to quantify and aggregate, but it can provide some useful insight. Qualitative data often answers the question "Why?" and deals substantially with emotions. When you are initially trying to understand your stakeholders and their needs, you deal in qualitative data.

Quantitative data is the numbers and statistics that we track and measure. They provide hard numbers that are easy to understand but do not always provide much insight. Quantitative data is good for answering the questions "What?" and "How much?"

Vanity versus Actionable

Vanity metrics make you feel good but don't really help you make decisions or take any actions. Vanity metrics usually do not have all the characteristics of good metrics listed in Table 3.6. An example of a vanity metric is total reviews.

Actionable metrics change your behavior by helping you pick a course of action. These types of metrics usually meet all the characteristics of a good metric. An example of an actionable metric is reviews per session.

In order to determine if you have an actionable or vanity metric, ask yourself, "What will I do differently based on this information?" If you are unable to think of any different behaviors, you are working with a vanity metric.

Exploratory versus Reporting

Exploratory metrics are speculative and help you discover new insights to ensure that you are solving the right problem. They result when you don't know what questions you should ask. An example of an exploratory metric is Arthur and his team in the commissions system case study in Chapter 8 looking for what aspects of commissions, if any, impact the behavior of salespeople.

Reporting metrics help you track day-to-day operations and identify when an established process is starting to stray from normal operation. Reporting metrics are helpful when you know what questions to ask but don't know the answers. An example of a reporting metric is velocity. Your team can use velocity to determine potential issues with your process.

Leading versus Lagging

Leading metrics (sometimes called leading indicators) help you try to predict the future. These types of metrics usually don't represent the ultimate outcome you are trying to reach but provide some indicators of how likely you are to reach that desired outcome.

Lagging metrics tell you what happened in the past. A lagging metric gives you an indication that there's a problem—but by the time you're able to collect the data and identify the problem, it's too late. This is the type of metric you would use if you were doing benefit realization. You deploy your solution, wait for it to have an effect on the organization, and then, after a preset time frame, you measure a select metric and determine the result, getting an indication of how successful the project was. The downside of this approach is that the project is already over, so if you find out it didn't generate the desired outcome, well, at least you know not to do it again.

Leading metrics are inherently better because they provide information that you can act on, and they offer a shorter feedback cycle.

Correlated versus Causal

Two metrics are correlated when they change together. Correlations between metrics may be interesting and can sometimes help you predict what is going to happen, especially if the change in one metric precedes the change in the correlated metric. This is a good situation.

If a change in one metric drives a change in another, they are causal. A causal relationship between metrics is much more helpful because it indicates what changes you can make to achieve a specific outcome.

Identifying a correlation can help you identify causation, but it's important to remember that many factors usually are involved to cause something. All the same, finding even a partial causal relationship between metrics can put your team on the path toward identifying a successful outcome.

When you are creating metrics for use with objectives, it's important that you use a metric that is at least correlated with your outcome, if not an outright cause. Without that kind of relationship you may end up identifying an outcome that is impossible for a project to deliver based on the objectives you are tracking to. For example, if the commission system replacement project were to establish an objective of increasing sales, that may not be a realistic goal if all the project is focusing on is improving the process of calculating and paying commissions. While commissions do have an influence on sales, improving the efficiency of the commissions process probably will not drive sales. However, it may negatively impact sales if the process slows down production of commission checks.

Creating Your Metrics

Good metrics are a powerful way to describe what you want to accomplish with an IT project and know how close you are to getting there, driving needed behavior change along the way. Bad metrics can change behaviors as well, but rarely in the way that you want. When you seek to create metrics for your project, keep the characteristics of good metrics in mind, and remember that different types of metrics are appropriate for different situations. Table 3.7 shows the types of metrics described previously that are best suited for different situations.

Eric Ries provides some suggestions on working with metrics (www .fourhourworkweek.com/blog/2009/05/19/vanity-metrics-vs-actionable-metrics/) that can help you make sure you are using them effectively.

Focus on a Very Few Key Metrics

More metrics are not necessarily better. There are most likely a small number of things that you can measure that tell you if your IT project is successful and will identify when your project is straying from the intended outcome. Keep the

Table 3.7 *Metrics for Different Situations*

	Project Objective	Discovery	Process Health
Qualitative/ quantitative	Quantitative	Qualitative	Quantitative
Vanity/ actionable	Actionable	Actionable	Actionable
Exploratory/ reporting	Reporting	Exploratory	Reporting
Leading/ lagging	Leading	Lagging	Leading or lagging
Correlated/ causal	Causal	Correlated or causal	Correlated or causal
Example	Paper claims/week	Impact on sales of different commission structures	Velocity (story points/ sprint)

number of objectives associated to a project small, say, one to three. The more objectives you have, the more likely they are to conflict and the more likely your efforts are to become scattered and unfocused. It's better to have a small number of metrics that provide a clear direction of what the project is supposed to accomplish than to have several potentially conflicting objectives that distract your team and make it difficult to decide the best course of action.

Croll and Yoskovitz suggest that startups should use **One Metric That Matters (OMTM)**, which is the idea that at any given time there is a single metric that the startup should focus on above everything else. That metric is usually determined by what stage of growth the startup is in, and the OMTM will change through the lifetime of a startup. The reasoning behind the OMTM is that by paying close attention to one key thing at a time, a startup can have clear focus on, as Croll and Yoskovitz say, "the right thing, at the right time, with the right mindset."

You can apply the idea of OMTM to IT projects as well. Identifying a single objective will allow your team to focus on the output that is needed to meet that objective and remove (or at least defer) everything that does not lead to meeting that objective. You can then move on to the next objective and meet that one. If you look at your project and say, "These objectives all have to be here," you could be facing one of the following scenarios:

1. Either some of the things you think are objectives are constraints, or they really describe outputs instead of identifying when you have reached a specific outcome.

2. You are trying to tackle too much in your IT project. This is a problem with the project paradigm. IT projects become dumping grounds for a bunch of different changes that an organization would like to make to a process or a system. The changes by themselves don't warrant an initiative to address, but if a bunch of them are grouped together, the sponsor feels as if the project is justified.

Controlling the scope of your project by limiting the number of objectives you tackle can help your team meet those objectives sooner and with potentially fewer outputs—a win-win all the way around.

Focus on the Macro

Those very few metrics should be things that the organization cares about and should be immediately identifiable as the way that you measure value for your project. This is why it's best to start with the goal you are trying to reach and use the objective(s) related to that goal to measure the success of the effort.

Keep the Micro Around for Reference

Even though you are focusing on the macro, it's helpful to have the detail that led to that macro information in your back pocket so you can do further research when you need to. That data is even better when it's tied to people. If you are looking at things related to how people use the result of your effort, you may find the best way to determine why something happened is to talk to the people who tried to use the system.

Keeping these ideas in mind will help you to stay focused on the important aspects of what you are trying to accomplish without getting distracted by the bright, shiny, and utterly useless vanity metric jumping up and down in the corner trying to get your attention.

If You Remember Nothing Else

- Validate assumptions early and often.
- Shorten your feedback cycle.
- Use metrics to help you determine whether you are on the path to delivering your desired outcome.

Chapter 4

Decision Making

Introduction

This chapter discusses decision making in more detail, specifically a structure for decision making, the idea of Real Options, and cognitive biases that can get in the way of effective decision making.

A Structure for Decision Making

Decision making is a fairly vague concept, so here's some structure to help explain what deciding wisely looks like:

- Determine the decision maker.
- Select a decision mechanism.
- Determine what information is needed.
- Make a timely decision.
- Build support with peers/stakeholders.
- Communicate the decision.
- Enact the decision.

Determine the Decision Maker

While this may seem like a no-brainer, it is difficult to make a decision if you don't know who is supposed to make it. People think differently. When people make decisions, some may rely heavily on how they feel about the options, whereas some may prefer to gather extensive data and rely solely on pure, unadulterated logic.

Knowing who is going to make a decision impacts the mechanism used to make the decision. Conventional wisdom suggests that a single decision maker is the most efficient model. This is similar to the situation where multiple people own a task and the odds increase that it will not get done because each owner assumes one of the other owners is taking care of it. I saw this firsthand a few years ago while working on a large, enterprise-wide **program** that was attempting to combine the operations of three previously autonomous business units. One of the primary indicators of the project's inherent dysfunction was its fairly substantial **organization chart**. Aside from the executive who reported to the CEO of the company, every key position on the organization chart contained a committee rather than a single individual. The project structure was built to allow everyone to claim plausible deniability. There was no clear decision-making accountability, and as a result, no clear decisions were made.

A key aspect of this program was a new credit policy that was intended to be a synthesized policy to be used by the new combined organization. However, the policy turned out to be a portion of each business unit's credit policy included together in a single document with no real effort to meld them into a cohesive whole. When the team came across situations where portions of the credit policy conflicted with other portions because they came from different business units, progress on the program would come to a grinding halt. Endless emails and discussions happened as the team tried to determine who was the appropriate person to make a decision on a credit policy matter.

Having a single decision maker is very helpful, but it may not always be realistic, especially if a project impacts several different stakeholders and there is no clear owner who has the ability to make key project decisions. This is often the case in IT projects such as a claims data warehouse project at a health insurance company. Because claims information is so central to many aspects of a health insurance company, it's difficult to find one person, or even one department, who has the final say on many critical decisions. In these situations, instead of a **decider**, you actually need a **decision leader**. The decision leader is responsible for making sure the right people make the decision with as much information as possible.

The product owner role is often looked to as a key decision maker in agile approaches and can be either the decider or the decision leader. When the person filling the product owner role on an IT project also has responsibility for the outcome of the project, he or she is usually the decider. This is the case in which Arthur, the commissions manager working on a commission system, found himself in the case study described in Chapter 8. On the other hand, when a product owner is identified from within IT to run a claims data warehouse project like the one I mentioned previously, that person is acting as a decision leader. This is the situation in which business analysts often find themselves when playing the product owner role on IT projects.

Select a Decision Mechanism

Ellen Gottesdiener wrote a great article about different decision mechanisms (www.ebgconsulting.com/Pubs/Articles/DecideHowToDecide-Gottesdiener.pdf)—actually it was more about how to decide how to decide. Here are my supplementary thoughts on when each of these items may be appropriate and how it works.

Arbitrary

This could also be described as the coin flip mechanism; it is the "just pick one" approach. **Arbitrary** decision making is rarely the best approach, but it can be used to some effect when the outcome of the decision makes no real difference. This may be closely related to the **decider decides without discussion** decision mechanism (discussed later), especially when the decider falls into the magazine product selection pattern—when a decision maker happens to read an article about a new product and decides to buy it soon afterward, without clearly understanding why that product should be used.

Decider Decides with Discussion

The **decider decides with discussion** approach is one you'll see product owners use effectively. This approach works when the decider (i.e., product owner) talks with key stakeholders to get their perspectives and understand the possible options, and then makes the decision based on a synthesis of the information gathered.

Consensus

Consensus decision making is slow but very collaborative. Some organizations pride themselves on being collaborative decision makers, but this can often lead to a dysfunction that results in no decisions being made.

Delegation

Delegation means that the primary decision maker identifies someone else to make some or all of the key decisions related to a project. The decision maker may identify specific decisions that the delegate can make, or he or she may allow the delegate to make all of the decisions. This approach is effective only if the person delegating the decision making fully supports the decisions made by the delegate. Later reversing the delegate's decisions undercuts any authority or responsibility (or confidence) the delegate may have had. Delegation may be the most appropriate decision mechanism in cases where a proxy product owner is used on a project, as long as the ultimate decision maker provides the delegate with useful decision filters and fully supports the delegate's decisions.

Decider Decides without Discussion

This is the dictatorship. It also can quickly lead to a very dysfunctional situation. The decision maker may make some good decisions initially without taking advice from others, but eventually the lack of input can lead to uninformed, and potentially disastrous, decisions.

Negotiation

In a **negotiation**, each party gives up something in an attempt to find a solution that everyone can live with but that no one finds ideal. The more that politics are prevalent in the organization, the more likely it is that this approach is used.

Majority Vote

Majority vote is a decision mechanism that involves counting the number of votes for two or more options. The option with the most votes wins. This approach has definite winners and losers and can lead to an adversarial environment or strengthen one that already exists. This is a sufficient approach for decisions that don't require complete support, because you generally won't get it. For most organizations, however, this is probably not the best mechanism to use.

Spontaneous Agreement

This decision mechanism is great when it happens, but **spontaneous agreement** is quite infrequent and potentially also a sign that there is too much **groupthink** going on.

Determine What Information Is Needed

By determining when you actually need to make a decision, you often create an opportunity to gather additional information about the options. Then, when the time comes, you can make the most informed decision possible. Figure out what you don't know and fill in as many knowledge gaps as you can. You may not be able to fill in all of the gaps, but you can at least fill them in partially and make intentional assumptions to get the rest of the way there.

At the SDC2011 conference in New Zealand, Nigel Dalton told a story about an approach he used to collect information to support a decision. He was working on one of the largest initiatives his company had ever faced. He was concerned about pulling the **business case** together, so he decided to take a different approach. He commandeered a conference room and painted the walls with whiteboard paint. Then he had his team write all the business case information on the walls. He then invited the stakeholders to go through the room and add their thoughts about the business case: "This is garbage." "We would never think about doing that." "That's a great idea."

The team and the stakeholders shared stories, benefits, and costs for three weeks.

When the time came for the stakeholders to make the actual decision on whether to fund the initiative, the discussion was fairly quick, and the initiative was funded.

How did Nigel manage to get the business case approved? He gave the stakeholders the data they needed to make an informed decision and gave them enough time to consider it, discuss it, question it, and resolve it in their heads. He knew when the decision was going to be made and used the intervening time to make the relevant information available to the stakeholders. In addition, he gave the stakeholders the time they needed to figure out their thoughts about the decision.

This is a pattern worth considering for use with your stakeholders the next time you have a fairly controversial decision that several people are involved in making.

When gathering information, get what you can, but don't spend an inordinate amount of time trying to come up with data that may not be available. Avoid the temptation to try to know everything before making a decision. Chances are you will not be able to obtain every piece of information you would like, so figure out what the key pieces of information are, expend the appropriate amount of effort to find that information, and then make assumptions to fill in the gaps. Just note your assumptions, so you can check their validity down the road.

Make a Timely Decision

Know when you need to decide. How do you know? Most decisions involve selecting from a set of options, each of which is available to you for only a certain amount of time. You have until right before the first option disappears to make your decision, gathering information in the meantime. Even then you may not need to make a final decision; you really have to decide only if you want to go with the expiring option, or if you would rather use a different option. This idea comes from the concept of Real Options, described later in this chapter.

The timing of decisions is all about information. People who decide too quickly lose the chance to make their decision with critical information because they did not take the time to gather it. People who decide too late have a smaller list of options to choose from—often because they have dithered too long trying to find every shred of information and their analysis paralysis cost them potentially elegant options.

There is a fine balancing point between gathering enough information and spending too much time trying to gather information that is not there, or is not helpful. You aren't going to know how much information is really available until you start seeking it, so the best thing to do is to determine when you absolutely have to make a decision, and use the intervening time to gather information.

One project I worked on was to implement a nurse line **service** for a health insurance company. The service required specially trained individuals to staff the phones, in this case, nurses. That activity was not a core competency of the health insurer, so we chose to work with a small company that focused on staffing nurse call centers. The vendor was very good at what they did, but they were small, and the health insurer's business was considerably larger than any the vendor had before, thus stressing their technical capabilities.

In order for the health insurer to analyze data from the nurse line service, the vendor had to provide information regarding the caller's membership in various employer groups based on the insurer's somewhat complex grouping scheme, requiring additional development work by the vendor.

Some insurer team members were concerned that the vendor would not be able to complete the necessary work in time. So while we would be able to operate the service, the data we received would not meet all of our analytical needs. We had a decision to make: we could trust the vendor to deliver the necessary functionality by the due date and be in a sad state if that did not happen, or we could add additional work internally to produce the necessary analytical data. We were still three months out from the targeted implementation point, but there was a burning desire to make a decision NOW!

As it turned out, we exercised a third option. We proceeded as if the vendor would deliver on their commitments and at the same time followed some design approaches that allowed us to react quickly if the vendor was not able to deliver. We deferred the decision in order to gather more information, in this case whether the team members' concerns were justified.

The vendor was very capable of delivering on their commitments, and we found that by deferring our commitment to a particular design approach, we saved time and money. The concerns about the vendor's ability to deliver were unfounded, but we were comfortable in our ability to mitigate that risk had it come to fruition.

Build Support with Peers/Stakeholders

Your method of decision making will impact how much time you will need to spend building support with your peers and other stakeholders once you make the decision. If you decided by consensus, you already have the support of everyone involved in making the decision. The only rub here is if you failed to include some key people in the decision.

If you are the sole decision maker, you have a bit more work on your hands. Deciding with the input of others will help you build support, especially if you listened to and considered input from the key people whose support you need. Nigel's conversation room actually served two purposes: it helped him gather information, and it also helped build support by including all the stakeholders in the information gathering.

If you make decisions in a dictatorial manner, you may have a harder time building support and may never fully win the support of everyone involved. Then again, you may feel that based on your position in the hierarchy you don't need to gather support. That may be true on the surface; however, failure to build support from your peers or stakeholders could lead to actions that subvert the decision. This is especially the case in passive-aggressive or highly politicized environments.

The way in which you communicate the decision may be a key aspect of how you build support, especially for those stakeholders who wouldn't normally expect to be involved in making the decision.

Communicate the Decision

The last two steps in making decisions might seem to fall into the "no kidding" camp, but I think they are important to mention. The first one is to make sure you actually communicate the decision. In other words, you've made the decision; now make sure those whom you expected to be involved in enacting the decision, and those impacted by it, know about it. I have lost count of the number of times I've been involved in a project and learned too late about a decision that directly impacted my work or those working around me. Having been on the opposite side of that fence and been the person who surprised a few folks, I also realize that most of the time (but not always) the surprise comes from forgetting to tell everyone. Don't do that.

There are also times when people have made a decision and are afraid to communicate it, often because they fear the reaction. That reluctance is to be expected, and it may be helpful to examine those thoughts briefly. If someone is going to be upset with the decision regardless of what it is, the question becomes, in effect, "Are we upsetting the right people, and will it drive the behavior we're looking for?" If you shouldn't expect people to be upset but you're still worried about it, that may be a sign that you made the wrong decision. You may want to reevaluate it quickly from that perspective.

Enact the Decision

This step also seems like a no-brainer. Yet again, I've had the experience far too many times of a decision being made and no one ever taking steps to make it a reality. The idea was there, but it lacked execution. The reasons for this are fairly similar to the reasons that decisions are not communicated: we either forget, or we're afraid to put them into action.

When making a decision, it's best to think about how it will be enacted at the same time. The execution of a decision can play a huge part in whether it produces the results envisioned by the person or people making the decision.

Real Options

People abhor uncertainty. When given a choice of whether to be wrong or to be uncertain, many people would rather run the risk of being wrong than continue in a state of uncertainty. Unfortunately, that tendency leads to uninformed decisions, without any good reason other than people were uncomfortable not knowing.

Chris Matts, Olav Maassen, and Chris Geary introduce the idea of Real Options in the graphic business novel *Commitment*. The idea can be summed up like this:

- Options have value.
- Options expire.
- Never commit early, unless you know why.

There are two subtle yet key points that make the idea of Real Options especially useful in everyday life. First, it's important not to confuse options with commitments. Options are things you have the right but not the obligation to do. Commitments are things you have to do. Many things that people think are commitments—such as tickets for airplanes, concerts, or sporting events—are actually options. When you purchase an airplane ticket, you are buying the option to get on the flight, but you don't have to. Sure, you will be out the price of the ticket, but you are not obligated to take the flight. The airline, on the other hand, has made a commitment to get you to your destination (although those of you who travel frequently may feel like that does not always happen). Understanding this key difference between options and commitments helps you keep a clearer head about many decisions, because you will no longer feel trapped into having to make a particular decision.

Second, the idea of Real Options can help you decide when you really need to make your decisions. When you are facing a decision, take a few minutes to figure out your options, and then identify when those options will no longer be available—when they expire. You can then use the time up to when the first option expires to gather more information that will help you make a decision. Even then you may not need to make a final decision. You really have to decide only if that option is the one you want to go with or if you would rather use a different option.

Let's look at an example from the Mercury space program. In February 1962, John Glenn was attempting to become the first American to orbit the Earth. The flight was planned for three orbits. At the end of the first orbit, Mission Control was just about to patch President John F. Kennedy through to Glenn when they received a "Segment 51" warning and Glenn began having altitude control problems. Mission Control told the president that they were a little busy at the moment and would have to call him back. The team then turned to figuring out what the error meant.

Segment 51 indicated deployment of the landing bag—a rubber bag inflated after reentry to keep the capsule afloat in the ocean. The landing bag was situated behind the heat shield that protected the Mercury capsule from the intense heat of reentry. If the landing bag had truly deployed, that also meant that the heat shield had been pried loose from the capsule, which was not a good thing for John Glenn. Based on the data they had, the Mercury capsule could burn up during reentry.

Mission Control immediately began reviewing options. Theoretically, instead of jettisoning the retropack used to slow the capsule for reentry, they could leave it in place to save the heat shield. But leaving the retropack in place to burn up might also damage the heat shield. And some team members thought the Segment 51 alert could be a false alarm caused by an electrical failure, which could mean that leaving the retropack in place was an unnecessary risk to Glenn and the capsule.

With two orbits left, Mission Control began a series of simultaneous activities. Some controllers tried to determine whether the indicator was an electrical issue or if the heat shield had actually dislodged. Others tried to figure out what would happen if the retropack stayed attached to the capsule, and still others figured out how the reentry procedures needed to change if they decided to leave the retropack on. Chris Kraft, the flight director for the mission, stalled deciding whether to leave the retropack on until the last possible moment so he could have as much information as possible.

Walter Williams, the operations director and Kraft's boss, finally made the decision to leave the retropack on, but only when the retropack rockets had fired, the team was sure the rockets were not at risk to explode during reentry, and there was still enough time to alter the reentry procedure to accommodate the change. Of course, Glenn returned safely.

Later analysis confirmed that the Segment 51 reading was invalid.

Kraft knew that his options started running out when *Friendship 7* was over Hawaii during its last orbit. He therefore postponed any decision until that point so the Mission Control staff could gather information and try to determine what was really going on.

You can use the idea of Real Options in your everyday life, including your software projects. When you are faced with a decision, find out what your options are, find out when they will no longer be options, and use the intervening time to uncover more information so that you can make an informed decision. Waiting to decide and putting the time to good use will improve your chances of making the right decision and help you to be a little more comfortable with uncertainty.

Cognitive Biases

For the longest time, economists have built many of their theories on the assumption that consumers exhibit strictly rational behavior. Research over the past 50 years by psychologists and behavioral economists such as Daniel Kahneman, Amos Tversky, and Dan Ariely has systematically disproved that assumption. In the process, Kahneman, Tversky, Ariely, and many others have identified many cognitive biases—patterns of deviation in judgment that occur in particular situations.

In a quick count conducted via Google search I identified over 100 known cognitive biases, and more seem to appear every day.

Acknowledging and identifying cognitive biases are important when working on IT projects. These biases impact the interactions between stakeholders and delivery teams and the decisions that delivery teams and sponsors make about projects, products, and initiatives.

I could write an entirely separate book on cognitive biases. In fact, many people already have. If you are at all interested in the topic, I recommend *Thinking, Fast and Slow* by Daniel Kahneman, which is the seminal work on the topic and is heavily referenced by all the others. Dan Ariely's *Predictably Irrational* is a good second choice. Instead, I want to focus on a few types of cognitive biases that are especially important when dealing with stakeholders and making decisions on initiatives. I've grouped them based on their impact on different types of analysis activities.

Elicitation

Cognitive biases that impact elicitation activities can be split into those experienced by the stakeholder and those experienced by the analyst.

Biases Affecting Stakeholders

Biases experienced by stakeholders include **response bias**—the tendency of stakeholders to answer a question based on what they think the analyst wants to hear, not what they really think. Response bias can be compounded if the analyst poses leading questions, making it clear what answer he or she seeks.

There are a variety of reasons that stakeholders provide the answer they think an analyst is looking for. Perhaps they genuinely want to help the analyst and be cooperative. Perhaps they just want the analyst to leave them alone. Whatever the reason, response bias can take on catastrophic proportions when it's compounded by groupthink.

Groupthink occurs when a group of stakeholders all convey the same information whether or not that's what they truly believe. One type of groupthink is the **herd instinct,** where stakeholders adopt the opinions of the majority to feel safer and avoid conflict. Herd instinct can be especially apparent when talking to a group of stakeholders at the same time. Another form of groupthink is the **bandwagon effect,** where different stakeholders profess to believe things because many other stakeholders believe the same thing, even if they don't share those beliefs.

A final cognitive bias that impacts stakeholders is **the curse of knowledge.** Knowledge of a topic can diminish a stakeholder's ability to think about it from a less informed and more neutral perspective (i.e., that of the analyst). The curse of knowledge can lead a stakeholder to leave out key pieces of information that "everyone knows."

A good way to diminish the impact of cognitive biases influencing stakeholders is to supplement what stakeholders say by observing what they actually do. You can do this by identifying ways to analyze existing data on stakeholder behavior, or figure out ways to collect data about their behavior in certain circumstances. Sometimes this may be a matter of delivering a particular feature that will provide insight into how your stakeholders interact with the solution and that is targeted toward validating or invalidating assumptions you've made when planning your solution.

Biases Affecting Analysts

The curse of knowledge can also impact the analyst, especially if the analyst is a subject matter expert in the area he or she is analyzing. In this case, domain knowledge prevents the analyst from taking a new, fresh perspective on the need and possible solution. This can also lead to a **confirmation bias**, which is the tendency of an analyst to search for, interpret, and remember information in a way that confirms his or her preconceptions. A variation of that is the **observer-expectancy effect**, when an analyst expects a given result and therefore subconsciously manipulates or misinterprets data in order to find it.

Analysts can also fall victim to the **framing effect**, which leads them to draw different conclusions from the same information depending on how or by whom that information is presented. This is most prevalent when the analyst places more stock in what a functional manager says about how a team uses a system, disregarding what the team says. In these cases, the team usually understands much better than the boss. But because the manager is in a position of power (and may be in a better position to help the analyst's career), the analyst who succumbs to framing effect bias tends to listen more to the manager than to the people who will have to use the system on a day-to-day basis. This is often what is behind the tendency to pay more attention to the people who are paying for the IT project, even though they may not use the resulting solution on a daily basis, than to the people who will actually have to use the solution. Framing effect bias is also a substantial difference between business analysts and user experience (UX) experts. Both skill sets are focused on figuring out what to build, but analysts typically focus on those stakeholders who are paying for the solution, whereas UX experts typically pay more attention to the people who will use the solution. Both perspectives are important, and it may not make sense to favor one over the other. That's why it's helpful to have both skill sets available, to help a team make sure they truly are delivering the right solution.

A final cognitive bias that analysts fall into during elicitation is **mirror imaging**. This happens when analysts assume that stakeholders think like they do, and hence assume that the stakeholders with whom they interact like to work, express ideas, and learn new information the same way they do. This can lead to a variety of other assumptions that end up being wrong. These mistaken assumptions often aren't validated until too late into the overall effort, which can often contribute to the confirmation bias.

An effective way to overcome these analyst biases is to include more than just the analyst in any substantial elicitation sessions. Having multiple team members, preferably looking at things from different perspectives, lessens the chances that all the information elicited about a particular topic is framed from only one point of view. I'm not suggesting that every time someone from the team wants to talk to a stakeholder, he or she has to take along a buddy, but I am suggesting that for sessions where the intent is to have substantive discussions about the project and its requirements, it's always helpful to have multiple perspectives.

Analysis

Additional biases can come into play when you are sifting through the elicited information, trying to make sense of it and figure out what it's telling you.

The **anchoring effect** or **focusing effect** is the tendency of an analyst to place too much emphasis on a particular piece of information when analyzing a situation. Related is the **survivorship bias**, where the analyst concentrates on people or things that successfully made it through some process, ignoring those that did not.

The **availability heuristic** is the tendency to overestimate the likelihood or frequency of an event because memories of that event are more recent. There are several variations of the availability heuristic. **Observation selection bias** is noticing things that were not noticed previously, and therefore wrongly assuming that the frequency of those noticed items has increased. **Recency bias** occurs when recent events are considered more important than earlier events. And the **frequency illusion** makes a word, a name, or a thing that has recently come to your attention suddenly seem to appear with increased frequency shortly afterward. For example, if you are at a conference and you meet an interesting person, chances are that you will surprisingly "run into" that person quite frequently for the rest of the conference. The truth is, you would have seen the person just as much had you not met him or her; you just notice more often because of your introduction.

The confirmation bias impacts how the analyst interprets information, again encouraging the analyst to find ways to reinforce preconceived notions. One variation of the confirmation bias is *Déformation professionnelle*, which is especially prevalent with the movement toward creating the "profession" of business analysis. This bias is the tendency to look at things according to the conventions of the observer's profession, forgetting any broader point of view, leading business analysts to overlook helpful techniques and ideas not normally associated with the business analyst profession. Another form of confirmation bias is the **Semmelweis reflex**, which is the tendency to reject new evidence that contradicts a paradigm. This particular bias occurs when an analyst is aware of information that disproves a preconception but ignores it specifically because it goes against that preconception.

Analysts are sometimes inclined to see patterns where they don't exist. One cognitive bias of this type is the **clustering illusion**. Another type is the **Texas sharpshooter fallacy**, where an analyst interprets pieces of information that have no relationship to one another as being similar and therefore pointing to the existence of a pattern. (This bias is named after the story of a man who fires his gun randomly at the side of a barn, then paints a bull's-eye around the spot where the most bullet holes cluster, implying his excellent marksmanship skills.)

The point is that you don't want to infer a pattern based on pieces of data that coincidentally happen to be close together.

An effective way to counter biases that impact analysis is to explicitly play the devil's advocate. As you are analyzing information you have elicited and find that you are starting to identify all types of patterns and find all kinds of confirming information that you hadn't noticed before, force yourself to stop and consider other possible explanations for the information you are seeing. Another technique that can be helpful to address these cognitive biases is the practice of **Break the Model**, which I describe in the "Feature Injection" section in Chapter 5.

Decision Making

As you may expect, there are cognitive biases that become apparent in groups that are trying to make decisions.

One type of bias has to do with group agreement, which can become readily apparent in IT projects where multiple stakeholders are responsible for making decisions (i.e., there is no clear decision maker). These types of biases include the **false consensus effect**, where people overestimate the degree to which others agree with them and don't bother to confirm whether that is in fact the case. This particular bias can also happen when there is a clear decision maker who wrongly believes that other stakeholders with some influence agree with what he or she has decided.

Another cognitive bias related to group agreement is the **group attribution error**, where a stakeholder assumes that the decision of a group—a steering committee, for example—reflects the preferences of the members of that committee, despite evidence to the contrary. For example, in situations where members of the group tend to work in a passive-aggressive manner, the stakeholders may say they agree, but their body language, attitude, and tone of voice convey a completely different perspective.

Sunk cost biases become particularly apparent where decisions regarding continuing an initiative are concerned. The biggest sunk-cost-related bias is **irrational escalation**, where decision makers justify continued and even increased investment in an initiative based on how much has already been spent, in spite of new evidence suggesting that the initiative should never have been started in the first place. Irrational escalation is often attributed to the decision maker's desire to avoid looking foolish for stopping work on an initiative he or she originally approved, even though there is no clear hope that continued investment will turn the situation around. This is often described as "throwing good money after bad." Usually, other initiatives that would be less expensive and have a better chance of success lose funding in favor of the failing initiative.

An offshoot of this type of bias is **loss aversion**, where decision makers would rather avoid a loss—a common view of canceling an initiative—than experience a gain by spending funds on a new initiative instead.

Common ways of counteracting these biases that impact decision making are the processes that you use for discussing and arriving at decisions. A simple technique such as the **fist of five** is a good way to gauge agreement with and support for a particular decision. By having members of a group indicate their level of support for and agreement about a particular decision, a decision leader can determine if there are people who are still concerned about a decision and discuss those concerns. Another technique that can be used to counteract sunk cost and related biases is to invite discussion about the opportunity costs of continuing the IT project—what other things the organization is not able to do because they are continuing the project in question. Another way to counteract the sunk cost bias is to welcome frank discussions about whether the IT project will still result in the outcome that it was intended to produce. In some cases, your team may also need to discuss whether the outcome is still worth the effort the IT project requires.

If You Remember Nothing Else

- Agree ahead of time who will make certain types of decisions and be aware of the approach taken to make those decisions.

- When you face a decision, your first question should be "When do I have to decide?"

- Be aware of your cognitive biases and those of your stakeholders, and take steps to reduce their effect in your elicitation, analysis, and decision making.

Chapter 5

Deliver Value

Introduction

A guiding principle that warrants some extra discussion is the principle of "Deliver value." It seemed appropriate to explain this principle in a bit more detail given how much lip service is given to the idea of delivering value in the agile mindset. In this chapter I discuss some key concepts surrounding value delivery, including Feature Injection, minimum viable product, and minimum marketable feature.

Feature Injection

Feature Injection is a term coined by Chris Matts for an alternative approach to analysis. This approach is derived from the idea that as we pull business value from a system, we inject the **features** that represent the work the team does (outputs) to create that value (outcome). The key aspects of Feature Injection are understanding the value the initiative intends to deliver, delivering the features that provide that value, and communicating information about those features primarily through examples.

Perhaps the biggest source of confusion about the idea is why it is called Feature Injection. I decided to go right to the source and engaged Chris in an email dialog (April 14, 2015) about the derivation. Here's the resulting explanation:

> "As we pull business value from the system, we inject the features that create that value" was my original mantra on [Feature Injection], and it is still an accurate description of the process. Feature Injection was a[n] homage to Dependency

Injection due [to] its vague similarities, but also because DI was coined as a name at ThoughtWorks when I was there.

One of the reasons for the name was a rejection of "pull" as an axiom of Lean Software Development. I participated in too many conversations where the discussion would go round and round until someone said "It's a pull system" and everyone would nod sagely as if that was all that was needed. Pull works for the items being produced, but the pull occurs because of the requested items [features]. The requests themselves are pushed, or rather injected (a more precise version of push) into the system. [Chris describes this as the information arrival concept.]

The big thing was that information flows in the opposite direction to value; i.e., "pull" in Lean was not universal. It's a poetic way of saying arbitrage. You give up information [the feature representing a request for an output] and in return you are rewarded with value.

I still stand by the metaphor in the 2009 comic [Real Options at Agile 2009, available here: http://www.lulu.com/us/en/shop/chris-matts/real-options-at-agile-2009/ebook/product-17416200.html]. Stand at the out door of a Toyota factory that is idle, empty, and with all the workers waiting. Then request a car. You would see the parts pulled to the out door, starting at the in door. If you watch carefully, you would see the Kanban cards flowing backwards against the flow of value.

Feature Injection provides the theoretical underpinnings for much of the rest of this book, so it's worthwhile to spend a little time explaining what it really means.

To help explain Feature Injection, let's examine the three key ideas:

- Identify the value.

- Inject the features.

- Spot the examples.

Identify the Value

Feature Injection begins by creating understanding about the business value an initiative is trying to deliver. That value is then expressed in the form of a model so the team can repeatedly test progress toward delivering that value as the initiative proceeds.

Business value is a vague phrase that has been thrown around quite a bit in agile circles, since those approaches put a particular emphasis on delivering business value as the ultimate outcome. But there is no clear definition of what business value really means. I have been most influenced by two particular definitions. The first is from Chris Matts: a project delivers business value when it increases or protects revenue or reduces cost in alignment with organizational strategy. Another favorite definition is the acronym IRACIS: Increase Revenue,

Avoid Costs, Improve Service. Both of these definitions generally focus on the same concepts, but I have found that they don't necessarily cover all organizations, specifically not-for-profit or government organizations that tend to measure success not by profit, but by service to their mission, their members, or their constituents. Steve Denning even suggests that value should not be focused on profit or shareholders, but on delighting customers.

With all these possible definitions of value, I wanted to find a general way of describing business value that can apply to all types of organizations. I landed on this description: the business value of an IT project can be gauged by whether it helps an organization meet one or more goals. Based on our earlier definition of goals, this is measured based on the project's impact on one or more objectives.

Organizational goals can be explicitly financial: a new product should (ideally) increase revenue, a project to address regulatory concerns can protect revenue (avoid fines), and a process improvement project can reduce costs (for example, labor savings). Often, however, there is no readily accessible tie between the outcome of an IT project and direct financial impacts. In these cases, objectives can measure something that the project *can* impact, which is then indirectly related to some financial measure or measures. These are the leading indicators described in the "Metrics" section in Chapter 3.

Take, for example, a financial services company's efforts to revise its Web presence for an outside sales force. This organization competes with other companies that sell the same type of financial products, so it has to find ways to stay front-of-mind with that independent sales force to build and maintain its relative market position. While changes to the website really don't have a direct, measurable impact on revenue or costs (the site mostly provides information about the company's products), there are intermediate objectives—such as a measure of satisfaction with the site and the number and length of visits to the site—that can be correlated to improved brand awareness and ultimately have an impact on increasing or protecting revenue.

Once you know how to define the business value in the context of your project, you need to figure out how to express those objectives using a business value model, rather than just as a static number. A business value model describes the impact of the project on your selected objectives so you can reevaluate your expectations based on new information throughout the course of the project. Describing business value this way gives you a way of assessing your project while it is still under way, so you can determine if it will drive the results you are looking for. This also means that if it appears that the project will not accomplish what you want, you can correct course sooner, rather than completing the entire project and then finding out it's not going to work.

Here are some examples of how this might work.

Over the past few years, I have organized several different conferences, mostly focused around agile or business analysis. These conferences tend to be a major source of revenue for the nonprofit organizations that put them on, so a key objective of each conference is to generate a certain amount of money to fund the remainder of the nonprofit organization's activities. There are certainly other objectives, but revenue generated is the best representation of business value for the nonprofit organizations for which I planned conferences.

In order to help assess the impact of decisions on the revenue objective, I use a budget spreadsheet that allows me to see those impacts, such as how many sessions to have, what kind of compensation to give the speakers, whether lunch is served every day, and other factors that influence the success of the conference. When I'm considering a change in some aspect of the conference, I can tweak some of the information in the budget spreadsheet and see the effect on the expected revenue. I can also test out assumptions about the anticipated number of attendees and sponsors and see the impact of those assumptions on the overall revenue. Modeling this information at various points during the planning period leading up to the conference allows me to determine whether the planning committee needs to do additional marketing for the conference or seek out additional speakers. The budget spreadsheet is a business value model.

Chris Matts and Andy Pols suggest another format for a business value model in a paper they wrote in 2004 (http://agileconsortium.pbworks.com/f/Cutter+Business+Value+Article.pdf):

> This project will generate an additional $15 million in profit. The model is based on the following assumptions:
>
> 1. We achieve 20% of the sales of existing product XYZ ($100 million a year).
> 2. The total cost of designing and producing the product is $5 million.
> 3. Our product is the first to market.
> 4. We are able to release the product two months before Christmas.

In order to express business value as a model, not just a number, this example both describes the target of the objective and explains the assumptions underlying the target. It also provides a way to test what happens to the objective if the underlying assumptions change.

Pascal Van Cauwenberghe provides another perspective on business value and business value modeling. His proposed model extends the idea of business value being in the eye of the beholder (http://blog.nayima.be/2010/01/02/what-is-business-value-then/):

- Identify the relevant stakeholders.
- Identify their needs and goals.

- Agree on how we measure/test the achievement of the needs and goals.
- Select the (few) most important measurements and tests, the "Value Drivers."
- Define the relationship between the Value Drivers.
- Use the Value Drivers to focus and prioritize our work, from start to finish.

He continues, "It's important to define the relationship between the Value Drivers. E.g. we may have both 'profit' and 'customer satisfaction' Value Drivers. Which comes first? If we find a way to increase our profit at the expense of reduced customer satisfaction, would that be acceptable? There is no right answer. It depends on the company, the project and the circumstances."

Inject the Features

Once you understand the value you are trying to deliver, and you have created a model of that value which allows you to test how different assumptions impact it, you can use that information to guide what you do next. You want to select the outputs (which are requested in the form of features) that allow you to make progress toward meeting the targeted goals or help validate assumptions made in your business value model. Which aspect you focus on first will depend on how far along you are in the initiative. At the start, you will most likely spend more effort on validating assumptions (you can also think of this as reducing uncertainty) and follow up with delivering features that you know will deliver the value you seek.

The key point here is that you identify value first, then iteratively identify the features that you need to deliver it. Don't brainstorm a big list of possible changes and try to figure out what each feature could contribute to business value. Measuring value at the granularity of a user story is very difficult and can generate wasted effort. Too often, the team spends time overanalyzing the **value points** associated with a story when they could have easily made a priority decision another way, which is really what value points are intended to help with. By working from value to features instead of in the other direction, you'll have fewer items to manage at any point in time, and you'll also avoid the tricky business of trying to assign value to any specific change.

Injecting features can work in a few different ways. If you are trying to achieve a specific business goal and have the freedom to identify different options for meeting that goal, a technique such as impact mapping (Chapter 14) can be very helpful for identifying possible options and determining which to try first.

You don't always have a clear-cut goal with options for achieving it. In some cases the method of achieving your goal is predetermined, at a high level at least. This is often the case when you are changing an existing process or system, or replacing an outdated process or system. The organization has certain capabilities, but you may have some freedom as to the order of implementation. In this case, a list of things to deliver—which are truly options when using impact mapping—becomes part of an overall solution. Implementing features iteratively can still be very helpful because it provides a way for the team to remove extraneous functionality. Story mapping (Chapter 14) is a helpful technique here, because you can determine the key activities that need to happen at a fairly abstract level but be very selective about what specific functionality you produce to support each of those key features. The team would define scope as measuring the established business goals and objectives, rather than as a specific list of deliverables. This can give you the latitude you need to remove features that are not truly needed by not injecting them.

This is the approach that we used for the conference submission system (Chapter 7). At the core of the matter, we were trying to support the submission process for the agile conference. We didn't have a lot of different options for completely different behavior; we had chosen a process we were going to use and we needed to support it. We found a story map helpful to organize the work because we were able to make some clear decisions about what aspects of the submission system we were and were not going to do.

So you may have several different potentially independent options to choose from, or you may have many dependent features, most if not all of which have to be included. In either case, once you have chosen to inject one feature, start with some representation of the output that represents the feature. Then, work backward to understand what you need to deliver that output.

Imagine you are working with a company that has decided to introduce a new payroll system. The new system can have a variety of outputs, including paychecks and reports. Depending on your perspective, different outputs generate value. If you are an employee, the check produced by the payroll system provides you with value. If you are the human resources manager, you may view the reports produced by the payroll system as protecting revenue. They give you information to help you take actions that reduce risk, such as discrepancies in your payment structure based on improper factors such as age, race, or sex.

It follows, then, that you need to determine who your stakeholders are and what outputs they expect from the system. Starting with stakeholders is helpful because it prevents you from generating outputs that aren't really needed. You can identify your key stakeholders by asking, "Who would care if this payroll system did not exist?" Table 5.1 shows a list you might come up with.

With this understanding of the stakeholders, you can identify the outputs that deliver the value they expect. This is where models come in handy, especially those representing displays of information or reports that stakeholders are looking for in order to answer some questions or make some decisions.

Table 5.1 *Payroll Stakeholders and Their Expectations*

Stakeholder	Expectations
Employees	If the payroll system did not exist, they might not get paid. This is probably not the case, but it certainly may be a more complicated process to get payroll completed. From the employees' perspective, the payroll system adds value because it generates checks. When employees get paid, they continue to work, so the value is in protecting revenue by keeping employees satisfied that money is still coming in the door. (Yes, I know this is kind of a stretch, but it's the one that seems to fit best.)
Payroll department	Assuming that the organization would still pay its employees even without a payroll system, the lack of a system would make the process inefficient and more prone to error; so creating a payroll system reduces costs. And to some extent, it protects revenue by reducing the risks of incorrect paychecks.
Employee relations manager	Even if you could pay employees without a payroll system, the lack of organized data makes it much more complicated to perform analysis on payroll information, which indirectly leads to increased risk for the organization, similar to the items described previously.

In the case of the commission system, the output can be something a bit more tangible, such as a paycheck, or starting a process that will result in something being shipped to a customer.

Once you understand the outputs, you can work backward to figure out what processes are needed to produce those outputs (including the rules that act in those processes) and the inputs the process needs to create the outputs. You are effectively performing analysis in the opposite direction of development, which tends to bring in the inputs of a system first, then build the process, and finally create the outputs. Said another way, because you are pulling value from the system via the outputs, you leave a hole at the beginning of the system into which features are injected.

Spot the Examples

We typically use models to describe the outputs and processes and the inputs used to create them. These models are helpful for creating a shared understanding with everyone involved in delivering the features, but they are rarely sufficient. In the words of George E. P. Box, "All models are wrong, but some are useful." One way to make the overall understanding of a model clearer is to add examples. Examples serve two purposes. First, they provide concrete guidance in very specific situations to people who tend to ask, "Yes, but what about this situation?" Second, examples give the team a way to test the models, make sure they account for different situations that may occur, and build a shared understanding about what a feature should do. Examples also describe requirements and tell when a feature has been delivered successfully, giving your team a head start on your tests. Examples tend to provide a more useful description of the requirements than other means, based on anecdotal evidence and my conversations with developers. If given a choice between a set of examples and a set of textual requirements, developers I have worked with almost always refer primarily to the examples.

In an approach that Matts calls "Break the Model," a team establishes a model they believe appropriately represents the domain in which they are working and use it to produce the desired outputs. Then examples are cited to determine whether the model, as it currently exists, will support that situation. If it does, great; we keep the example around as a convenient way to describe the desired behavior of the system. If the model does not support the example and the example is actually relevant (meaning the example is actually likely to happen, and it's a situation we are interested in addressing), we revise the model to represent the new understanding of the domain to account for that example. We then provide both the relevant examples and the model to the rest of the team as a description of what needs to be built for that particular feature. One thing to keep in mind here is the Key Example pattern described by Gojko Adzic in his book *Specification by Example*. That idea is to focus on key examples and avoid repetitive examples that do not show anything new. Don't keep examples that don't add any new information to the set you already have.

When we built the submission system, we described all of our features in terms of examples. Those examples were used as the basis for automated acceptance tests, and I still use them as a reference for what was and was not accounted for. For example, recently a question came up from the current conference chair about what he could control with respect to whether the submission system was "open" or "closed." I was able to go into our source code repository and find the pertinent examples (shown below). The examples indicated that the conference chair can control when people can submit new session proposals, edit their session proposals, or edit their accepted session proposals.

```
Feature: Edit conference dates
  As a conference chair
  I want to change session submission deadlines

  Background:
    Given I am logged in as "Connie"
    Then session submissions should be open
    And session edits should be open
    And accepted session edits should be open
```

```
Scenario: Update Open Date
  When I change the session submission start date to 1 day from now
  Then session submissions should be closed

Scenario: Update Close Date
  When I change the session submission end date to 1 day before now
  Then session submissions should be closed

Scenario: Update Edit Date
  When I change the session submission edit date to 1 day before now
  Then session edits should be closed

Scenario: Update Accepted Session Edits Start Date
  When I change the accepted submission edit start date to 1 day from now
  Then accepted session edits should be closed

Scenario: Update Accepted Session Edits End Date
  When I change the accepted submission edit end date to 1 day before now
  Then accepted session edits should be closed
```

The thought process surrounding Feature Injection is a huge influence on how I approach analysis on all projects, and while I very rarely mention the name to the teams I'm working with, I'll often introduce the ideas. Most of the people I talk to say things like "Yes, that makes a lot of sense. Why didn't we do that before?" or "Yeah, we do that, with these few tweaks." Starting with the value you want to deliver, using that value to decide what feature to build next, and describing that feature through the use of real-life examples proves to be a simple, effective way to build the right thing, and not build things that are not right.

Minimum Viable Product

Eric Ries introduced the concept of minimum viable product in his writings on Lean Startup. This is the most straightforward description he provides (*The Lean Startup*, Chapter 6):

> A minimum viable product (MVP) helps entrepreneurs start the process of learning as quickly as possible. It is not necessarily the smallest product imaginable, though; it is simply the fastest way to get through the Build-Measure-Learn feedback loop with the minimum amount of effort.

> Contrary to traditional product development, which usually involves a long, thoughtful incubation period and strives for product perfection, the goal of the MVP is to begin the process of learning, not end it. Unlike a prototype or concept test, an MVP is designed not just to answer product design or technical questions. Its goal is to test fundamental business hypotheses.

The main purpose of MVPs as defined by Ries is learning what customers find valuable, not necessarily delivering value to customers. Additionally, learning is trying to figure out business as well as product design and technical questions, and in the early stages it is most likely focused on the business questions.

MVPs are a technique that your team can use to carry your discovery activities forward through your delivery process. It's a key component of the Build-Measure-Learn loop because it's the thing that teams build in order to gather feedback and learn from it.

That's all stated from the startup context. What value can the MVP concept bring to IT projects? Primarily, the MVP can be used when testing solutions. We may find that we get a lot of information from our stakeholders about what they believe their needs are, and we may even pull some data from a variety of sources that tells us how our stakeholders behave, but at the end of the day the most effective way we may find to see if our solution is really going to satisfy our stakeholders' needs is to build it, try it, and see what happens.

The idea of the MVP, even in the IT project context, means that the purpose of an iteration is to either learn or earn. Initially your team is trying to learn about the problem and solution by doing things to validate assumptions, address risks, or make progress toward your desired outcome. Your team produces some output that while not a complete solution does provide information for the purpose of testing your hypothesis. In effect, you're saying, "We think this is going to work, but we won't know until we try it, so let's see what happens."

Your team may be able to provide something for stakeholders at the end of an iteration, get feedback, and have a pretty good idea of whether it will work or not. The benefit of this approach is that you can get feedback sooner because you don't have to build a solution that's conceptually complete, just enough that you can get feedback on it. It's important when the intent of a sprint is learning that you have a specific question in mind that you are trying to answer. This can be stated as your sprint goal so that it's clear to your entire team.

What does an MVP useful for feedback in an iteration setting look like? I worked with a team recently that was building new analytic capabilities for an organization that traded securities. The team was working on an effort to incorporate a new source of data into an existing data warehouse, and one of the first things they needed to do was verify that they could successfully merge data from the new source into an existing source. They selected a view of the data that represented a simple listing of securities but contained attributes from multiple sources. Instead of worrying about creating a pristine report or moving the data through all the various architectural layers, they chose to start by associating data from the new source into the existing data and generating a query using Excel. They were able to show the data they expected to see in the final report without spending a lot of time designing the report or building all of the background infrastructure perceived as necessary to automatically integrate the data in the long run. They had to determine whether they could combine data from the disparate sources correctly. Doing it in this manner let them immediately identify where they had some logic corrections to make, and they were able to find that out in a couple of weeks. Had they taken the typical approach to building up a data warehouse, they might not have uncovered the issues they found until months down the road, because they wouldn't have been able to isolate where the problem occurred. In addition, they were able to quickly get meaningful feedback from their stakeholders about which attributes were really needed and specific rules on how to match data from the disparate systems.

On the other hand, your team may figure out that the only way to truly know whether an MVP will work is to let stakeholders use it in actual day-to-day business. In this case, the MVP may represent a more complete change than the version that was demoed at the end of a sprint.

In the preceding analytics example, this type of MVP happened when the team released one full-fledged report to its stakeholders. Here, they were trying to find out if the reporting interface was helpful to the stakeholders and if the organization of the reports made sense. This one report would still be useful, but real value would be generated when multiple reports were available. However, by delivering this one report first, the team learned a great deal about the stakeholders' needs, and the stakeholders gained a better understanding of their needs and the reporting capabilities.

Either way, understanding the MVP idea keeps teams from feeling compelled to define too much information up front and encourages them to see delivery as a way to validate assumptions and test hypotheses.

The other important aspect of the MVP concept is the implied focus on speed. You seek the minimum viable product (or change to an asset) because it means you can get it done sooner, get it in front of stakeholders sooner, and get feedback sooner. All of that means that you aren't wasting time heading down a road that leads nowhere; and if you are, you aren't wasting nearly as much time on that dead end.

Minimum Marketable Features

Minimum marketable feature (MMF) is a similar concept that came out a few years before the idea of MVP. While the ideas are similar, there are some significant differences.

Given our focus on delivering value, we may find it helpful to organize our work based on how much value we're providing. In 2004, Mark Denne and

Dr. Jane Cleland-Huang came up with a way to do that called the minimum marketable feature (MMF):

- Minimum—the smallest possible group of features that deliver significant value to the user
- Marketable—provides significant value to the customer
- Feature—something that is observable to the user

Their ideal MMF is a small, self-contained feature that can be developed quickly and that delivers significant value to the user. Denne and Cleland-Huang define MMF in the context of a software product (again, externally focused) where the concept of marketability makes sense. Since I am examining internally focused efforts here, our definition of MMF needs a slight adjustment. In this case, "marketable" means "provides significant value to the stakeholder," where value is measured as progress toward a specific objective. We still want to group the work we're doing in terms of MMF for our stakeholders to sequence, though we may not necessarily use the rigorous analysis suggested by Denne and Cleland-Huang to do so. When I talk about features and user stories later, I expect the features to have the characteristics of MMFs. I chose not to label them that way because I am not talking about the context of building a product for sale.

Another good tidbit of information from Denne and Cleland-Huang is that MMFs make the best unit of planning for releases. Since this is the concept of when we are deploying to our stakeholders, we want what we are deploying to be a conceptual whole, but we may build up parts of those features in separate iterations and deliver those to our customers for the purpose of getting feedback. Features are the main planning unit for releases, and user stories are the main planning unit for iterations.

Context is a final important difference between MMF and MVP. MMF grew up in the world of established organizations that were building large products or maintaining existing ones. In this book, I am extending MMF to IT projects. MVP meanwhile was created for use in the context of starting a new business. While many people (including me) would like to apply Lean Startup ideas to established enterprises—and there are places where that does work—it is often the underlying principles these ideas embody more than the direct application of the ideas themselves that are important to understand. So when deciding when to use MMF or MVP, consider your context and choose appropriately.

Some people tend to confuse minimum marketable feature with minimum viable product because they both happen to have "minimum" in their name. The MMF is the smallest set of functionality that provides significant value to a stakeholder, whereas MVP is the version of your product that lets your team complete the Build-Measure-Learn loop as quickly as possible with the least amount of effort. In other words, MMF is definitely about delivering value to stakeholders, whereas MVP is about learning more about the ultimate product. The MVP could range anywhere from not having any MMFs, to having a single MMF, to having several MMFs. They are not the same concepts, but both reinforce the idea that we should be seeking, in Alistair Cockburn's words, "barely sufficient" functionality.

Both concepts are also often misinterpreted to mean "crap." They don't. Whatever functionality is deployed should work, should be supportable by the organization, and should be something that you would be proud to put your name on. It's just limited functionality that focuses on the core of what you are trying to accomplish, be that satisfying a particular need (MMF) or learning more about how you may be able to satisfy a particular need (MVP). Remember that the names are minimum *marketable* feature and minimum *viable* product for a reason.

If You Remember Nothing Else

- Effective analysis starts with the outcome and works its way backward through output, process, and input.
- Minimum viable products are intended to get information.
- Minimum marketable features are intended to capture value.

Chapter 6

Analysis with an Agile Mindset

Introduction

Chapters 1 through 5 described some important concepts that underlie analysis with an agile mindset. This chapter is intended to describe a typical approach to analysis on IT projects where teams exhibit an agile mindset. It provides a framework that's used to tell the case study stories in Chapters 7 through 10. It also places into context most of the techniques described in Chapters 11 through 15. This approach to analysis happens in four steps, illustrated in Figure 6.1:

1. What is the need?

2. What are some possible solutions?

3. What should we do next?

4. What are the details of this part?

These steps do not necessarily happen in quick succession. Often you will return to some steps again and again as you develop a deeper understanding of the project.

One of the primary reasons for breaking this approach into steps is to remind your team to evaluate your project on a regular basis and determine what to do next. After each step you should ask whether you should continue working on the project as it is currently envisioned, change the direction of the project, or stop the project. This is the "Commit to, Transform, or Kill" question for portfolio projects that Johanna Rothman describes in her book *Manage Your Project Portfolio*.

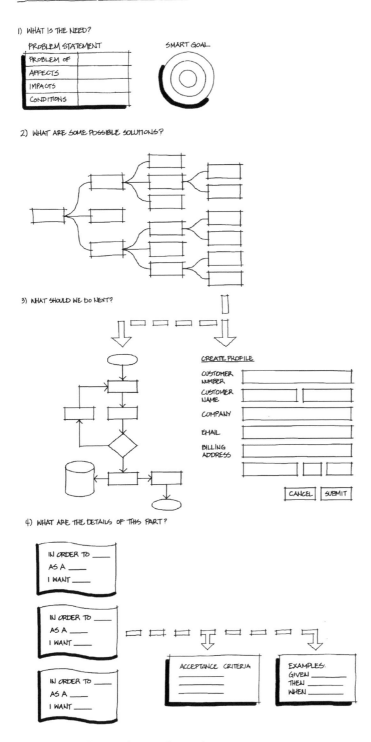

1) WHAT IS THE NEED?

PROBLEM STATEMENT   SMART GOAL

PROBLEM OF	
AFFECTS	
IMPACTS	
CONDITIONS	

2) WHAT ARE SOME POSSIBLE SOLUTIONS?

3) WHAT SHOULD WE DO NEXT?

CREATE PROFILE

CUSTOMER NUMBER

CUSTOMER NAME

COMPANY

EMAIL

BILLING ADDRESS

CANCEL   SUBMIT

4) WHAT ARE THE DETAILS OF THIS PART?

IN ORDER TO ____
AS A ____
I WANT ____

IN ORDER TO ____
AS A ____
I WANT ____

IN ORDER TO ____
AS A ____
I WANT ____

ACCEPTANCE CRITERIA
_____
_____
_____

EXAMPLES:
GIVEN _____
THEN _____
WHEN _____

Figure 6.1 *Analysis with an agile mindset*

As a lead-in to this approach your team will want to make sure everyone understands their stakeholders (using the techniques described in Chapter 11) and the context in which they're working (using the techniques described in Chapter 12). You may not need to analyze these aspects in detail for every project and may just need to confirm that your current understanding is still applicable.

Let's take a closer look at how this actually flows, what techniques are helpful, and what kind of evaluation needs to occur at each step.

What Is the Need?

In this step, your team is trying to understand your stakeholders, their needs, and which of those needs, if any, are worth satisfying. In other words, what problem are you trying to solve or what opportunity are you trying to exploit? This evaluation has two aspects: stating the need, and ensuring that everyone involved has a shared understanding of the desired outcome.

Techniques your team can use for identifying the need and building a shared understanding include the problem statement and the project opportunity assessment (Chapter 13). The true value of these techniques is the way they are created. When done collaboratively, they not only describe the need but also steer the process in a way that builds a shared understanding.

Also extremely helpful at this point is the clarification of goals and objectives, which helps your team answer the question "Do we know what success looks like and how to measure it?" In addition, **decision filters** (Chapter 13) give the team a way to stay on track and tie the effort back to strategic direction or the objectives themselves.

These techniques are best applied when an effort is getting off the ground, but it never hurts to revisit them when new team members come aboard or the team senses that conditions have changed in a way that may change the need itself.

During this step your team answers the question "Is this need worth satisfying?" This may be better stated as "Is this need a big deal regardless of the time and money we need to spend to satisfy it?" If so, move forward. If not, stop right here.

What Are Some Possible Solutions?

It's rarely a good idea to assume that there is only one solution for a given need. Identifying multiple possible solutions is important, but it is helpful to note the differences among those options and understand ways of identifying and assessing them. If you find yourself in a situation where you have a need to satisfy and you've defined a goal to know when you have satisfied it but you don't have a specific solution in mind, you have a great deal of flexibility. Impact mapping (Chapter 14) can be very helpful in identifying what solution(s) you should work on and in what order. This is especially true when the solution depends on altering stakeholder behaviors.

In other cases, you know the general solution, but you could take different paths to get there. These situations are more a matter of implementation decisions: build versus buy, which packages to purchase, and so on. If you are facing an effort with uncertain implementation, an analysis similar to impact mapping may have been done at a more organization-wide level to determine whether the goals of that particular effort were important to address for the purposes of a greater strategic goal. So, either you identify a possible solution and then decide on the desired implementation, or you focus solely on the implementation.

Story mapping (Chapter 14) can also be helpful to supply some context for the various things that need to be done and when they should occur. It also provides a starting point for the next step in analysis.

When your team is trying to figure out the possible solutions, or lands on a solution you would like to explore further, there's a good chance that you will perform some collaborative modeling (Chapter 14) to understand things better. Common models used at this point include a **context diagram, process flows, business domain models, wireframes,** and **storyboards.**

During this step, your team may identify features as placeholders for the big changes necessary to implement the eventual solution.

Your team will ask, "Is this need worth satisfying with this solution?" about every potential solution, pushing aside solutions that do not make sense.

What Should We Do Next?

This step is where your team gets down to deciding which solution, or part of a solution, to deliver to stakeholders next. You may reference existing models and create new models to start pinpointing the specifics of the solution. Your team will use current-state and future-state models to identify specific changes that are necessary, and they will start breaking the features already identified into more granular user stories for planning purposes.

Your team usually does this during **release planning** which results in a subset of work that your team focuses on for the next delivery. You use decision filters to determine which user stories should be included in the **release backlog.** Your team revisits the backlog on a regular basis to incorporate revised understanding of the need and how you believe the solution is working to solve it.

In this step your team compares the solutions that made the cut, with special attention to the cost effectiveness of specific solutions. You also evaluate how well the identified solution satisfies the project's objectives.

What Are the Details of This Part (i.e., Telling the Story)?

Once your team selects the next part of the solution you are going to deliver, you begin the work to further understand and describe the solution for purposes of delivery. User stories are typically best explained through the use of models, examples, and acceptance criteria (Chapter 14). The nature of each user story and your team's definition of ready (Chapter 15) dictate how extensively your team uses each technique. When completed, models, examples, and acceptance criteria should convey all the information the team has agreed they need in order to begin delivery, as detailed in the definition of ready. Progress toward the definition of ready may be tracked using a discovery board (Chapter 15) so that your team can see which items are coming up next for delivery.

Once items are brought into a sprint, the progress of delivery may be tracked on a delivery board (Chapter 15). Both discovery and delivery boards are examples of **visualization boards** (or **information radiators**). The delivery board in particular is used to track each item's progress from definition of ready to definition of done (Chapter 15) and eventual deployment to stakeholders. A definition of done may include updating system documentation intended to support the next effort on the asset by providing an updated reference of the current state of the asset.

Evaluation done at this point includes "Is this user story ready?", "Is this user story done?", "Should we deploy?", and other questions of that nature.

If You Remember Nothing Else

Analysis with an agile mindset allows your team to gradually dive into detail about your solution, taking advantage of the learning you received from delivering earlier output. This iterative approach to analysis also provides your team with regular opportunities to decide whether to commit to, transform, or kill your project.

Part II

Case Studies

Chapter 7

Case Study: Conference Submission System

Introduction

The Agile Alliance is a nonprofit organization with global membership committed to advancing agile development principles and practices. One of the organization's main programs is the annual North American conference (Agile2013 was the conference held in 2013). In order to find program content for the weeklong conference, the Agile Alliance runs an open submission process so that anyone can submit a presentation idea. A committee of volunteers then reviews the proposals, provides feedback, and selects the 240 sessions that will be part of that year's program. To facilitate this process, the Agile Alliance uses a conference submission system where submitters can submit session proposals, and the program team can provide reviews and manage the selection process.

I have been the product owner for the conference submission system since preparations started for Agile2011 in the fall of 2010. During the first two years, my main focus was maintaining and making periodic updates to an existing submission system built in 2008. This is the story of building the submission system for Agile2013 and then maintaining it for Agile2014.

The Need

In the fall of 2012, the Agile Alliance executive director and I realized that we had to replace the existing submission system, because it was based on an outdated version of the Drupal content management system that was no longer supported. Every year we would make revisions to the process based on our experiences planning the previous year's conference. Those changes were getting more difficult to make because of the mix of an out-of-date framework and the large amount of customized code that had gradually been added over the previous four years. In effect, the submission system was a kinder, gentler version of many legacy systems that most organizations deal with sooner or later. The straw that broke the camel's back was when we found out that the team that originally built the submission system and had been supporting it was no longer going to be able to provide that support.

Put simply, our goal was to provide ongoing support for the Agile Conference submission process. We found that the best way to build a shared understanding around what we were trying to accomplish was to use the decision filter "Will this help us run a community-based submission process?"

The Possible Solution(s)

When we realized we were losing support for the existing system, we started looking at our options. We narrowed them down to the following:

- Update our Drupal installation and make the corresponding revisions to the submission system.
- Start from scratch with a purchased solution.
- Start from scratch with a custom-built solution.

Updating our Drupal installation ended up not being a viable option because every developer we talked to who was experienced with Drupal said that by the time we updated our instance of Drupal, we would pretty much have to rebuild the submission system anyway.

We looked to see if there were any existing systems out there, and we found that our submission process was unique enough that there were no prepackaged solutions that provided the community-based aspects we were looking for. It's important for the Agile Alliance to maintain our community-based and feedback-rich submission process because it is closely aligned with the values of the organization. The submission process is a **differentiating activity** for the organization (see the section on Purpose-Based Alignment in Chapter 12), which indicated that creativity and innovativeness (read custom-developed system) were warranted.

That left rebuilding the submission system from scratch. Brandon Carlson and Darrin Holst with Lean TECHniques developed the submission system. Brandon had previous experience with the submission process, both as a submitter and as someone involved with the program team; Darrin is an experienced developer with a great deal of expertise in Ruby on Rails and acceptance test driven development (ATDD).

The Deliveries of Value

Brandon and I got together and established an overview of what we needed to build. We referenced the existing system as a guide for what functionality we needed. This discussion started with me identifying a bunch of features—I wrote them on index cards. Brandon and I met for lunch one day during a conference. We spread the cards out on a table and began organizing them into groups. Brandon proposed using a story map to organize the features, so we started one in Google Docs. In the top row of the story map, we identified the key **user roles:**

- Conference chair
- Track chair
- Track reviewer
- Submitter
- Attendee

Then we identified the key activities that each of the roles needed to be able to perform using the submission system.

Then we started talking about the specifics of what we needed to do for each activity and, just as important, when we were going to deliver the capabilities. We had two overriding constraints: the budget available to develop the system, which was based on an initial guess from Brandon, and a time frame that had about a week or two worth of wiggle room. We had to make sure that we could accept sessions and allow people to review them by early December 2012. The initial meeting took place in October 2012.

The time constraint was the most pressing, so as we discussed what would be in the first release, Brandon constantly asked, "Do you really need this right away?" On several items, when I answered yes, Brandon's next question was "Why?" or "Is it more important than this?" Constantly keeping in mind our time constraint and the bare minimum functionality required at that point in time helped me decide what was really necessary. It also helped to have the cards in front of us so we could physically move a feature "in" or "out" based on our conversation. The story map also helped ensure that we weren't leaving anything out, because it provided more context and structure than a mere list would have provided.

We ended up with a story map that looked like Figure 7.1.

Note that our story map did not use the familiar "As a . . . I want . . . so that . . ." structure so common to user stories. Instead, we used simple titles such as "Add session proposal," "Edit review," and so on. The more detailed

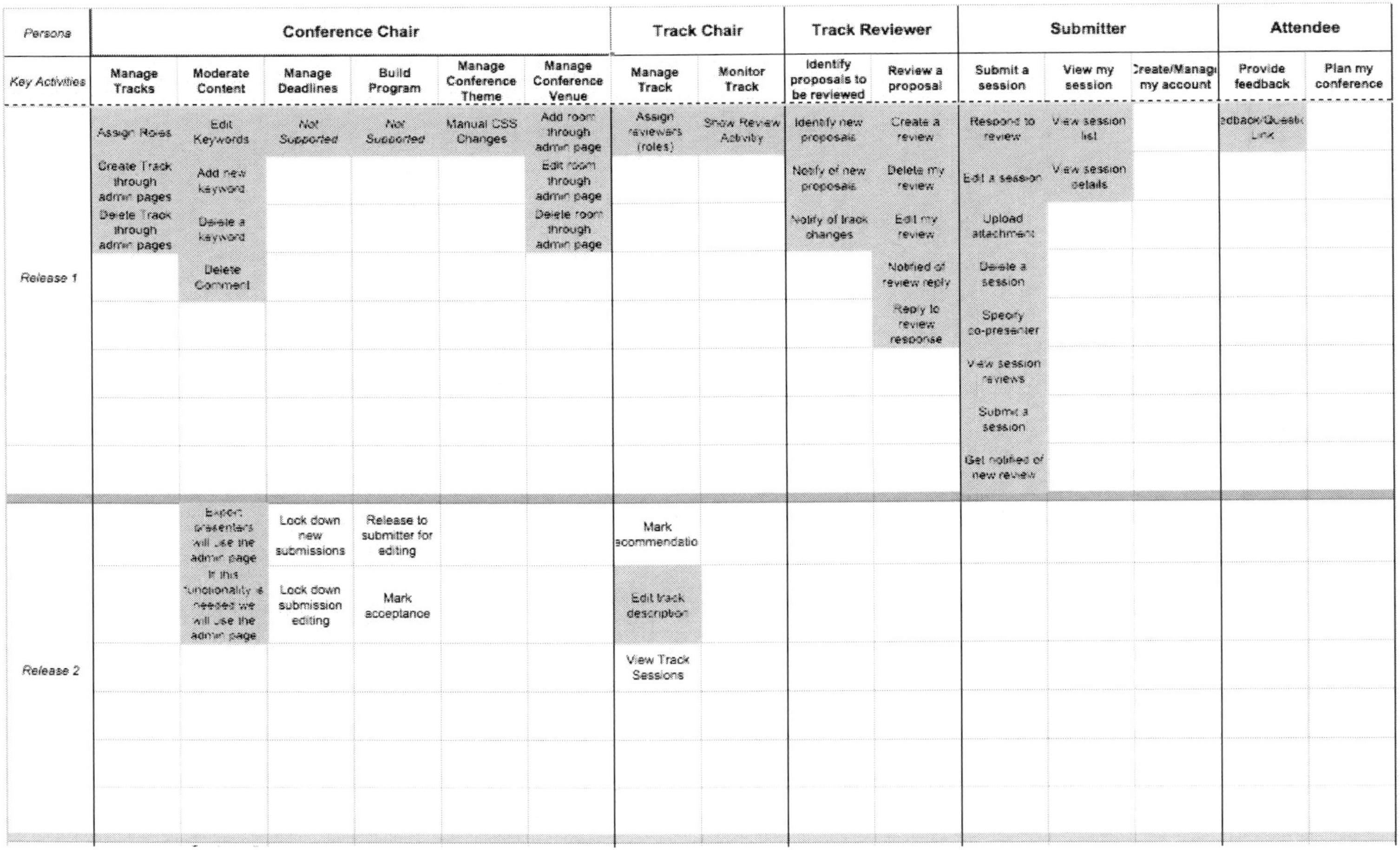

Figure 7.1 *Conference submission system story map*

descriptions often included stories in the more familiar format, primarily when it was important to note specific context such as which role should be able to do some activity. Generally speaking, our hierarchy of user roles went from most permissions to least: conference chair, program chair, track chair, track reviewer, submitter, and attendee. The attendee has general viewing rights as well as the ability to create a proposal. Submitters have those rights plus additional rights when related to their session proposals. Track reviewers have even more rights when dealing with session proposals in their track, followed by a track chair who has even more rights with session proposals in his or her tracks, followed by the conference and program chairs who have the most rights.

I also found myself adding the "so that" portion of a user story when it was particularly important to convey why we wanted a particular feature. But as often as not, I just provided that information in the description of that user story in our backlog.

Even though we did not use the traditional format, we tended to stick with the generally accepted good characteristics of user stories, normally described as INVEST (Independent, Negotiable, Valuable, Easily Sized, Small, Testable). We kept the stories as small, discrete packets of valuable functionality. Each user story was backed up with examples, and eventually automated acceptance tests, to ensure that the functionality created from them worked as it was supposed to. Again, we were able to work in this way because we had a great deal of trust among team members, and we all were pretty much on the same page when it came to what we were trying to do.

Define-Build-Test

Once we had our story map, Brandon and Darrin launched into development. We did not organize work into time boxes with a planning meeting every couple of weeks. For this particular project and this particular team, that would have been overkill. Instead, Brandon and Darrin would pull an item off the story map, build it in our QA environment, have me take a look at it, and when I said it looked good they would move on to the next item. In the early days before we released the submission system out into the wild, Darrin would move changes up to our "production" location (submissions.agilealliance.org). Once the submission process started, we were a little more intentional about when we moved changes, but we were still able to move them up anytime we needed to, and there were a couple of times when we had to make fairly quick changes.

Brandon and Darrin created a development/QA environment and a source code repository. They gave me access to both applications so I could check progress along the way. I would go into the QA environment to review development they had just finished to give it the OK to move to production. A nice aspect of the QA environment is the "stubbed identity service" which let us quickly switch from one user role to another to see how the submission system behaved for a conference chair versus a submitter. In the stubbed identity server we used informal personas (Chapter 11) such as Reed the Reviewer and Sam the Submitter and also referred to these personas in our examples. In addition to version control, we used the source code repository to track which stories we were working on and any issues that came up, and also as a repository for documentation.

When we first started working on the submission system, we talked about a couple of different ways to convey requirements. I had initially sketched some screen mockups to reflect how I wanted to rearrange something, but we found we didn't refer much to those mockups. It helped that Brandon had experience with previous conferences, so he had a fairly good idea of what was needed and had some ideas about how to improve screen layouts. We finally landed on the following general approach: Brandon or Darrin would select a user story from the story map and create an item in the repository to track any conversation about it. Any questions they had were noted in the item. I received an email notification whenever a new item was created or a comment was added to any item with which I was associated. When there were questions, I would provide an answer as a comment to the item. This simple workflow (see Figure 7.2) helped us keep all the information and conversations about user stories in one place instead of being strung across multiple email chains.

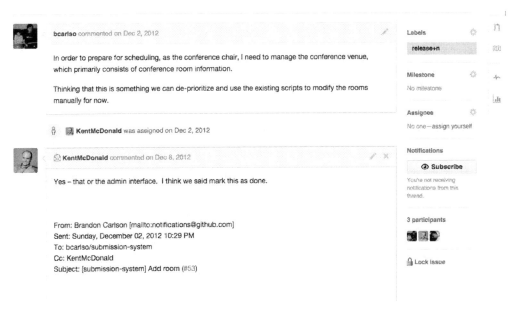

Figure 7.2 *Repository item*

Most questions were resolved with just one or two comments back and forth. Only a couple of times did Brandon and I end up talking on the phone about a particular issue.

Brandon and Darrin would take my fairly general answers and create examples for them. They organized and stored these examples by role, and then by feature. The examples served initially as a way for us to agree to what the submission system should do. After development was finished, they provided a great reference to the scenarios the submission system was built to handle. When a question came up about weird behavior the submission system seemed to be exhibiting, I was able to check the examples—stored in feature files, as we call them—to see what the system was built to handle. In every case, the "weird behavior" was the result of a situation that we had not accounted for. (As I told the team, these cases occurred not because the system was working improperly, but because I was.) This experience also reinforces the fact that no one can possibly think of everything ahead of time.

I had confidence that these examples appropriately described how the system behaved, because every feature was converted into an automated test that Brandon and Darrin would create before writing the code to make it pass. These tests run every time a change is committed, so Brandon and Darrin would know right away when something was not working as it should. This freed me to focus on determining whether the most recent changes met the needs of the submission process and to determine if we had missed any scenarios.

Here is an example of one of the feature files. This set of examples is for the Add Review feature, which allows reviewers in a given track the ability to provide feedback to submitters by adding a review to their session proposal. Note that the names that appear in these examples refer to the personas we created and used in the QA environment.

```
Feature: Add Review
  As a track reviewer
  I want to add reviews

  Background:
    Given I am logged in as "Reed"

  Scenario: Review a session
    Given a session exists on my review track
    When I add a review to that session
    Then the review should be added to that session

  Scenario: Unable to review for other tracks
    Given "Sam" has created a session on another track
    When I try to add a review to that session
    Then I should not be allowed
```

```
Scenario: Unable to review my own session
  Given I have created a session on my track
  When I try to add a review to that session
  Then I should not be allowed

Scenario: Unable to review sessions I'm a co-presenter on
  Given a session exists on my review track
  And I am the co-presenter on that session
  When I try to add a review to that session
  Then I should not be allowed

Scenario: May only review a session once and must respond to existing review
  Given a session exists on my review track
  And I have already reviewed that session
  When I try to add a review to that session
  Then I should be taken to the "Existing Review" page
```

Several rules may be inferred based on this set of examples:

- Reviewers can review only session proposals submitted to a track on which they are a reviewer.

- Reviewers cannot review a session proposal on which they are a presenter or co-presenter.

- Reviewers can review a session proposal only once.

We did not need to create a lot of requirements documentation because there were only three of us, because the domain was fairly simple and straightforward, and because Brandon and I had a great deal of experience with the submission process and Darrin was a quick study. We found that sharing information via repository items and referring back to the feature files when necessary was sufficient for recording the information we needed.

The Incident of the Themes

Of course, there were some cases where the questions could not be answered adequately by exchanging messages. One example is the addition of **themes,** which we incorporated fairly early in the development cycle. As part of the submission process, we ask submitters to identify a particular track to which their session belonged. The Agile Conference usually has about 15 to 20 topic-based tracks that are used primarily to organize the 1,000-plus submissions that the reviewers have to sift through in order to review and select sessions. Going into planning for 2013, the program chairs felt it would be helpful to group the tracks together so that each of the three program chairs could focus on a subset of tracks. This grouping was added after Brandon and Darrin started work on the submission system, and conveying this request was actually the first time

Figure 7.3 *Add Themes item*

we used the repository to convey information about a user story. I conveyed the program chairs' request to Brandon, and Figure 7.3 shows how he wrote it up.

He followed that with a comment indicating his true feelings about that change (see Figure 7.4).

Notice his last sentence: "What problem are we really solving with the theme concept?"

Brilliant.

Figure 7.4 *Add Themes item part 2*

Here I was, a product owner who should know better, detailing a solution: "The selection of the Theme filters the Track list. Add this field above the Track field. It is required." Brandon—a developer at heart but one of the best analysts I know (that was meant as a compliment, Brandon)—was keeping me honest, trying to figure out what I was really trying to accomplish so we could find the best solution. I exchanged emails with Brandon and Darrin outside of the repository (we hadn't quite smoothed out our process yet) and indicated that the important bit was to group the tracks together so that one of the program chairs could easily keep an eye on a group of tracks. Based on that, Darrin mocked up a different approach to achieving that same goal using a capability of HTML that I was not aware of—a single, grouped list in a drop-down box, shown in Figure 7.5.

Perfect. We went with that approach, the idea of theme was fairly seamlessly interwoven into the application, and I was reminded how important it is to think about what you are trying to accomplish rather than suggesting how to accomplish it, leaving that determination for team members who understand the capabilities of the technology. We had the great advantage of not getting too concerned about roles.

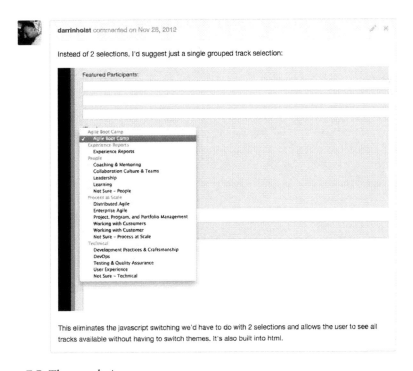

Figure 7.5 *Theme solution*

That was pretty much the groove we hit while getting ready for Agile2013. Once we passed our first hurdle—getting the submission system up and running to accept session proposals and reviews by early December—Brandon and I met and discussed what features the next release should contain. We updated the story map to reflect the items that had to be addressed in the second release. In this release we found we needed to focus primarily on the functionality to support the submission process milestone dates and the activities that occurred after the session proposal period was over. Having learned my lesson from the theme instance I described previously, I merely indicated that we needed some way of preventing people from submitting sessions after a given date, and then prohibiting them from editing existing sessions after a later date. It would have been easiest to hard-code the dates that sessions could no longer be accepted; however, we had a little bit of time to get these changes in, and we knew we were going to be using the submission system for several years, so we built the ability for the conference chair to change those dates (see Figure 7.6). This would also come in handy if for some reason the conference chair decided to extend the submission period or the edit period.

Some issues also came up as people began using the submission system. We added these as repository items, and I indicated whether we should address them. Once the submission process started, we began experiencing the outcome of my prioritization decisions. Because we had replaced an existing system and also were working under a tight time frame, I had to make some pretty hard decisions about what would and would not be included. Two main features that we excluded from the first release, and for the entire version supporting Agile2013, were public commenting and reporting.

Public commenting allowed people who had access to the submission system but were not reviewers, track chairs, program chairs, or conference chairs to provide feedback on a session proposal. This feature was also available on the old submission system, and we found it was mostly used by spammers and by friends of the submitter posting glowing comments about the session. With previous submission systems, we even had to be sure the submitters knew the difference between reviews and public comments. I decided to leave public comments off the Agile2013 version based on our budget constraints, and in order to see how many people missed it. We did receive some emails asking why there

| New Sessions: | 12/07/2014 00:00 COT | - | 02/23/2015 00:00 COT |
| Sessions Edits: | 12/07/2014 00:00 COT | - | 02/23/2015 00:00 COT |

Figure 7.6 *Conference date user interface*

was not a public commenting capability, and there was some chatter on Twitter as well. Since the audience of users are all used to agile approaches, I replied to let them know that we did not include public commenting because it wasn't as high a priority as other features, and that seemed to satisfy just about everybody. I also paid attention to the amount of feedback we received, for future consideration.

The other feature that we left off was reporting. This impacted a smaller group of people—namely, the program team—but it did have a fairly large impact. Several of the track chairs often want to have the session proposal information available to analyze outside of the submission system, generally using Excel. I knew that our focus in this first year was to provide ways to get the information into the submission system, indicate which sessions the track chairs recommended and which sessions the conference chairs selected, and indicate where and when the sessions would play. But I also knew that many members of the program team relied on reporting capabilities. I decided to use the simplest thing that would work. I asked Brandon to set me up with direct access to the database supporting the submission system and proceeded to fulfill any data requests through ad hoc queries. I reasoned that this would allow us to meet the immediate reporting needs everyone had and at the same time learn what actual reports were needed so we could provide reporting capabilities when we had the budget and time to do so.

In both cases, I used an inherent decision filter to determine whether or not we should add a particular feature. The decision filter for the first release was "Will this help us to accept and review session proposals?" The decision filter for the second release was "Will this help us to build a program?" Public commenting clearly did not meet either of those decision filters, so it was an easy call to leave it out. Reporting was a harder decision. I could make a case for it helping the program team to build a program, but it came down to the fact that there were other, more essential features that came first, and by the time we got to reporting, we had run through our budget.

The story map provided one additional benefit. When we had run through our initial budget and realized we still had some additional items to deliver, we wanted to reconcile what we thought we were going to do, what we actually had done, and what we still had left to do. This would provide some basis for requesting additional development money. I went through the story map and color-coded it to reflect two perspectives: whether items were not started, in progress, or done; and whether they were included in the original estimate. As you would expect, we discovered some additional requirements as we started work, and other features became obsolete because Brandon and Darrin found a different way of addressing the needs the features were originally intended to satisfy. This analysis was done strictly for financial reasons. It had no impact on the actual system functionality because we made decisions during development to create the functionality that was needed. Rather, the analysis was an exercise to explain why not everything was delivered from the original list that was the basis of the original guess. We knew why in general terms, but conveying the information this way helped us tell the story. If I had to do it over again, I probably would have tried to keep the story map up-to-date as we proceeded through it.

For features that weren't either "in estimate" or "done" I explained why the feature was in the state it was in. This accounted for differences that arose from establishing a budget based on an estimate, and then making decisions based on the most current information. In addition, we were more concerned about the outcome supporting the submission process in the best way possible, rather than sticking rigorously to an initial list of scope items created at the point of maximum ignorance. I think this approach is relevant to other, more complex projects in larger organizations, provided the team also maintains an ongoing record of the differences between planned and actual instead of trying to rationalize it after the fact. I was able to do a look-back analysis because we didn't have very many features. It would have been more difficult on a larger system.

As another example of why you should express requirements in the form of what you want to accomplish instead of how to do it, there were several features that we ended up not having to specifically build. These features all had to do with the capability of adding conference-specific information that was used to set the program, such as creating tracks; deleting tracks; creating, editing, and deleting themes; creating, editing, and deleting rooms; and creating, editing, and deleting time slots. We originally thought we would have to build pages to allow the conference chair to do this type of editing, but Darrin found an administration framework that provided several maintenance features for data out of the box, as it were. By implementing this admin framework, we were able to save a lot of development work building special admin screens. We did not know about the existence of this framework when we put the initial feature list together, but because we were measuring progress against outcome, not output, we were comfortable using the framework.

It was very fortunate that Brandon and Darrin found the admin framework, but they didn't find it right off the bat, yet we were able to move forward without having the capabilities to maintain a lot of that descriptive data. A session proposal is kind of the "hub entity," if you will, where most of the relevant data for the submission system provides further description of the session proposal (much like a claim is the "hub entity" for an insurance company). Some of the pieces of information that are associated to a session proposal and are necessary for a complete session proposal are theme, track, duration, and session type, all of which can change from year to year and therefore are not good candidates for hard coding. Brandon and Darrin created structures that allowed these attributes to be dynamic and then manually populated them (i.e., mocked up the data). This allowed us to create new session proposals without building the capability to create or edit the descriptive data first. This simple trick sped up the availability of the really important functionality—the ability to create session proposals.

The day before Agile2013 started, the program team held a retrospective on the selection process. The session provided a lot of great feedback on what we could improve in the submission system for the upcoming year. Most of the information was not new, but there were a few good insights, and we also gathered some information that helped put things in their proper perspective and shed some light on the appropriate priority for various items. We used that information to influence how we approached work for Agile2014.

Agile2014

Going into the Agile2014 submission period, we knew that we wanted to make several changes to the submission system, but the changes didn't fit into the same broad categories we used in Agile2013. A straightforward product backlog made sense for organizing the information for Agile2014, so we generated a new list in the spreadsheet we had used for the Agile2013 story map. The 2014 backlog included our remaining open issues from the repository, as well as new items from the retrospective and other conversations. The spreadsheet allowed easier sorting and filtering than the repository.

Our first task was to identify a budget. The executive director of the Agile Alliance assumed a dollar figure in his conference budget for the year but indicated that I should let him know if that amount was sufficient.

Since there was already a number in the budget that was not provided by Brandon, I decided it was probably representative of what was considered reasonable. In effect, it was the target. So I treated that dollar figure as a constraint. We were also working with a time constraint, although it was not as pressing as in the previous year. There was minimal work necessary to get the submission system ready for Agile2014, and most of the items on our list were improvements. I compiled the backlog and sent it to Brandon for estimating.

Brandon estimates using a range representing a 90% confidence interval, which means that 90% of the time the actual time to develop a feature would fall into the range provided. I asked Brandon and Darrin to estimate every feature on the list while I grouped the features into A, B, and C buckets. The A bucket represented the things I felt were absolutely necessary to finish for Agile2014, the B items would be really nice to have, and the C items were everything else. When I got the estimates back, I added up how much each feature would "cost" (using the high end of the range for each item) and summed up all the As. The total for all of the As was a little bit more than the budget item, so I moved a couple of items down into the B category until I was below budget.

I could have asked for more money, but that would have required explaining why it was needed, and it didn't seem worth it. After all, these were estimates, and if I could get everything we needed using the existing budget assumption, we were better off getting started than arguing over a small percentage of the total budget. Plus, since I used the upper end of the estimate scales, there was a fairly good chance that some of the features would not take as long as Brandon and Darrin thought (and yes, I also realized some would take longer), and in the long run we would be able to get some of the B items done.

I got the idea for this approach from Todd Little's ABC approach to software prioritization that he wrote up at http://toddlittleweb.com/wordpress/2014/06/22/the-abcs-of-software-requirements-prioritization/. Focusing on budgeting rather than estimating allowed me to treat money like a design constraint. This meant that our conversations could center around what was possible to accomplish within our constraints rather than arguing about how "right" the estimates were.

I told the director that we could use the budgeted number and asked Brandon and Darrin to get started using the prioritized backlog and to let me know every so often how much budget they had left. (Since they invoiced by the hour, they would have a fairly good idea of where they were.) Brandon and Darrin figured the easiest approach would be to indicate how many hours they ended up spending on each item, and I added a calculation to keep a running total of how much they had spent. Using this approach, anytime a feature was completed we could all tell whether we could "afford" to pick up another item. As it worked out, we were able to get halfway through the B list.

As I was preparing the backlog, I found that I needed to produce some new documentation. Specifically, I created a matrix of which actions should generate notifications and which roles were allowed to add, edit, view, or delete specific pieces of information. This helped me to ensure that functions were working correctly, but based on questions from this year's program team, I realized that others would find this useful as well.

I also still needed to document concise instructions for the program team. As much as possible, we made the submission system intuitive enough that instructions were not necessary, or were available within the system already. But there is a new conference chair every year, and many of our "intuitive" features aren't as obvious to the new chairs. In several cases when a conference chair asks for a specific change, I ask what he or she is trying to accomplish, and then show how the submission system already provides that capability. This pointed to the need not only for documentation for the people maintaining the system, but also for a bit more instruction for those using it.

Yes, I know you are saying, "Well, duh, Kent," but I bring that up to emphasize that documentation certainly has its place, as long as it is documentation with a specific purpose and it is created specifically to fulfill that purpose. We did not need to create a great deal of requirements documents for use during discovery and delivery, but we do find some system documentation (Chapter 15) helpful to support future development.

Lessons Learned

The submission system experience, although relatively simple compared to other projects I've been involved with, continues to provide a lot of great opportunities to learn about good and not-so-good project approaches. This project team enjoys a short duration; a small team of engaged, skilled people; and a fairly clear idea of what we're trying to accomplish. If anything, the experience has helped me to see that context is important not only when expanding processes to deal with complex projects, but also for stripping out all but the bare essentials when dealing with simpler ones. Following are some of the lessons I have learned, so far, from this experience.

The more trust and transparency that exist on a team, the less need there is for process and project documentation. I have never met Darrin in person, and during the past two years I spoke to Brandon in person only a handful of times. Yet we were able to keep **project documentation** to a minimum because we trusted each other and our ability to sufficiently convey our thoughts using email or other means. We weren't interested in justifying our position, or covering our assets; instead, we focused on building a useful submission system.

In some cases, even the minimal practices suggested by Scrum can be overkill. As I mentioned earlier, we did not approach this project with structured sprints. It was much more of a flow approach, primarily because the rituals of planning meetings, daily standups, and demos were unnecessary overhead. Once we settled on an approach (quite organically, as it turned out), we got into a nice rhythm. Darrin or Brandon would pull something off the list, set it up in the repository, and if any questions came up we communicated via the repository so answers were recorded in-line with the issue itself. They let me know when something was ready to check out, and we didn't have to wait for a specific demo for me to try out functionality or tell them if it was what we needed. (That's not to say that I didn't occasionally look at a bunch of changes all at one time, but that was my choice based on how I organized my work, not on any particular team ritual.) Find the techniques that work best for your team and get rid of the rest. Context is king. If your team is much larger than five to nine people, first figure out if you really need that many people, then realize that with more people come more communication channels and a greater need for daily coordination and additional technology to aid collaboration.

Automated testing is invaluable. When I compare this submission system to the previous one, the difference is like night and day. I was working with a different team on the previous submission system, but I don't attribute the difference to them; they were also great to work with. The main difference is that the new submission system was built on top of a suite of automated tests, and I was able to establish a great deal of trust and comfort that when a change was made, it would work. I found myself doing a lot less double-checking than I had before, and what testing I did do was either to understand how the new system worked, or to check out very unique situations.

One potential downside of automated testing is that it is very easy for the people reviewing the system functionality to get a little lazy. Once I got comfortable with the new system, I got a little lax reviewing various pieces of functionality and probably did not anticipate as many infrequent but important scenarios as I could have. As I said before, when we ran into problems, it wasn't because the submission system wasn't working, it was because the product owner wasn't working. I attribute this primarily to being a part-time product owner for the submission system. It is one thing I do on the side, in addition to my day job. It does not warrant being full-time, but I suspect if I were focused entirely on the submission system, I would be a lot more attentive to those types of things.

Let your approach dictate the tools you use, not vice versa. One question I get asked quite frequently is what tools teams should use. My first suggestion is usually to irreverently hold up a marker and a pad of sticky notes. More seriously, I tell teams to use whatever tools they currently have. I have seen too many teams adopt a tool first and then design a very inefficient process based on the dictates of the tool. In the case of the submission system, we first used Google Docs simply because it was free, and it worked for a distributed group of people. Fairly early on we switched to using the issue functionality in the repository because it allowed Darrin and Brandon to work in one place, and it provided us with all the functionality we needed (which was not much). Again, this approach will not work for everyone, but it worked in our particular situation, and that, frankly, is all that really matters.

Working as a distributed team is not all bad in certain circumstances. Brandon, Darrin, and I have never all met face-to-face. Yet we all live near the same town. Doesn't that go against the whole ideal of agile? Not really. We were able to make it work because email and communication via the repository worked just fine for us. We were all mature and were able to communicate properly using those means. The few times we were dealing with a complex problem, Brandon and I would jump on the phone and chat, or meet for lunch somewhere. It also helped that we were not spread across multiple time zones, but even that was not too critical in this instance because there weren't that many things that required a lot of in-depth synchronous collaboration. It also helped that Brandon had a good understanding of the process in general and was very clear on what we were trying to accomplish. The only time he and I had to discuss specifics was when I was making a change to the process going forward, or we were trying to address issues that previous program teams had. Again, this will not be the case for many projects. But one lesson I can take from this experience is that building shared purpose and understanding at the beginning of the project can make distributed collaboration go much, much more smoothly.

Use budgeting instead of estimating. Treat time and money as design constraints similar to the number of users a site needs to support. You establish these constraints and then let the team determine the viable solutions or tell you that it's not possible to drive the outcome within the stated constraints. As I mentioned earlier, this allows for much more productive conversations when you are trying to decide which features to produce, and it keeps the conversation away from how low you can go to estimation limbo.

Chapter 8

Case Study: Commission System

Introduction

McMillan Insurance is a midsize health insurance company located in a midsize city in the middle of the United States. McMillan has grown through acquisition, and until recently one of its practices was to let each company keep its own identity when dealing with anyone outside the walls of headquarters. This included the relationships with independent agents and the resulting commission structures. This meant that Arthur, the manager of the commissions area, had to deal with a slew of different very unique commission rules down to the individual agent level, and the resulting hodgepodge of commission "systems" required to administer those different commission plans. McMillan has finished its acquisition binge and now realizes that some commonality needs to be introduced in many areas, including commissions.

Arthur was charged with making the commissions area more efficient, so his first instinct was to find a new commission system that would allow him to administer all the various commission plans in one place, while still maintaining all the unique commission structures. He sat down with a couple of more experienced members of his staff, and they started scouring the Internet for possible products. A quick search revealed several options. (Of course, this should have been obvious just from the seven different software applications McMillan had inherited from the acquired companies, only one of which was built in-house.)

It was at this point that they reached out to IT for some help figuring out what to do. Arthur was a little hesitant to do that at first because he was concerned that IT would want to build something in-house. He was pleasantly surprised when Heather, a business analyst from IT on the team, suggested that instead of immediately going out and looking for specific products they should step back and think about what need they were trying to satisfy. Heather and Arthur sat down to discuss the current situation and what Arthur hoped to accomplish.

The Need

As a result of their conversation, Arthur and Heather identified the following objectives:

- Reduce the time it takes to produce commission payments from one week to two days.

- Reduce the time required to set up a new commission plan from six weeks to one week (needed every time a new product is created).

- Reduce the time required to set up a new agent from one day to one hour.

They then discussed the characteristics of a desirable solution. As they were talking, Heather used the Purpose-Based Alignment Model (Chapter 12) to identify commissions as a **parity activity**, and Arthur realized that trying to have unique commission rules for every agent was, in effect, overinvesting in commissions. Data from the existing commission payments indicated that the unique rules did not have a direct impact on what the agents sold, so they were probably not worth the effort that Arthur's area spent in creating and administering them. Arthur made a note to talk to the sales managers about reducing the complexity of the commission rules.

At this point a team was formed that included Arthur and some of the more experienced members of his staff as well as Heather and a few others from IT. Arthur and Heather described the objectives they had put together and then worked with the team to create decision filters for the project, to make sure everyone was on the same page.

Here are the decision filters they came up with:

- Will this reduce the cycle time for commission payments?

- Will this help us set up a commission plan faster?

- Will this help us set up a new agent faster?

The Possible Solution(s)

Once the team had a good understanding of what they were trying to accomplish, they decided they needed to identify options for realizing those objectives, starting with reducing the time required for commission payments. They used

Table 8.1 *Desired Characteristics of New Commission Software*

Characteristic	Required/ Optional
Accept inputs from multiple policy systems to determine commissions.	Required
Create unique commission rules for each individual agent.	Required
Support multiple hierarchies: some sales channels are organized based on product, others are based on geography, some are based on both product and geography.	Required
Allow for adjustments to occur in the calculated commission rules.	Required
Allow for manual determination of commission payments.	Required
Create unique commission rules based on free-form attributes and specific values of those attributes.	Optional
Support multiple commission rules unique to the individual, unique to the policy.	Optional

impact mapping (Chapter 14) to help them identify options. Several options came up, including simplifying the commission rules and consolidating the multiple commission systems into one. The team also identified multiple options for dealing with the existing systems:

- Build something in-house.
- Revise the existing conglomerate.
- Purchase something.
- Outsource all commissions activity.
- Do nothing.

The team decided that the best route was to start with simplifying the rules for commissions in one of the acquired companies to see if there was any impact on sales. At the same time, they started the search for software to replace all of the existing commission systems. Table 8.1 lists the characteristics that served as criteria for the search.

The team included the optional characteristics as a way of seeing if any commonly used applications used complex rule logic, in case they found data to support the need for unique commission rules.

The Deliveries of Value

The team split the work into a series of rounds. (They chose that term instead of *releases*, because not every round involved deploying software.) They weren't

Table 8.2 *Rounds of Work*

Round	Contents
1	• Simplify the commission rules for Southern Comfort Insurance (SCI).
	• Identify a commission system to purchase.
2	• Implement a commission system in-house.
	• Use the commission system for McMillan agents (who already had straightforward commission rules).
	• Simplify the commission rules for Western Amalgamated Insurance (WAI).
3	• Use the new commission system for SCI.
	• Phase out the existing commission system for SCI.
	• Simplify the commission rules for Eastern Agrarian Insurance (EAI).
4–N	• Roll out the commission system to the remaining units.
	• Simplify the commission rules for the remaining units.
	• Phase out the existing commission systems.

sure how many rounds they would have at the beginning, but they knew they would be organized along the lines shown in Table 8.2.

The team figured that after the first couple of rounds they would simplify rules and move the units to the new commission system at the same time. They staggered the first few so that they could isolate the changes and get a sense of what impact those changes had on sales.

Lessons Learned

The effort is still going on at the time of this writing, but the team has already learned several lessons:

Not all problems require a technical solution. The team found that simplifying the commission rules helped reduce the amount of time required to process commissions a great deal and confirmed their suspicions that unique rules did not have a large impact on sales agent behavior. Even so, the team decided it would be good to consolidate all the processing on a single system.

You may not realize how good you have it on your side of the fence. As the team started their search for a new commission system, they decided to include the five purchased systems they were already using to administer parts of their commissions. They found that as a result of simplifying commission rules, one of the systems they already had fit the bill nicely for what they were trying to do. They had to upgrade that commission system several versions, but once they did, they found that their work mainly consisted of creating new interfaces for any data they didn't have in that system already.

Commercial off-the-shelf (COTS) systems often contain good industry practices. When the team picked the commission system, they found they could use that unit's commission process for all the other units as well. That process was one suggested by the developers of the existing commission system. Switching to that process for all the units provided even more improvement in overall commissions processing and eased the transition effort since the team didn't have to come up with new processes for each unit.

Don't forget change management. Just because the team didn't have to come up with new processes didn't make the change completely turnkey. The commissions team did not have much trouble with the change, since over half of the team was involved on the project to switch commission systems, but they had a bit of change management to do with the agents. When they found out that commission structures were changing, most of the agents complained. Loudly. The team found that the best way to help the agents adapt to the change was to give them examples of their own commissions under both the old and the new structures. Most of the agents found that their commissions would stay consistent, or even increase. The only agents whose commissions decreased were those few who had studied the old plans enough to use loopholes to maximize their revenue. These agents were among the highest compensated but were only middle of the pack in terms of actual sales.

Don't overlook interdependencies with other efforts. The team originally thought they would have to do a lot of work to interface with a new set of systems for each unit they brought onto the new commission system. Shortly into the project, the team caught wind that the accounting and new business systems were also undergoing projects to make things more uniform. The commissions team got together with the other two teams and synced their rollout plans so they affected the same units in the same order, though not necessarily at the same time. That meant that the commissions team did not have to build new interfaces for every additional unit; they just had to revise the ones they had already built.

Chapter 9

Case Study: Data Warehouse

Introduction

Data warehousing and business intelligence projects provide some interesting challenges to teams adopting agile approaches, such as large data sets, complex integrations, and the thought that you need all the data for any of it to be useful. This case study aims to provide some insight into how you might approach the analysis effort for such a project.

McMillan Insurance, introduced in Chapter 8, is a member of an association of loosely affiliated health insurance companies that have established agreements to process claims for each other's members when they are not in their home areas. For example, if Tricia lives in New York and gets sick while visiting Kansas City, she can visit a doctor there and still be covered as if she had visited a doctor in New York. (One of my reviewers from outside the United States thought it was important to note that this is a specific characteristic of the U.S. health care system and may be interpreted as another sign of how messed up U.S. health care appears to Europeans.)

The Need

The health plans in the association transfer claim and membership information to each other using the Interplan Claim System (ICS) created and maintained by the association. The association uses data from ICS to calculate a set of 30 performance metrics, which it uses to gauge how each of the plans performs, and to identify opportunities for improvement in interplan communication. The claims processing department at McMillan Insurance has been struggling with their performance on several of the metrics and is facing the possibility of fines if they do not improve their performance soon.

The claims processing department realized that the updates they get on the performance metrics—monthly reports printed from their instance of ICS—are not frequent enough for them to proactively manage their work. They decided that if they could get the data from ICS on a more frequent basis, they would be able to assess the performance metrics on a daily basis and plan their work accordingly. If they could see how they were doing on the metrics from one day to the next, they could get quicker feedback on how their actions impacted claims processing cycle times.

As a result, McMillan started a project to get updated ICS data on a daily basis and calculate the performance metrics daily. As the team discussed the initial scope of the project, they realized they might have to associate the claims information from ICS with information in their own claims processing system. Their claims processing system is affectionately known as EDDIE, although no one knows what EDDIE stands for now, if it ever stood for anything.

Getting the project approved was anything but easy. There were plenty of other projects competing for the limited funding available, and since McMillan Insurance didn't subscribe to a "fund it and it will get built somehow" approach to portfolio management, they had to find a time when this project was deemed important enough to supersede several other projects vying for funds. A complicating factor was the project's lack of any financial objectives with a clear tie to improvement in the bottom line (apart from avoiding fees from the association). By the time the project was finally approved, the need was acute.

Even though the portfolio management process did not require specific objectives other than impact to the McMillan Insurance bottom line, the team decided they needed some clear objectives in order to gauge whether they were heading in the right direction. Luckily, the nature of the project presented a prime candidate for objectives: the performance metrics. The 30 performance metrics were aggregated into a composite score that added up to 100, so on a monthly basis the team could see any impacts to McMillan's overall score and plan future work accordingly. Although a stated aim of the project was to calculate the performance metrics on a daily basis, the real measure of success was what the metrics actually showed.

The Possible Solution(s)

The team decided that they couldn't afford to wait to get all 30 performance metrics completed before they rolled out the new data. They had to get something up and running for the claims processing team as soon as they could. Fortunately the performance metrics built on one another; the first five metrics on the list were fundamental items that were needed for determining the following metrics and would provide a good basis for the claims processing unit to get started. The team decided that they would organize their releases around groups of the performance metrics. The first five metrics were included in the first release, the next ten were in the next release, and the final 15 were in the final release.

In addition to functionality necessary to calculate the performance metrics, the team decided to expose the data elements used to calculate those performance metrics in an ad hoc reporting environment so that the claims processing area could identify the claims that were impacting the performance metrics and make sure they were making their way through the process. This way, not only could the claims administration area see what the performance metrics were, but they could also see the specific claims that were causing less-than-desirable scores.

Since the performance metrics were based on ICS data, in order to make the individual claim data really helpful, they needed to associate the claim records in ICS with the claim records from EDDIE. The good news was that EDDIE claims data was already in the data warehouse. The bad news was that it was spread out over several different collections. One collection represented the claims that were still being processed, cleverly labeled "In Process" claims. Once claims were finished processing, the information about those claims was stored in two collections—a "Completed" collection, which contained all the processing information about the claim, and an "AU" collection (sometimes referred to as the "Heart of Gold"), which contained several additional data elements calculated for the actuarial and underwriting area.

The team figured that they would eventually have to associate ICS data with all three of the collections. It seemed infinitely improbable that the actuarial and underwriting area would ever have any reason to use it, but they would ask for it anyway because that was how they rolled. Regardless, the team knew that for the first release it was most important to link ICS data only to the In Process claims collection because that would provide the most useful information.

The Deliveries of Value

So the team had a good handle on what their releases needed to look like, roughly speaking. They identified three releases and a set of decision filters for each release, as shown in Figure 9.1.

These decision filters provided the team with quick, clear ways to determine whether to work on particular features and also to identify how much architectural work they needed to do. There were aspects of the architecture implied in the various releases that were not explicitly called out in the decision filters. The biggest piece of this was in Release 1, which would involve considerable work to read ICS data and get it into a usable format.

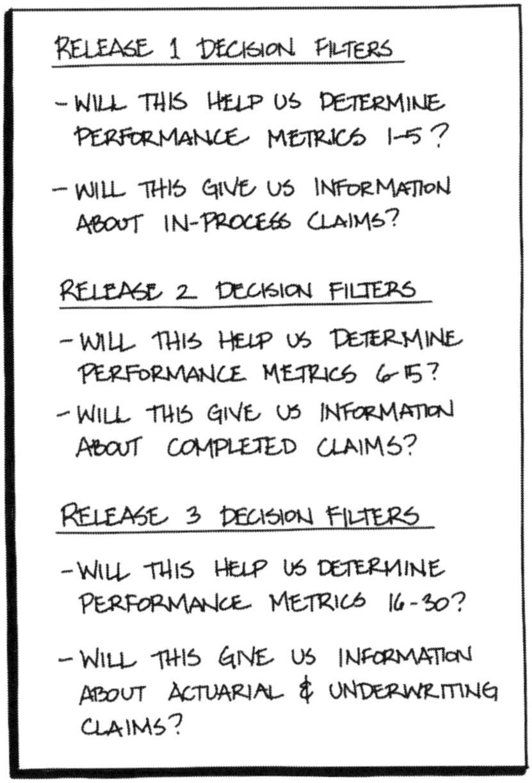

Figure 9.1 *Data warehouse release decision filters*

Because the team wanted to avoid unnecessary entanglements with outside organizations, they decided to intercept the files that were sent to McMillan's instance of ICS. While this seemed like a good way to avoid all that tedious mucking about with an outside entity, the team realized once they dug into the files that the data was not being transmitted in a terribly friendly format.

Since ICS was a mainframe system, the data was transmitted in a set of fixed-length text files where the first few characters of each record indicated what kind of record it was and thus determined the layout of the rest of the record. The data was organized into four main types of records called formats:

- Submission Format (SF)

- Disbursement Format (DF)

- Reconciliation Format (RF)

- Notification Format (NF)

As a claim progressed through the lifecycle from one plan to the next, it would gradually collect first an SF, then a DF, then an RF, and potentially multiple NF formats. On top of that, the information for each format for a claim was broken into multiple records (SF05, SF10, etc.) with specific pieces of data showing up on specific record types.

The first challenge, which was pretty uncomplicated, was to be able to identify a particular record. That was simply a matter of reading the first few characters of each line to determine what claim the information corresponded to and what particular record type the line was. Easy.

The hard part was associating all of a given claim's multiple lines. For the SF, DF, and RF formats this was not too challenging, since a claim would have only one SF format, one DF format, and one RF format. The NF formats weren't so accommodating since any given claim could have multiple NF formats, and there was some fairly complicated procedural logic that occurred to link the NF format data up with the right claim.

The team initially hoped that they didn't need to worry about the NFs right away, but a couple of the performance metrics they had identified dealt with NF data, and there were pieces of information in the NF format that were necessary for tying an ICS claim to an In Process claim from EDDIE.

Luckily, the ICS team for the association did a good job of documenting the information about ICS and keeping it up-to-date. Unluckily, at least for the ICS 2 DW team, the association did not think it necessary to share the logic used to tie the various formats together. To do that, the team had to reverse-engineer the COBOL code used by their instance of the ICS system to read in the data files.

Several of the first few iterations became exercises in trial and error and pair development, where the analyst who had tried to sift through the COBOL code (learning how to read COBOL in the process) sat down with a developer who was working on the Extract-Transform-Load (ETL) code. Most of the work was easy enough until the team hit the NF formats. This is where the trial and error really began and where the pair development was the most effective. The analyst had written up the rules that he thought were relevant, but the developer found it much more helpful to have the analyst sit with him as he tried several variations on rules to see which ones worked. It took several trials to get a process that seemed to work, an effort slowed by the processing time required every time they tried a different version of code. By the time they were done, they referred to the code as the "duct tape module" because it had the feeling of very fragile code that would cause great problems if anyone ever touched it and broke it. This was definitely a pile of technical debt, but they decided to live with it for the moment so they could move on to getting some useful data to their stakeholders.

Upon later reflection, the team felt they would have been much more effective if they'd had a set of examples to use along with their development efforts.

The demos in these early iterations felt a bit anticlimactic, because they weren't able to show a lot of meaningful reports. Instead, it was often, "Well, we figured out how to identify the various SF records. See, here's an input file, and here's the resulting output." But it was a start.

Next the team had to start extracting data from the various formats and saving the key pieces of information they needed to calculate the performance metrics and make meaningful comparisons for the same claim in the EDDIE data. A big reason the team chose to do only a few performance metrics is so they would not have to extract all the data in the records at once. At first blush this wouldn't seem like a big deal once they figured out how to identify the record. But the fact that the files were written in EBCDIC made it much more challenging than it otherwise might have been. The team decided that the best path was to extract only the data elements needed for the features they were working on and leave the rest of the data in what amounted to a holding area until it was needed.

The team organized their work for the first release as shown in Table 9.1. They decided based on the nature of the ETL challenges that they could get some value from being able to even read the data.

Table 9.1 *First Release Backlog*

Feature	User Stories
Read ICS data	• Read SF data (broken down into a story for every associated record type that contains data needed for performance metrics 1–5)
	• Read DF data (broken down into a story for every associated record type that contains data needed for performance metrics 1–5)
	• Read RF data (broken down into a story for every associated record type that contains data needed for performance metrics 1–5)
	• Read NF data (broken down into a story for every associated record type that contains data needed for performance metrics 1–5)
	• Link format data (the goal being to associate information for the same claim together)
Performance metrics	• Performance metric 1
	• Performance metric 2
	• Performance metric 3
	• Performance metric 4
	• Performance metric 5
	Note: Some of these stories were broken into smaller bits when getting the appropriate data and calculating the metric proved too large for a single story. The first place the team looked to break things down was a story to get the data and a separate story to do the calculation.
Link ICS claims to In Process claims	• Associate ICS claim to In Process claim
	• Various stories to add additional pieces of information

This collection of stories changed quite a bit during the course of the release as the stakeholders identified pieces of data from either ICS or EDDIE that would be helpful for answering specific questions and as they got a chance to view the data as it was forming and starting to identify how they would use it.

The team did not bother to break the second and third releases down too much while they worked on the first release, but they at least identified the key features they thought would be in each release, as shown in Table 9.2.

The team did not specifically know what, if any, items would be included in the expanded In Process claims and expanded Completed claims when they created these features, but they figured it was good to have placeholders, if for no other reason than to reassure their stakeholders that they didn't have to get every piece of information for In Process claims in the first release and could safely decide to postpone delivery of some items.

While it was very tempting to have the stories specifically call out the data elements being added, and the team actually started out that way, they quickly found that they had difficulty prioritizing the stories because they didn't know the context in which the elements were being used. Their coach suggested that they try expressing the stories in terms of the questions their stakeholders were trying to answer or decisions they were trying to make. This provided a bit more context that at least made the prioritization discussions with their stake-holders more meaningful. They were able to focus on which questions were asked most often, or if there were questions that needed to be answered before other questions could be answered.

As the team finished the first release, they began refining the features for the second one, focusing primarily on the second set of performance metrics. At that time, the team thought they could establish the connection between ICS and Completed claims in order to support the few questions that required that type of information. Unfortunately Completed claims were useful only if historical information about the claims was available. This involved more complicated processing than In Process claims, which required only a point-in-time

Table 9.2 *Features in Subsequent Releases*

Release	Features
Second	Performance metrics 6–15
	Expanded In Process claims
	Completed claims
Third	Performance metrics 16–30
	AU claims
	Expanded In Process claims
	Expanded Completed claims

view of the data. This discussion led the team to realize that while they knew there was some need for Completed claims information, they weren't confident about how much need there was, so the team decided that they would do the work necessary to build a history of the ICS data and connect it with Completed claims but not expose a great deal of historical information for reporting until they had a handle on what needs might really be out there.

The team was able to satisfy all the information needs related to In Process claims, so they decided not to include the expanded In Process claims feature in the second release. When they made that decision, they also discussed that it would have been nice to be able to release the In Process/ICS link earlier than other parts of the first release because they realized that the best way to identify further needs for In Process–focused claims was to give people a chance to use the available data. Think of it as a case of you don't know what else you need until you have it.

The team liked the idea of waiting to see what was needed based on actual experience, but they hated that they had to wait so long to see. The first release took only four months, but it still seemed too long once they realized how much information they could get from stakeholder reactions to that release. The team decided that in the future they would try to decrease the time between releases so they could get that needs information sooner.

Decreasing the time between releases seemed like a good idea until they ran through their first build of historical data at the beginning of work on the second release. They had to run the process on the weekend to ensure that they had sufficient processing bandwidth on the test machine and wouldn't interfere with work that other teams were doing. It took an entire weekend to process the files. What was worse, this first run required quite a bit of babysitting. If every release required that level of processing, more frequent releases didn't seem like such a great idea after all.

One of the team members joked that at least if they had to do it over and over again, they'd get really good at it. There was wisdom in that wisecrack. There is a saying in some parts of the agile community: "If doing something is hard, do it more often." That seems counterintuitive, but when actions like releasing are done sporadically, a lot of difficult manual approaches can be acceptable because the team figures they won't have to do them very often. If that task becomes more frequent, the practice you get from repeating it more than a couple of times a year will make it easier. You also can't help but find refinements that make the process easier—sometimes dramatically so.

As the team discussed the situation, they realized that a lot of the babysitting activity came from manually kicking off processes or validating results. It made sense initially because they wanted to get the historical data processed as soon as they could during the second release, and automating processes would have delayed the processing. Once they realized they would like to be able to do historical loads frequently, "their laziness spurred them to action," as one team member said. In addition to automating the historical processing scripts, they split things up so they could run only selected parts. This came in handy if they had recently run a historical load and then decided to add a couple more fields. Both of these steps saved a lot of time in the long run and gave the team a great deal more flexibility and responsiveness to stakeholder requests.

Once the stakeholders began using the joint ICS and In Process claims data, they started identifying a lot of potential new questions they needed to answer. The claims department realized they could now investigate cases where the data on an incoming ICS claim did not match the data in EDDIE. In some cases, long-standing, undocumented, nearly forgotten business rules indicated which ICS fields would be loaded into the claim record on EDDIE and occasionally were used to transform the data before loading it. In other cases, data was changed in ICS by claims administrators somewhere in the process. Having the information from ICS and EDDIE side by side was invaluable for tracking these items down and identifying what corrective actions were necessary.

Some stakeholders also realized that the performance metrics themselves were not nearly as important as the information used to calculate them. The performance metrics told the stakeholders that there was a problem, but the detailed information was more helpful in identifying the specific claims that were causing the problem. Once the stakeholders figured out queries to identify the problematic claims, the performance metrics themselves became much less important.

In fact, halfway through the second release the stakeholders and the team sat down and talked through the calculations for each of the remaining performance metrics. They decided to forgo building the automated capability to calculate the last remaining performance metrics, preferring instead to expose the data used to calculate the performance metrics and using their understanding of how the metrics were calculated to identify troublesome claims. In most cases, the performance metrics were some measure of cycle time, so once claims that were increasing cycle time were identified, the claims administration staff could prioritize them. At that point, seeing the performance metrics on a monthly basis was sufficient, because the claims administration area was fairly confident that they had addressed the key problems.

It was also around this time that the stakeholders decided that they did not have to tie the ICS information to AU claims after all. It turned out that ICS did not provide any meaningful information for actuarial and underwriting purposes. The ICS data proved to be very helpful for operational purposes (primarily In Process) and for some historical investigation of processing and trends that could be done using the completed claims and didn't require the cleansed data contained in AU claims.

Lessons Learned

Sometimes a project can produce changes that can get the organization close to the desired result, but other changes have to occur for the organization to get all of the way there. In this particular case, the real value was derived not from being able to see the metrics on a daily basis, but from the ability to associate ICS data and EDDIE data to reprioritize claims. Luckily, the team picked an objective that would point them in that direction, and once they realized which features were providing benefits, they altered their approach to focus on features that helped smooth the association of data. Eventually, they even chose not to build the last five performance metrics and not associate the new data with the AU claims.

The value realized here is a value often proposed for using an agile approach—responding to changing requirements. This example proves the point that while changing requirements often introduce new things, they can at the same time make some of the original requirements irrelevant.

This project team also learned the value of learning. Shortly after the first release, the team realized that by paying attention to how their stakeholders were using what they delivered, they could alter their plans to deliver only what their stakeholders found helpful. This also meant that they did not need to deliver other features that were no longer needed.

Chapter 10

Case Study: Student Information System

Introduction

IT projects are not limited to organizations with IT departments. They also exist in small nonprofits such as Deep Thought Academy—a small, nonprofit, private school. Deep Thought Academy enrolls children from preschool through eighth grade and boasts small class sizes that allow personalized instruction for all students. This case study describes how Deep Thought Academy sought to use a purchased product to help them address issues they had with enrollment and communication.

The Need

The school tries to keep the students up-to-date with respect to technology, including a curriculum that relies heavily on the use of laptops and tablets. The technology used for the running of the school, as in most nonprofits, seemed to lag a little bit. Every year parents had to fill out the same forms to provide enrollment information, often providing the same information every year. Payment of enrollment fees was handled through the normal invoicing process, which included invoices generated as PDF files sent out by the school's bookkeeper and emailed to the parents. The parents then had to send back a check, arrange for automatic withdrawals from their checking account, or make automatic payments by credit card.

The yearly enrollment process was paper based, and it was a pain. In addition to the repetitive but necessary address updates for the students and their parents (with all the complications that modern families present in the form of divorces, remarriages, etc.), the school had to collect state-required health information about the students and information about extra services the families might require such as before-school care, after-school care, and hot lunch.

The information came into the school office handwritten on paper forms, so it took a while to transfer all of the key information to a format that could be easily accessed when it was needed. Filling out the forms was time-consuming for families, and processing the forms was time-consuming for the staff.

The school administration had gradually adopted email to communicate with families, and all teachers had email accounts as well as technology at the school with which to access them. Communication between parents and teachers was not hampered as much by technology as it was by the use habits of parents and teachers.

Keeping the online directory up-to-date was a little bit of a challenge, but families usually found a way to keep the pertinent contact information current.

The school tended to have several events during the year. Most were set at the beginning of the school year, but some sprang up throughout the course of the year. The staff usually provided email reminders of upcoming events through the weekly newsletter and signs at the school where parents picked up their children.

While the board was deciding what to do about their enrollment process and communication, the school was undergoing a major facilities upgrade. A few years previously, the school board at the time had decided to expand the school by enrolling two classes per grade. (Up to that point there was only one class per grade, with an average of 15 students per class.) They started with kindergarten, and as that class proceeded through the elementary years, a second class was added to each grade.

This progression worked fairly well for a few years, but about the same time as discussions were going on about the enrollment process, the board realized that they would run out of classroom space in their current leased building. The only way to make more space available was to either move to a new building or add on. Everyone in the school liked the current pastoral setting, so they preferred to add onto the existing building. This endeavor would require a large capital investment that meant extensive fundraising and would also add to operating expenses.

So of all these things, the one that was not served terribly well was enrollment, something that happened once a year and was a mild irritant. In isolation, a solution to automate this process would probably be helpful, but it couldn't be too expensive because it did not add a tremendous amount of benefit. Nor was it something that was going to go a long way toward increasing enrollment at the school—another important consideration given the drive to add onto the school and the corresponding need to fill all the classes that were being created from one year to the next.

To put this in perspective, the board and staff of the Deep Thought Academy should consider their organization through the lens of the Purpose-Based

Alignment Model (see Chapter 12). A Purpose-Based Alignment Model for the Deep Thought Academy would look something like Figure 10.1.

This model indicates that all the activities described previously are parity activities. They are important for Deep Thought Academy to do, but only as well as their competitors. In this case, their competitors are other public and private schools competing to attract the same students. Having a really great enrollment process generally will not attract new students, but having a really awful enrollment process might encourage families to look elsewhere. An effort to improve things that are parity activities is warranted only when there is a gap with other players in the market; and even then, you are only looking to close the gap.

So Deep Thought Academy's first decision is whether they have gaps in the activities of parent-teacher communication, enrollment, and school directories. The gaps could be that those activities are not occurring at all—not the case here—or the activities as they are occurring are painful—which is probably the case for enrollment but not the other items.

If the board feels it is important to address that gap in the enrollment process and not necessarily the others, they should favor solutions that do enrollment fairly well, as long as that capacity is not exceedingly high-priced.

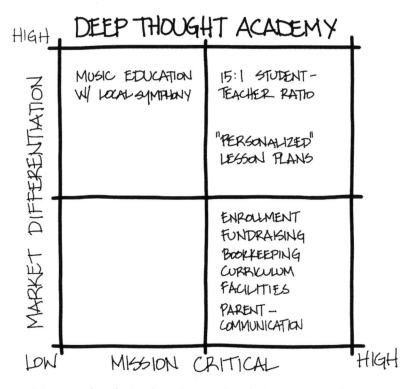

Figure 10.1 *Deep Thought Academy Purpose-Based Alignment Model*

The school administrators also tried many different ways to keep parents up-to-date and help them connect with the teachers and each other. Mostly, they found themselves reverting to handing out very helpful notebooks called *The Parent's Guide to Deep Thought Academy*, or "The Guide" for short, and then providing paper updates from one year to the next. Naturally, the update included a school directory that was out of date shortly after it was printed and handed out.

The school board and school administrators decided that they wanted to find a technology solution that would help them automate the enrollment process and improve the communication among parents, faculty, and staff.

The Possible Solution(s)

Because Deep Thought Academy did not have an internal IT department, they decided that the only viable way to provide enrollment and communication capabilities was to purchase a system. They started the search for a student information system (inevitably abbreviated as "SIS") that could streamline the enrollment process and keep families informed about school activities on a regular basis. The school board's director of technology put together the following RFP for a student information system:

Background of School

Deep Thought Academy is a nonprofit education community for preschool through eighth grade.

Purpose

Deep Thought Academy is currently in search of a "student information system" that is Web/software as a service (SaaS) based. The software will be used to manage student and parent data, enable interactive communication between teachers and parents, and handle online enrollments. The software needs to fulfill all functional requirements as described in the section titled "Functional Requirements." The purpose of this document is to describe the requirements of such software and request pricing information.

Infrastructure

The software needs to be hosted by the vendor and offered as a service accessible through any modern Web browser (IE/Safari/Firefox/Chrome). The vendor must have a redundant architecture with fail-safe processes and mechanisms in place such that

- The data hosted on the system is backed up daily and archived remotely.
- The Web-based software is hosted over multiple load-balanced servers and/ or on a cloud-based architecture such as Amazon AWS.
- SSL connection should be provided where sensitive information is being transferred over the Internet.

Audience

The users of the system will be parents and staff members. We currently have 190 students enrolled and 20 staff members.

Functional Requirements

1. **Authentication, Roles, and Permissions**

    The system must authenticate the user and allow for flexible roles and permissions allocation of various parts of the system (e.g., a parent may not update the information of another parent).

2. **Student/Parent Directory**

    The student and parent directory is a searchable database that allows parents to browse by grade. Parents may choose to

    a. Update their contact information such as their address, phone numbers, and email addresses.

    b. Mark their information as private such that only school staff members may view it.

    c. Export the directory to CSV, Excel, or PDF based on criteria such as classroom.

3. **Staff Directory**

    Staff and parents should be able to search by name, or browse the directory by grade and job function.

4. **Calendar**

    The system must allow for the creation of multiple calendars (i.e., a calendar for each classroom). Each calendar needs to have permissions support such that only specific staff member(s) and/or parent(s) may update or edit its events. Last, it must support the standard format of iCalendar/iCal such that staff members and parents may subscribe to the calendar using their preferred calendaring software.

5. **Online Enrollment**

    The system must allow for online enrollment. It must support the acceptance of credit card and/or ACH transactions via an SSL connection. QuickBooks integration is preferred but not required. In the event that the system does not have QuickBooks integration, online enrollment data must be exportable to CSV or Excel format.

6. **Parent/Classroom Portal**

    Teachers for each classroom have access to a parent portal for posting classroom information and notes. Parents must have access to this portal upon authentication. It is preferable but not required that there be a forum format for parents and teachers to communicate, interact, and share ideas.

The director of technology distributed the RFP to the other board members for comments and then sent it to a variety of suppliers of these types of systems. Some board members asked whether it made sense to take on adding a SIS at the same time that they were trying to raise millions of dollars for a facility addition. Other board members pointed out that most of the student information systems on the market were subscription based—typically a certain fee per month per user—so the cost addition would be operational in nature. The school might even see some savings (though certainly not enough to counteract the cost of the SIS) through reduced staff time dealing with enrollment and communications.

The board also discussed how the decision would be made about which student information system to use. (These board members already assumed it was going to happen and were mostly focused on which solution would be used.) They asked if there were certain features that were more important than others. The director of technology commented that all the systems they were looking at already had most of these features so it would probably come down to a matter of cost.

Let's assume the board at Deep Thought Academy does determine that getting a SIS makes sense. Let's examine their RFP to find opportunities for improvement and locate potential problems they could run into with their current version.

Purpose

Deep Thought Academy is currently in search of a "student information system" that is Web/software as a service (SaaS) based. The software will be used to manage student and parent data, enable interactive communication between teachers and parents, and handle online enrollments. The software needs to fulfill all functional requirements as described in the section titled "Functional Requirements." The purpose of this document is to describe the requirements of such software and request pricing information.

The purpose falls into a common trap of documents initially describing a project: they jump all over describing the solution without fully explaining the problem. Granted, most vendors love this particular approach, especially if the RFP was written with their product in mind. But it does a disservice to Deep Thought Academy, because it narrows down their options. For some written RFPs, this is intentional. The downside is that Deep Thought Academy may go down the route of buying a very expensive, all-encompassing solution when all they really need is a way to expedite the enrollment process.

The request for the solution to be Web/SaaS based at the core makes sense because the school does not really have a staffed IT department, but again, they are limiting their options. What they are really asking for here is a system that they do not have to maintain technically themselves. While Web/SaaS-based technologies are usually the way that capability is delivered, it's unnecessary to specify that. The RFP should specify what the school really needs.

The next paragraph in effect describes nonfunctional requirements, but again it's too specific:

Infrastructure

The software needs to be hosted by the vendor and offered as a service accessible through any modern Web browser (IE/Safari/Firefox/Chrome). The vendor must have a redundant architecture with fail-safe processes and mechanisms in place such that

- The data hosted on the system is backed up daily and archived remotely.
- The Web-based software is hosted over multiple load-balanced servers and/ or on a cloud-based architecture such as Amazon AWS.
- SSL connection should be provided where sensitive information is being transferred over the Internet.

Instead of being this specific, the RFP could say:

- Our audience typically uses Internet Explorer version 9 or above, Safari, or Chrome.
- We want the system to be secure.
- We want backups on a nightly basis.
- We want the system to be available 24 × 7 [with perhaps some stipulations about downtime for maintenance].

There are probably other missing conditions, such as how many total users and how many concurrent users the system must support. In reality, the performance requirements of this particular application should not be too taxing since the total population of users is fewer than 1,000 people. Also, while the functionality is important, it is most likely not mission critical in the same way that air traffic control systems are to an airport, so availability requirements need to be set accordingly.

Finally come the functional requirements:

Functional Requirements

1. **Authentication, Roles, and Permissions**

   The system must authenticate the user and allow for flexible roles and permissions allocation of various parts of the system (e.g., a parent may not update the information of another parent).

2. **Student/Parent Directory**

   The student and parent directory is a searchable database that allows parents to browse by grade. Parents may choose to

   a. Update their contact information such as their address, phone numbers, and email addresses.

   b. Mark their information as private such that only school staff members may view it.

   c. Export the directory to CSV, Excel, or PDF based on criteria such as classroom.

3. **Staff Directory**

   Staff and parents should be able to search by name, or browse the directory by grade and job function.

4. **Calendar**

   The system must allow for the creation of multiple calendars (i.e., a calendar for each classroom). Each calendar needs to have permissions support such that only specific staff member(s) and/or parent(s) may update or edit its events. Last, it must support the standard format of iCalendar/iCal such that staff members and parents may subscribe to the calendar using their preferred calendaring software.

5. **Online Enrollment**

   The system must allow for online enrollment. It must support the acceptance of credit card and/or ACH transactions via an SSL connection. QuickBooks integration is preferred but not required. In the event that the system does not have QuickBooks integration, online enrollment data must be exportable to CSV or Excel format.

6. **Parent/Classroom Portal**

   Teachers for each classroom have access to a parent portal for posting classroom information and notes. Parents must have access to this portal upon authentication. It is preferable but not required that there be a forum format for parents and teachers to communicate, interact, and share ideas.

These present a mixture of very specific requirements—which, again, reduce options—and more general requirements. At this point, the RFP should express things that the audience would like to accomplish in each of these cases and provide enough background information to allow the vendors to indicate how their product does or does not help the user accomplish those things. User stories can be very helpful to convey this type of information. In some cases, the user stories may need to be backed up with specifics, such as what pieces of information the school needs to collect for online enrollment, or what different classes of users there may be (I can foresee Teacher, Student, Parent, and School Administrator in this case).

Lessons Learned

Deep Thought Academy is still in the process of finding a SIS, but already it provides some great lessons learned in dealing with IT projects in a nonprofit, where you do not always have a fully staffed and skilled IT department and are often reliant on purchased solutions for most of your IT needs.

The Purpose-Based Alignment Model can be used for nonprofits. Differentiating activities in that case are things directly related to the nonprofit's mission. Deep Thought Academy's mission is to educate students. The Purpose-Based

Alignment Model may also tell them that if a solution that handles enrollment well also helps with personalized lesson planning, the bonus could put that particular solution over the top. Personalized lesson planning is a differentiator, meaning that if Deep Thought Academy does that particular activity well, they may just attract more students than their competitors.

Consider projects in the broader perspective of the entire organization. In the case of Deep Thought Academy, the board should consider whether it makes sense to undertake a substantial technology project at the same time the school needs to pay for and build substantial additions to the facility.

Watch out for solutions looking for problems. In this case, the first question to ponder is "What exactly is the need?" The project started as a search for a solution to deal with yearly enrollments. But it was unclear whether the paper-based enrollment process was onerous enough to warrant investing in a student information system. In all likelihood this was the case of the technology director seeing a bright, shiny SIS and thinking, "I've got to get me one of those" without really understanding the problem it was meant to solve, or, if it did solve a problem, whether that problem was worth solving.

Not all projects generate direct financial benefits. Let's assume for a second that this project does solve a problem. Even though this effort is being undertaken to close some process gaps, the project itself may or may not drive any real cost savings. Since current staff handles the enrollment process now, any improvements to the enrollment process will not drive direct cost savings, since the enrollment process itself is not a full-time job. It will free up the staff to do other things, so there are definitely benefits, but the bottom line will most likely see an impact that only partly balances out the cost of the SIS, unless you factor in avoiding the costs of having to hire additional help. I mention this to point out that a straight cost-benefit calculation is not going to show that this project makes sense, and it most likely will not generate a payback. Instead, cost information is helpful for comparing alternatives. It certainly does not allow the staff and board to be as objective as they might like, but it still provides information that can be used in a decision.

That's not to say a cost-benefit analysis is not helpful, but it's not going to tell the board mathematically whether or not to get the SIS. It will only present a specific piece of information that is helpful for comparing options in conjunction with more subjective information. Of course, one of those options is to do nothing.

Be careful how you write requests for proposals, and requirements in general. If your requirements are too specific, you may unintentionally eliminate viable options by overspecifying your desired solution.

Part III

Techniques

·

Chapter 11

Understanding Stakeholders

Introduction

I have heard it said, and have probably said it many times myself, that IT projects would be so much easier if people weren't involved. That's not the case—people are involved, and they are the most important aspect of the projects. The main purpose of IT projects is to change the work people do or the way in which they do it, so it makes sense to figure out how best to work with them.

This chapter describes some techniques that are helpful for understanding the people you are working with. The first two techniques are useful for understanding the people whose needs you are trying to satisfy—better known as stakeholder analysis. The other two techniques in this chapter will help you better understand the people who are actually going to use the solution you deliver; let's call this user analysis.

Stakeholder Analysis

What do I mean by "stakeholders"? Remember the BABOK version 3 definition of stakeholder: a group or individual with a relationship to the change or the solution. That's a pretty broad definition that includes, well, just about everyone who has anything to do with a solution. In this book I focus on a subset of that group with the needs that a solution is trying to satisfy—in other words, project sponsors, subject matter experts, users, regulators, service providers, and anyone else who could impact or is impacted by the solution. Keep in mind that these can be people from both business and IT areas. Technology people have needs, too, and can often provide a different perspective on possible solutions.

For example, IT support often has different interactions with end users than the rest of IT and may have some very helpful insight with respect to problems that end users face.

So stakeholder analysis is the act of understanding those stakeholders better, usually with the goal of figuring out the best way to communicate, engage, and work with them. The two techniques I cover here are ways to guide the conversation about your stakeholders on the way to establishing a plan for working with them.

- The stakeholder map takes a look at the relative influence and interest of your stakeholders so you can decide how to engage them.

- The commitment scale guides a conversation about how much your stakeholders support your project. This discussion provides ideas on how to engage them and what type of change activities you need to conduct to get the stakeholder support you need.

User Analysis

A special subset of stakeholders is the people who are actually going to use the solution you deliver—your users, for lack of a better term. User analysis helps you understand who uses your solution, what they can do, and the environment in which they use it. You can use that information to guide design decisions and structure permissions so that people can do what they are supposed to and can't do what they aren't supposed to. The two techniques I describe here help to structure conversations around those ideas and persist information going forward.

- User modeling structures a conversation about the user roles involved with your solution in order to arrive at a consistent list that can be used to organize work and identify functionality gaps.

- Personas help the team understand the context in which the solution's users work, which helps guide design decisions.

Stakeholder Map

What It Is

The stakeholder map is a technique commonly used for stakeholder analysis. Using the stakeholder map to guide conversations helps a team understand who the stakeholders for the project are, understand key characteristics about those stakeholders, and identify plans for engaging the stakeholders on an ongoing basis.

Primary outcomes from a stakeholder map include

- A comprehensive list of the stakeholders involved with the project
- An understanding of how to interact with those stakeholders

An Example

Figure 11.1 is an example stakeholder map for the commission system replacement project. Note that the rest of the team (aside from Arthur) did not put themselves on the map. Had they done so, they would ideally all fit in the upper right quadrant—high influence, high interest.

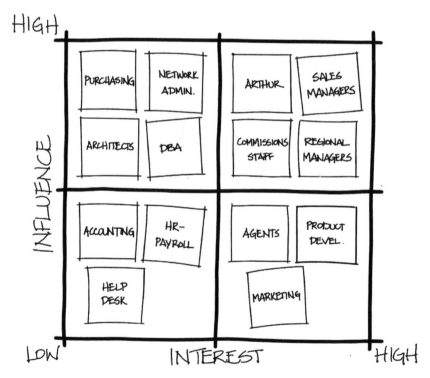

Figure 11.1 *Stakeholder map for commission system*

When to Use It

Stakeholder maps are appropriate in all situations; however, the extent to which you use one depends on whether the current initiative involves new stakeholders or a group the team has been working with for quite a while. New stakeholders will generally prompt more rigorous and intentional map creation.

Why Use It

By explicitly discussing stakeholders using a stakeholder map, the team reduces the chance that they have forgotten someone who is impacted by or who can impact a project. The team also stands a better chance of having effective and efficient interactions with their stakeholders.

How to Use It

1. **Generate a list of stakeholders.**

   Gather the team together, provide them with sticky notes, and encourage them to think of as many stakeholders as they can. You may want to do some affinity grouping of the identified stakeholders before moving to the next step so you can remove duplicates and arrive at a manageable number of stakeholders.

2. **Map the stakeholders based on their characteristics.**

   There are a variety of different sets of characteristics that can be used to understand your stakeholders, but they typically represent some variation on the influence of the stakeholder (often referred to as their power) and the interest of the stakeholder.

   Create a two-by-two matrix with one axis representing influence and one axis representing interest. An example is shown in Figure 11.2.

3. **Establish plans for engagement based on the characteristics.**

   Each quadrant provides guidance on how to engage the stakeholders with those characteristics. The team considers which quadrant the stakeholder was placed in and establishes the corresponding approach to engagement (see Figure 11.3).

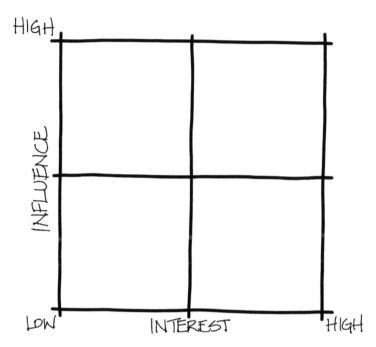

Figure 11.2 *Blank stakeholder map*

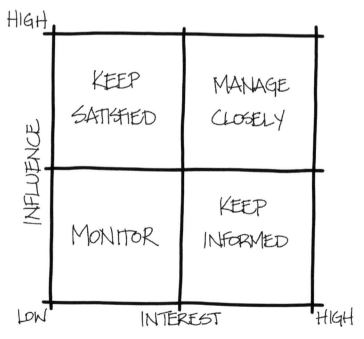

Figure 11.3 *Stakeholder map with actions*

Low Influence/Low Interest—Monitor

These stakeholders are usually only partially impacted by the solution. An example from the commission system (Chapter 8) is accounting. General information is sufficient for these stakeholders, and it may be appropriate just to let them know where information is available and leave it up them to decide if they are going to take advantage of it. It can be helpful to keep an eye on these stakeholders to make sure that their interest or influence does not change throughout the course of the project.

Low Influence/High Interest—Keep Informed

Stakeholders with these characteristics are a very good source of detailed information about your project, so it's important to understand their needs and solicit their input. Stay aware of their perspective on the project; if they feel their concerns are not being addressed, they may engage more influential people. Some subject matter experts and end users are often in this quadrant. In the case of the commission system, agents fit into this category because they have a high interest in the commission system working properly (else they may not get paid), but their influence is limited because the main focus of the project is determining how the process runs.

High Influence/Low Interest—Keep Satisfied

This group usually contains people with an important position in the organization who are not directly related to the project. In the commission system case, purchasing, the architects, the DBAs, and the network admins fall into this category because even though they are not directly involved with the project, they can exert a great deal of influence on it. Your team should engage with stakeholders in this group to understand and satisfy their needs when they are in alignment with the overall goal of the project. It also often pays to consult with these stakeholders on critical issues, but not on every single decision. You may also consider whether the project would benefit from having these stakeholders be more interested in the project.

High Influence/High Interest—Manage Closely

Teams should fully engage the stakeholders who fall into this category, which usually includes sponsors and highly influential subject matter experts. Whenever possible, these stakeholders should be explicitly part of the team.

Caveats and Considerations

Discussions using a stakeholder map should definitely be held at the beginning of the effort, but it's just as important to revisit the map on a regular basis, especially if there are changes in the business environment or project goals, or major new insights that could change stakeholders' interest in a project. Any change in organization structure is also a good reason to revisit the analysis, because it may drive changes in stakeholder influence.

Often, the best way to gauge stakeholder interest is to talk with them directly about their perspectives on the project. Determining their influence can be a little trickier, as individual stakeholders may have inflated perceptions of their own influence. Those discussions are best held within the core project team.

Additional Resources

Gamestorming. "Stakeholder Analysis." www.gamestorming.com/games-for-design/stakeholder-analysis/.

MindTools. "Stakeholder Analysis." www.mindtools.com/pages/article/newPPM_07.htm.

Note: These two resources describe the same activity with two major differences. The Gamestorming article provides more detail on how to do stakeholder analysis in a highly collaborative manner, and the axes are switched between the two approaches. But both approaches provide a means of understanding your stakeholders to establish communication plans for them.

Commitment Scale

What It Is

The commitment scale is a stakeholder analysis technique. This technique gauges the current level of stakeholder commitment to a project, as well as what level of commitment is needed to ensure the project's success.

An Example

After the commission system team created their stakeholder map, they also thought it would be a good idea to discuss the commitment of the various groups to the project. Figure 11.4 shows the resulting scale that they came up with.

LEVEL OF COMMITMENT	COMMISSION STAFF	SALES MANAGERS	REGIONAL MANAGERS	AGENTS	NETWORK ADMIN.	ARCHITECTS	DBAs
ENTHUSIASTIC SUPPORT	●	●	●				
HELP IT WORK				●	●	●	●
COMPLIANT							
HESITANT	X						
INDIFFERENT					X		X
UNCOOPERATIVE			X			X	
OPPOSED		X		X			
HOSTILE							

Figure 11.4 *Commission system commitment scale*

When to Use It

The commitment scale is most applicable when a team is starting a new project that does not have clear, unanimous support from all stakeholders or on projects that are introducing significant organizational change. It may also be helpful when a team is working with a set of stakeholders with whom they have not worked before.

It's a good idea for the team to have a discussion surrounding the commitment scale when they are first getting started (during iteration zero, for example) so they can establish their plans for engaging with stakeholders early on.

Why Use It

The commitment scale is best suited to guiding team conversations about how they will interact with their stakeholders. Members of the team may have various assumptions about some stakeholders' impressions of the project. This technique provides a means of getting those assumptions out in the open and helps the team determine a course of action to increase support for their project.

How to Use It

1. Gather the team together and explain that you need to discuss how you will work with the various stakeholders.

2. Draw a chart on the whiteboard as shown in Figure 11.5.

   Here are the definitions of the various levels of commitment:

   Enthusiastic support: Will work hard to make it happen

   Help it work: Will lend appropriate support to implement the solution

   Compliant: Will do the minimum acceptable and will try to lower the standard

   Hesitant: Holds some reservations; won't volunteer

   Indifferent: Won't help; won't hurt

   Uncooperative: Will have to be prodded

   Opposed: Will openly state opposition to the solution and act on that opposition

   Hostile: Will block implementation of the solution at all costs

LEVEL OF COMMITMENT							
ENTHUSIASTIC SUPPORT							
HELP IT WORK							
COMPLIANT							
HESITANT							
INDIFFERENT							
UNCOOPERATIVE							
OPPOSED							
HOSTILE							

Figure 11.5 *Blank commitment scale*

3. Identify the key stakeholders the team needs to discuss. Start with groups, but the team may identify some influential individuals who need to be discussed separately.

4. For each stakeholder, discuss as a team the stakeholder's current level of commitment and where the stakeholder needs to be in order for the project to succeed. It's helpful to use sticky notes to represent current and desired levels of commitment, because the perspective of the team may change frequently throughout the discussion. See the example above.

5. After identifying the current and desired levels of commitment, identify the actions needed to move the stakeholder from the current commitment level to the desired level. These actions will influence how you engage with that stakeholder going forward.

Caveats and Considerations

Some people consider the nature of the information on the commitment scale to be controversial, so it's best to use the commitment scale to guide a conversation and determine action plans, but not necessarily persist the scale itself.

The information contained in the scale is not of the type that teams would directly ask their stakeholders. Because of this, teams using this technique as a discussion starter may find that most of their information comes from observation or discussions with people who have good insights into the various stakeholders such as the project sponsor.

The focus of this technique will be on stakeholders who are not already part of the team, but through this discussion the team may identify additional people they need to add to the team because those people need to be very supportive and engaged in the project.

Not every stakeholder needs to be brought all the way up to "enthusiastic support" in order for a project to be successful.

Additional Resource

Rath & Strong Management Consultants. *Rath & Strong's Six Sigma Pocket Guide*. Rath & Strong, 2000.

User Modeling

What It Is

A user is anyone who receives value from a solution. Users include people who directly interact with the solution as well as those who do not directly interact with the solution but receive some value from it.

User modeling is a technique used to establish a commonly agreed-upon list of user roles for a solution. This list of user roles and their descriptions provides helpful context for user stories and other backlog items.

You can think of user modeling as one aspect of stakeholder analysis that is specifically focused on people interacting with a solution or receiving value from it.

An Example

The team working on the conference submission system modeled the user roles and used those user roles as an organizing concept for the story map. Following is a description of how we arrived at our list of users using the steps described previously. We did this as an exercise leading up to our creation of the backlog.

Brainstorm an Initial Set of Users

Each of us took a stack of index cards and wrote user roles on them, throwing each card into the middle of the table after we wrote it. This was to make sure that we didn't get hung up too much on specific user roles too early. We ended up generating the list of user roles shown in Figure 11.6. At this point, we also included systems

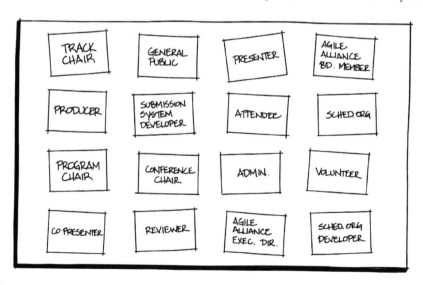

Figure 11.6 *Conference submission system initial user roles*

and roles on the team because we weren't worried about filtering our thoughts yet. We figured those items might spark other user roles that should be included.

Organize and Consolidate the Users

Next, we organized the cards into groups that seemed to make sense, as shown in Figure 11.7.

We also threw the following cards away:

- Submission system developer
- Agile Alliance executive director
- Agile Alliance board member
- Sched.org
- Sched.org developer

The reason? For the purpose of user stories, we don't want the people who are actually building the solution to be one of the user roles. Generally, if they are going to use the solution, they'll be filling some other role. We only want to include people who are expecting an outcome from the solution in the user roles. If there is another system involved, it's because there is someone who is accomplishing something as a result of that interface. Finally, we didn't include the executive director and board member because when those folks use the solution, they would fill an existing role.

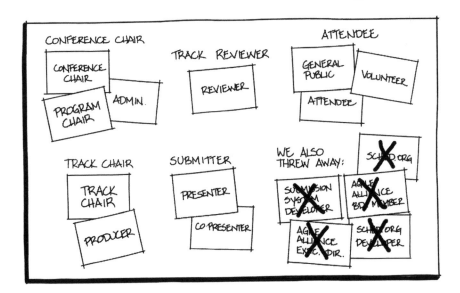

Figure 11.7 *Conference submission system consolidated user roles*

Table 11.1 *User Roles and Descriptions*

User Role	Description
Chair	Has overall responsibility for the conference program. The chair also acts as the administrator for the conference submission system.
Track chair	Has responsibility for selecting sessions for a given track in the program. Provides a final track recommendation to the chair. Also coordinates the review committee for his or her assigned track.
Track reviewer	Reviews submissions for one or more tracks and provides input on which sessions should be included in that track as well as provides feedback to the presenter on improvements to the session.
Submitter	Submits sessions to be included in the program and if selected will be the main presenter of the session. Can submit and edit his or her own sessions as well as respond to feedback posted to the session.
Attendee	General viewer of the submission information who may or may not attend the conference. Can view some session proposal information.

Refine the User Roles

Finally, we put together the short descriptions shown in Table 11.1 for each user role so that we had a shared understanding of the characteristics of each user.

When to Use It

User modeling is especially helpful when working on solutions with a significant amount of user interaction and where there are different types of users who are able to perform different activities or access different functionality.

It's generally best to do user modeling when first starting work on a solution. The discussions that occur during user modeling help to establish the range of potential users and can provide needed context. User modeling discussions can also provide some very helpful information for establishing scope. If your team is using one of the familiar formats for user stories, the list generated by user modeling provides selections for the "as a . . ." portion of those stories.

Why Use It

Consistent definition and use of user roles in user stories reduces confusion and helps to ensure that all cases are covered. The output of user modeling can also help with gap analysis.

If there are any user stories that have a user role that was not identified during user modeling, it could mean several things:

- There is a user role you forgot (new user).
- That user story is really not part of the effort (actual scope creep).
- You have the wrong user role in the user story.

If there are user roles without an associated user story, that raises different possibilities:

- You haven't gotten to that user role yet.
- You are missing user stories.
- You have identified an extraneous user role.

How to Use It

There are three primary steps in user modeling.

1. **Brainstorm an initial set of users.**

   Gather your team and ask them to write any users that come to mind on index cards (or sticky notes) and put them on a table (or wall). Don't judge any of the suggested user roles at this point.

2. **Organize and consolidate the users into user roles.**

   As a team, organize the cards into similar categories using whatever arrangement rules seem appropriate.

   - Arrange the groups of cards spatially to indicate similar and overlapping users.
   - Remove cards that represent users who are not relevant to the solution. This includes users who are not impacted by the solution, or whose roles do not have any relation to the goal of the IT project. They could also be users whom you have explicitly removed from the scope of the project.
   - Create a header card for each grouping that represents a user role for the solution.

3. **Refine the user roles.**

   Once you have settled on a list from the brainstorm, look it over and determine if any user roles seem to be missing. It may help to think of the kinds of user roles to "harden" the solution against:

   - Abusers: Think of people who may try to abuse the system and features to prevent these abuses.

- Nonadopters: Think of people who will resist using the system and whether there are any features worth adding that may encourage them to use it.

When the team thinks they have identified all user roles, prepare a brief description of each user role so that the team will have a shared understanding of the characteristics of users. Your team may decide to create some lightweight personas as a way of structuring the descriptions.

Caveats and Considerations

User roles should not be specific people but groups of people; for example, instead of "Fred" it should be "Claims Administrator." If your team chooses to use personas, you may see names showing up in the persona descriptions.

User roles should always represent people, not other systems. If there is a need for an interface between the solution and some other system, someone is receiving value from that interface. Represent those people with a user role. Remember, you are modeling user roles to identify the key roles that gain value from or can accomplish something with the solution. The intention of identifying user roles is not to identify all the external agents that interact with a solution (in which case identifying systems would be useful).

When creating user roles it may be helpful to think about what permissions they may have in the solution. Your user base may have many different titles that can do the same thing, such as Junior Claims Administrator, Senior Claims Administrator, and Claims Administrator First Class. In this case all of those users could be represented by the same user role. On the other hand, if there are people with similar titles who do different things—Claims Processor, Claims Entry, Claims Adjudicator—each of those may be represented by a different user role with different permissions.

You'll generally want to include as many of the team members as possible in the user modeling activity. They may have some perspective that the rest of the group does not, and the discussions that go into deciding what to ultimately call the users and how to group them together provide a great deal of information that's helpful later in the project, during define, build, and test activities.

Additional Resources

Cohn, Mike. *User Stories Applied: For Agile Software Development*. Addison-Wesley, 2004, Chapter 3, "User Role Modeling."

Patton, Jeff. "Personas, Profiles, Actors, & Roles: Modeling Users to Target Successful Product Design." http://agileproductdesign.com/presentations/user_modeling/index.html.

Persona

What It Is

Personas define a typical user of a solution. They are helpful for understanding the context in which user roles use the solution to help guide design decisions. Personas originated from Alan Cooper's work on user-centered design.

An Example

Figure 11.8 is an example persona for the conference submission system.

REED THE REVIEWER

"REVIEWING SESSIONS IS A GREAT WAY FOR ME TO SEE WHAT PEOPLE ARE TALKING ABOUT & WHAT I MIGHT WANT TO HEAR MORE ABOUT."

☐ AGILE PRACTITIONER

☐ REVIEWS ON A SOLELY VOLUNTEER BASIS IN HIS SPARE TIME

☐ LIKES TO REVIEW AS MANY SESSIONS AS POSSIBLE, SO DOESN'T WASTE TIME WITH PARTIALLY FILLED OUT PROPOSALS, OR LOOKING AT SESSIONS HE HAS ALREADY REVIEWED THAT HAVE NOT CHANGED

☐ LIKES TO KNOW WHEN NEW SESSIONS ARE POSTED

☐ FINDS VALUE IN BACK & FORTH DISCUSSIONS WITH SUBMITTERS

Figure 11.8 *Reed the Reviewer persona*

When to Use It

Personas are especially helpful when working on solutions with a significant amount of user interaction where the context in which those users work can greatly influence how they use the solution.

Personas are often a good technique to use in conjunction with user modeling.

Why Use It

Personas provide context for your users to help guide design decisions by providing a name, face, and story for each user role and helping team members understand the jobs users do and the environment in which they work. Personas do not have to be elaborate. A short description is sufficient. Keep them posted in the team space to remind team members who their users are.

When the team proposes various personas, they establish a shared understanding of who they are building the solution for. As a result, they're more likely to build a solution that more closely meets the users' needs.

How to Use It

Once you have identified the user roles that are relevant for your solution, create a persona for each. Jeff Patton suggests the following characteristics as helpful for a persona:

- Name
- A role or job title
- Quotes in the persona's language
- Relevant demographics
- Description that reveals goals, motivations, pain points
- Description of primary activities this user type will engage in

Following is one collaborative way to create personas. This approach is especially helpful for reducing the influence of loud voices in the room and to ensure that everyone on your team gets a chance to provide input.

1. Divide the team into small groups of three or four each.

2. Place flip chart paper around the room, with each page representing one of the personas.

3. Have each group start at a flip chart page and give them 20 minutes to create a draft persona.

4. At the end of the 20 minutes, have the groups rotate clockwise, but have one person stay behind to describe what the previous group came up with. The groups then have five minutes to discuss and revise the persona.

5. Repeat the rotations until the groups come back to their original persona.

Caveats and Considerations

The personas originally envisioned by Alan Cooper in describing user-centered design can be quite involved. My suggestion is to use the idea behind personas to provide simple yet helpful descriptions of the two or three key user roles. The goal is a bit of needed context for the team when making decisions about how to design and build the solution.

To be truly effective, the personas should be developed based on observations of people who fill those user roles in their actual environment.

Personas help prevent teams from designing solutions for themselves, which is important except when the team members building the solution are actually the main users.

Alliteration between the name of the persona and the role is frequently used (e.g., Reed the Reviewer, Sally the Submitter). It's not necessary, but it can help people remember whom they are talking about.

To make personas truly helpful, they should be publicly posted and available to the teams for reference when they are working on a specific story. It's a sign that the team has latched onto the personas when they ask, "What would Reed like in this situation?" instead of "What would a reviewer want in this situation?"

Additional Resources

Ambler, Scott. "Personas: An Agile Introduction." www.agilemodeling.com/artifacts/personas.htm.

Cooper, Alan. *The Inmates Are Running the Asylum: Why High-Tech Products Drive Us Crazy and How to Restore the Sanity.* Sams Publishing, 2004, Chapter 9.

Patton, Jeff. "Personas, Profiles, Actors, & Roles: Modeling Users to Target Successful Product Design." http://agileproductdesign.com/presentations/user_modeling/index.html.

Chapter 12

Understanding Context

Introduction

"It depends" is an often-overused phrase, especially by consultants or those seeking to avoid answering a question (some may say that was a redundant statement). The fact of the matter is that appropriate techniques really are dependent on the context in which work is being done. And one of the biggest contributions to context in IT projects is the characteristics of the organization itself and its strategy. Your team working on an IT project may need some discussions to understand the strategy of their organization if it is not clearly stated. The techniques described in this chapter can also be used to understand the strategy of parts of an organization more directly impacted by your particular IT project.

This chapter provides a set of techniques that are helpful for understanding the team's organizational context:

- The Purpose-Based Alignment Model: used to determine how to approach your project based on the organizational activities you are supporting

- Six questions: useful for identifying an organization's purpose

- The Context Leadership Model: helps you identify key risks your projects face and suggests analysis and documentation approaches to address those risks

These techniques are complementary, and you will often get the best results when you use them together.

Purpose-Based Alignment Model

What It Is

The Purpose-Based Alignment Model (see Figure 12.1), created by Niel Nickolaisen, is a method for aligning business decisions, process, and feature designs around purpose. The purpose of some decisions and designs is to differentiate the organization in the market; the purpose of most other decisions is to achieve and maintain parity with the market. Activities that do not require operational excellence either call for finding a partner to achieve differentiation or do not deserve much attention.

In practice, purpose alignment generates immediately usable, pragmatic decision filters that you can cascade through the organization to improve decisions and designs.

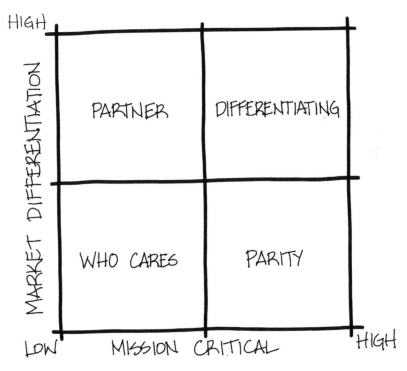

Figure 12.1 *The Purpose-Based Alignment Model*

The Quadrants Explained

Differentiating

The purpose of differentiating activities is to excel. Because you use these activities to gain market share and to create and maintain a sustainable competitive advantage in the marketplace, you want to perform them better than anyone else. These activities are or should be your organization's claim to fame and should link directly to your strategy. Be careful to not underinvest in these activities, as doing so would weaken your market position. In fact, you should focus your creativity on these processes.

What are the differentiating activities for your organization? It depends. It depends on the specific things you do to create sustainable competitive advantage.

For example, Deep Thought Academy's differentiators are their small class sizes and personalized lesson plans. Keeping these sustainable competitive advantages should be a strong consideration in all of the school's key decisions.

Parity

The purpose of the parity activities is to achieve and maintain parity with the marketplace. Your organization will not generate any competitive advantage if it performs these activities better than its competitors. However, because these activities are mission critical, you must ensure that you do not underinvest in them or perform them poorly. Parity activities are ideal candidates for simplification and streamlining; complexity in this quadrant implies that you are over-investing. While there might be value in performing the differentiating activities in a unique way, performing the parity activities in a unique way will not generate value and could actually decrease the organization's value if your overinvestment in parity processes limits the resources you can apply to differentiating processes.

Partner

Some activities are not mission critical (for your organization to do) but can nevertheless differentiate your organization in the marketplace. The way to exploit these activities—and generate increased market share—is to find someone who can perform them for you and combine efforts to create differentiation. In the following example for Deep Thought Academy, music education with the local symphony is something that the other schools in the area do not offer, so the partnership could be viewed as a differentiator in terms of attracting students.

Who Cares

Finally, some business activities are neither mission critical nor market differentiating. The goal for these activities is to perform them as little as possible. We refer to these activities as the **"who cares"** activities. Because these activities are neither market differentiating nor mission critical, you should spend as little time and attention on them as possible. Who really cares?

An Example

Figure 12.2 shows the Purpose-Based Alignment Model for Deep Thought Academy.

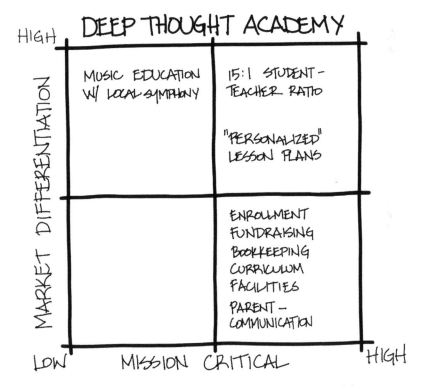

Figure 12.2 *Deep Thought Academy Purpose-Based Alignment Model*

When to Use It

Purpose alignment works well when you need to do these things:

- Define business and IT strategic and tactical plans
- Align IT with business priorities
- Evaluate, plan, and implement large system projects
- Filter and design features and functionality
- Manage project scope
- Reduce resistance to process improvements
- Reduce waste by improving focus and resource allocation

Why Use It

The Purpose-Based Alignment Model provides a simple way to determine what activities to concentrate on and how to deliver them. Through the characteristics of mission critical and market differentiating, it removes factors that distract from decision making and helps the team focus.

How to Use It

Follow these steps to engage in purpose alignment:

1. Present and explain the model.

2. Identify the business decisions and activities that differentiate your organization.

3. Once you have identified the differentiating activities, you should be able to write a simple filtering statement or question that you can use to quickly evaluate future decisions and designs. Before moving on, determine whether any of the differentiating activities can best be delivered via a partnership.

4. Once you have defined the differentiating activities, almost all other activities will fall into the parity category.

5. If you are using the Purpose-Based Alignment Model for strategic and tactical planning, you can next perform a gap analysis on the differentiating, parity, and partnering activities. Your plans should fill the gaps.

6. If you are using the Purpose-Based Alignment Model to design projects, features, and functionality, you can now design around purpose. Design

differentiating project elements, features, and functionality to help you win in the marketplace. Design parity project elements, features, and functionality to be good enough. Remember that the parity activities are mission critical and therefore cannot be done poorly. Nevertheless, they can be simplified and standardized so long as they deliver operational excellence.

Caveats and Considerations

Remember the mission-critical nature of the parity activities. Culturally, we associate our self-worth and value to the organization with the process and business rules we control and use. This creates a natural tendency to want our process and business rules to be "differentiating." If you don't emphasize and communicate the mission-critical nature of the parity activities, people will resist the use of the model and its associated decision filters. Alternatively, they may attempt to contort their processes so they fall into the differentiating category. This defeats the effective use of the model.

What is a differentiating activity changes over time. As soon as you unleash improvements to your differentiating activities on the market, the market can mimic what you have done. Therefore, you need a focused, working innovation process that constantly updates your roadmap with new improvements to your differentiating processes, business rules, functions, and features.

Parity activity classifications change over time. Good practices for your parity activities can change. As soon as a process improvement becomes the new standard, it creates a parity gap that you need to fill. Of course, to fill the gap, you can then mimic what someone else has already invented rather than invent it yourself. This requires an internal process to find and implement best practices.

Treat parity activities like parity activities. It's important that you do them well, but doing them better than anyone else is essentially a waste of money. Too many organizations overengineer processes or systems because they fail to realize that they are working to support a parity activity. For instance, companies buy COTS timekeeping products, then try to customize the products to accommodate their unique process for tracking time. The software already contains industry-wide leading practices for timekeeping, yet the organization is convinced that "we are special and unique." They may in fact have a unique timekeeping process, but chances are there is no good reason for them to have a unique process. It certainly does not earn them any additional business.

Purpose is not priority. Purpose identifies the design goals of a process, business rule, function, or feature. It does not define the sequence in which the work on that process, rule, function, or feature must occur. That being said, purpose can provide a framework for strategic and tactical planning.

Analytics can be differentiating. If you can make better decisions, particularly about your differentiating processes, you improve your ability to compete in the marketplace. Analysis that seeks to better understand your differentiating processes can also be differentiating. Not all analytics are differentiating, however. For example, a large retailer that differentiates itself through its superior supply chain management focuses its unique and differentiating analytics on the supply chain, not necessarily on sales data.

Treat exceptions like exceptions. Automating processes to handle exceptions generally adds nothing but complexity to your organization and very rarely differentiates the organization in a meaningful way. Avoid codifying the handling of exceptions to business rules.

Additional Resource

Pixton, Pollyanna, Niel Nickolaisen, Todd Little, and Kent McDonald. *Stand Back and Deliver: Accelerating Business Agility.* Addison-Wesley, 2009.

Six Questions

What It Is

The six questions listed below help guide your discussion about your organization's differentiating activities. These six questions represent two different perspectives.

You can use the first four questions to identify differentiating activities in your organization:

1. Whom do we serve?

2. What do they want and need most?

3. What do we provide to help them?

4. What is the best way to provide this?

The final two questions prompt you to think about the implications of your differentiating activities for your organization.

5. How do we know we are succeeding?

6. How should we organize to deliver?

Table 12.1 *Six Questions for Deep Thought Academy*

1. Whom do we serve?	Families located in the metro area where Deep Thought Academy is located with children in grades K through 8
2. What do they want and need most?	A secular school where their children can receive the best possible education
3. What do we provide to help them?	Small class sizes and personalized lesson plans
4. What is the best way to provide this?	A combination of Montessori, a traditional teaching model, and individual guided learning styles combined with experienced faculty
5. How do we know we are succeeding?	Based on average student rank in the Iowa Test of Basic Skills
6. How should we organize to deliver?	Nonprofit school with a board composed of parents; small central staff who also serve as faculty. Target 15:1 student-teacher ratio.

An Example

Table 12.1 shows the six questions applied to Deep Thought Academy.

When to Use It

These questions are best suited for discussions when an organization is trying to formulate or revise its strategy. Organizations ranging from small nonprofits to Fortune 500 corporations have used these questions as a way to guide strategy discussions. Your IT project team can also use these questions to guide discussions about what your organization's strategy actually is and whether your project aligns with that strategy.

Why Use It

These questions place the focus on the value the organization provides to its customers. They also ensure that the organization structures itself and its efforts around that purpose, rather than getting distracted by activities that don't promote progress toward the end goal of delivering value to customers. The six questions also drive the conversation around how to measure that progress. For IT projects, the value in discussing these questions is so that your team can identify your organization's differentiating activities based on how it actually behaves.

This can be especially helpful if your team is not receiving explicit guidance from your organization's leadership. The six questions are helpful because they emphasize the aspects of an organization's sustainable competitive advantage, which ties into its differentiating activities.

How to Use It

Pull a cross section of people together (the composition of the group depends on the purpose of the discussion), and guide them through the six questions. Sticky notes, fine-tipped permanent markers, flip chart paper, and flip chart markers are helpful for these discussions. You may want to identify several ideas individually, then discuss the ideas as a group in order to converge on one response, or just a few. The questions build on one another, so you want to identify the desired answer for the first question before moving on to the second.

Here's a brief description of what each question seeks to identify:

1. **Whom do we serve?** This question encourages a discussion about your organization's target markets and market segments. You'll want to narrow this down to a very small number—preferably three or fewer—so your activities will be focused. Discuss the following questions for each target market you identify.

2. **What do they want and need most?** This question identifies the needs each target market is seeking to address.

3. **What do we provide to help them?** This question identifies the products and services the organization provides to satisfy those needs.

4. **What is the best way to provide this?** The answers to this question can often help identify an organization's differentiators.

5. **How do we know we are succeeding?** This question helps identify overarching organizational objectives.

6. **How should we organize to deliver?** This question sparks conversation around how the organization should structure itself to most effectively satisfy the needs of the target market.

Caveats and Considerations

These questions help identify differentiating activities in an organization. If you are working on a project that does not address something identified by these questions, that is a good indication that you are working on a parity activity.

These questions focus on how your organization meets the needs of your customers. The answers to these questions are still useful for internal IT projects because they provide a better understanding of how your project relates to your organization's strategy.

The six questions are applicable at multiple levels of your organization. At a company level the answers to the questions are fairly abstract. At a product level the questions focus on your specific product offering. For an IT project, you could ask these questions from the perspective of the business stakeholder that you are representing. If you shift the focus in that way, you could switch the question "What do they want and need most?" to "What problem(s) do they [your stakeholders] have that they would pay to have removed?" It's an important shift. They may want several things, but what they really need is for a particular problem to go away. Even if they have a problem that they would like to go away, asking if they would pay to have it removed focuses even more on whether the problem is worth solving.

Additional Resource

Pixton, Pollyanna, Paul Gibson, and Niel Nickolaisen. *The Agile Culture: Leading through Trust and Ownership*. Addison-Wesley, 2014.

Context Leadership Model

What It Is

The Context Leadership Model, created by Todd Little, was introduced in *Stand Back and Deliver* as a tool for determining the appropriate project leadership style given a project's uncertainty and complexity. The Context Leadership Model can also be used to understand the risks inherent in a project and determine how to approach analysis and documentation in a way that will address those risks. (See Figure 12.3.) Todd chose to represent each quadrant with an animal whose characteristics mirror those of the projects that fit into that quadrant.

Table 12.2 shows a sample set of attributes and scoring model described in *Stand Back and Deliver* that you can use to determine where your project fits on the complexity scale.

Figure 12.3 *The Context Leadership Model*

Table 12.3 presents a sample set of attributes and scoring model described in *Stand Back and Deliver* that you can use to determine where your project fits on the uncertainty scale.

Tables 12.4 through 12.7 provide additional explanations of each quadrant.

Table 12.2 *Complexity Attributes*

Attribute	Low Complexity (1)	Medium Complexity (3)	High Complexity (9)
Team size	2	15	100
Mission critical	Speculative	Established market	Safety critical or significant monetary exposure
Team location	Same room	Within same building	Multisite, worldwide
Team maturity	Established team of experts	Mixed team of experts and novices	New team of mostly novices
Domain knowledge gaps	Delivery team knows the domain as well as SME.	Delivery team requires some domain assistance.	Delivery team has no idea about the domain.
Dependencies	No dependencies	Some dependencies	Tight integration with several projects

Table 12.3 *Uncertainty Attributes*

Attribute	Low Uncertainty (1)	Medium Uncertainty (3)	High Uncertainty (9)
Market uncertainty	Known deliverable, possibly defined contractual obligation	Initial market target is likely to require steering.	New market that is unknown and untested
Technical uncertainty	Enhancements to existing architecture	We're not quite sure if we know how to build it.	New technology, new architecture, some research may be required
Number of customers	Internal customer or one well-defined customer	Multiple internal or small number of defined customers	Shrink-wrapped software
Project duration	0–3 months	3–12 months	>12 months
Approach to change	Significant change control	Moderate control over change	Embrace or create change

Table 12.4 *Sheepdog Explained*

Characteristics	Simple project with low uncertainty
Description	Activities the organization does on a regular basis, such as annual updates, maintenance, small revisions to an existing system
Nature of project team	Small, most likely colocated
Useful approaches	Build a shared understanding on the team, then stand back and let the team deliver. Kanban can be useful in this setting.
Nature of analysis	• Resolve known unknowns. • Build shared understanding with team and stakeholders.
Impact on documentation	• As requested by stakeholders • Minimum needed to aid project delivery
Analysis expertise helpful	Domain knowledge

Table 12.5 *Colt Explained*

Characteristics	Simple project with high uncertainty
Description	Solutions that introduce new products or services or support new business processes. Little to no impact on existing systems or teams.
Nature of project team	Small, most likely colocated
Useful approaches	Customer development techniques as described in Chapter 3 and agile development techniques
Nature of analysis	• Iteratively discover unknown unknowns. • Resolve known unknowns. • Build shared understanding with team and stakeholders.
Impact on documentation	• As requested by stakeholders • Minimum needed to aid project delivery
Analysis expertise helpful	Familiarity with area of uncertainty

Table 12.6 *Cow Explained*

Characteristics	Complex project with low uncertainty
Description	Revisions to existing, often legacy systems that may impact other systems and teams
Nature of project team	Large, dislocated, may involve multiple teams
Useful approaches	Agile development techniques combined with additional practices to ensure proper communication among multiple teams and impacted stakeholders
Nature of analysis	• Resolve known unknowns. • Build shared understanding with team and stakeholders.
Impact on documentation	• As requested by stakeholders • Sufficient to communicate intent to dislocated team members (more detailed specifications) • As needed to aid shared understanding with dependent teams (published interfaces)
Analysis expertise helpful	• Familiarity with impacted stakeholders • Domain knowledge

Table 12.7 *Bull Explained*

Characteristics	Complex project with high uncertainty
Description	Introduction of new product or business process that relies heavily on existing systems or substantial changes to/replacement of systems that support existing products/processes
Nature of project team	Large, dislocated, may involve multiple teams
Useful approaches	Approaches that allow for iterative techniques at the team level and coordination among multiple teams. Customer development techniques may be helpful in these situations but you may need longer learning cycles.
Nature of analysis	• Iteratively discover unknown unknowns. • Resolve known unknowns. • Build shared understanding with team and stakeholders.
Impact on documentation	• As requested by stakeholders • Sufficient to communicate intent to dislocated team members (more detailed specifications) • As needed to aid shared understanding with dependent teams (published interfaces)
Analysis expertise helpful	• Familiarity with area of uncertainty • Familiarity with impacted stakeholders • Domain knowledge

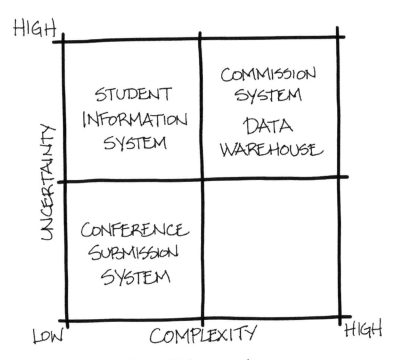

Figure 12.4 *Context Leadership Model for case studies*

An Example

Figure 12.4 shows the Context Leadership Model reflecting where the four case study projects fit.

When to Use It

The Context Leadership Model can be helpful for the following:

- Performing an initial risk assessment of a project and determining the best way to approach analysis
- Identifying potential opportunities to restructure a project so as to lower risk
- Examining the entire portfolio to get a sense of the aggregate risks faced by an organization in its portfolio

When starting a project, complexity and uncertainty analysis can help the team determine its initial risk profile. Subsequent reevaluations of the risk profile can be helpful for deciding whether existing risks have been addressed and new ones have arisen.

Why Use It

The Context Leadership Model is a quick way to assess a project in relation to common risks that all projects face and determine appropriate process and analysis approaches to address those risks.

How to Use It

Follow these steps to implement uncertainty and complexity management:

1. Identify the attributes and the scoring that you will use for complexity and for uncertainty. A sample set of attributes and scoring model are summarized in Tables 12.2 and 12.3.

2. Score the project and compute the average scores for complexity and uncertainty.

3. Identify the quadrant in which the project falls. Is it a sheepdog, colt, cow, or bull? Determine appropriate analysis approaches based on the suggestions in Tables 12.4 through 12.7.

4. Look at the individual attributes to determine if any represent a significant risk that you need to address in your project. Use Tables 12.8 and 12.9 for some suggestions for how to address those risks.

Table 12.8 *Addressing Complexity Risks*

Attribute	Ways to Reduce Complexity and Risk	Process Steps to Mitigate Risk
Team size	Split teams into smaller cohesive groups.	Make sure teams have a shared understanding of their purpose and the overall project success criteria. Bring teams together at regular intervals. Define, communicate, test, and manage project interfaces.
Mission critical	Not easy to reduce	Make critical decisions and overall project status visible to all stakeholders. Ensure that stakeholders understand the consequences of key decisions.
Team location	Colocate the team if possible.	Bring team members into face-to-face contact often. Invest in high-bandwidth communication and collaboration tools.

Continues

Table 12.8 *Addressing Complexity Risks (Continued)*

Attribute	Ways to Reduce Complexity and Risk	Process Steps to Mitigate Risk
Team maturity	Keep experienced teams whole, and leverage them from one release to the next. Integrate new members into the team early.	Make sure that time is allocated for mentoring of new team members, and invest in training and improvement for the entire team.
Domain gaps	Staff the team with members who have strong domain knowledge and use them to mentor other team members. Ensure that customer needs are constantly represented.	Educate and expose team members to the domain. Have team members sit with users and experience how they use the product.
Dependencies	Eliminate dependencies of work with static versions of dependencies. Build automated tests to check dependencies.	Invest in communication with teams that depend on you. Understand their needs and be clear about your progress.

Table 12.9 *Addressing Uncertainty Risks*

Attribute	Ways to Reduce Uncertainty and Risk	Process Steps to Mitigate Risk
Market uncertainty	Target a specific market segment that is better understood.	Deliver iteratively, use prototypes, and elicit customer feedback on a regular basis.
Technical uncertainty	Accept proven technologies. Design flexibility into situations to enable decisions to be made in the future.	Delay decisions where the uncertainty will resolve itself. Conduct experiments that will provide information to help resolve the uncertainty.
Number of customers	Target a specific customer segment or group of customers.	Use a product champion to solicit multiple customer voices and move them in a unified direction. Use the Purpose-Based Alignment Model as a filter.
Project duration	Shorten the duration or deliver functionality in incremental releases.	Deliver incrementally and maintain high quality throughout the project.
Change	Exert control over change where it has the biggest impact. Delay decisions so changes can be made without major impact.	Use incremental delivery and feedback to enable change to be absorbed into the project. Avoid committing to too much detail early.

Caveats and Considerations

While colt projects are ideally suited for agile approaches, that should not be taken to mean that agile approaches do not apply elsewhere. Even the lightly prescriptive agile approaches would most often be overkill for sheepdog projects;

as long as the team has a clear picture of what they are trying to accomplish and a simple way to stay coordinated, that is probably all the process ceremony needed. Cow projects can use agile approaches, but those approaches need to be supplemented by additional coordination activities between impacted teams and stakeholders. Agile can also be used for bull projects, but since the best way to address those projects is to split them into colts and cows, the thoughts for each of those projects apply.

Sheepdogs can use agile approaches, but many of the agile approaches are too complicated for these types of projects. Use only the techniques that you need to use, and resist the urge to make them any more complicated than necessary. As Todd Little suggests, "Sheepdogs are fine as agile projects, but just feed them dog food. And make sure you empower the dog to bite the project manager if they ever try to make it too complex."

It is possible for projects to move from one quadrant to another based on changes in their risk profile. Colts become bulls when the organization cannot properly control scope and ends up involving other projects and systems in what should have been a fairly isolated effort. Cows become bulls when the product owner cannot make decisions at the appropriate time, thereby adding excessive uncertainty.

Additional Resource

Pixton, Pollyanna, Niel Nickolaisen, Todd Little, and Kent McDonald. *Stand Back and Deliver: Accelerating Business Agility.* Addison-Wesley, 2009.

Chapter 13

Understanding the Need

Introduction

Most projects start because someone has an idea. Often, it's an idea to develop a new product or service, update an existing product or service, or make some change to a part of the organization. From an organizational perspective, projects can be started based on strategy, the desire for operational efficiencies, or in reaction to some change in the environment. But projects can also be started when someone has enough influence to launch an effort that supposedly helps the organization but really furthers his or her own ends. These are often referred to as "pet projects," and as much as organizations like to claim they don't exist, they do.

This chapter is not about pet projects. Not directly at least. This chapter is about building a shared understanding of the need that must be satisfied and determining whether the project is worth doing. The techniques described in this chapter provide a variety of collaborative ways to build shared understanding among teams and their stakeholders. The results of these techniques are helpful, but the conversations that they spark are even more helpful.

Even though I won't specifically address pet projects here (although I keep mentioning them), organizations that use these techniques may just spark the kind of conversations that put a stop to pet projects, or at least keep them on a leash.

A shared understanding of vision is important because it provides a common base for the success of the effort. If a team does not have a shared understanding of the effort's goals and purpose, odds are fairly good that the effort will not be successful. Why? Because even if team members don't consciously realize it, each individual on the team will have a different basis for day-to-day decisions about work. These differences will drive suboptimal results.

The goal of this chapter is to describe how to build a shared understanding of the vision, not necessarily how to create the vision. The difference is subtle but important. Projects inevitably come from individual people (we'll call them sponsors for ease of reference), either because those people initially conceive the project, or because they're responsible for the impacted portion of the organization. This is good and proper, because at the end of the day you still need a specific decision maker for those few extremely critical decisions that can greatly impact the success or failure of the effort. At the same time, you don't want all project decisions falling to a single person, so you need clear, uncomplicated guidelines for everyone working on the effort. Building shared understanding is more about communication and clarification than creation. Of course, the vision may be refined during discussions that create shared understanding; new information may come to light that changes the sponsor's perspective or maybe even convinces everyone that the project just should not happen.

These are the techniques described in this chapter:

- Decision filters
- Project opportunity assessment
- Problem statement

These techniques can be used individually or in conjunction with each other, depending on the nature of the project. That said, I strongly recommend establishing decision filters and objectives for every project.

Decision Filters

What It Is

Decision filters are simple questions used to guide decision making. They provide a quick way to communicate goals and objectives to everyone involved in realizing those goals and objectives. To put it in the words of Niel Nickolaisen, who originally created the concept: "Decision filters help teams do the smart stuff better and stop doing stupid stuff." In effect, they tell you when to say no to a project that does not truly align with strategy.

An Example

The project-level decision filter for the conference submission system is "Will this help us have a community-based submission process?"

The decision filter for our first release of the conference submission system was "Will this help us receive submissions and provide reviews?"

When to Use It

Decision filters can be used for

- Ensuring strategic alignment
- Aligning key product features
- Aligning key project objectives
- Aligning release goals
- Aligning iteration goals
- Determining the design approach (to determine if an activity is differentiating)

Why Use It

Decision filters make the goals and objectives of an organization very clear and accessible and are a quick way to check whether the team's current actions are aligned with those goals and objectives.

Every day, organizations are impacted by decisions made by people at every level. Even seemingly minute tactical decisions can impact the overall organization. Successful organizations realize this and look for ways to align decision making in all parts of the organization so the people who are in the best position with the most up-to-date information are making decisions. These are usually the people who are closest to the immediate impact of the decision. Blocks put in place by politics and corporate culture mean that those higher up are inherently less well informed than those next to the action.

While this type of distributed decision making is ideal for many reasons, organization leaders still look for some way to align decisions so that the people making those decisions apply the available information in a way that is beneficial to the organization and consistent with its chosen direction. The balancing act becomes providing enough guidance to decision makers without restricting their ability to use the information available as a result of their direct work with the project.

How to Use It

1. **Create the decision filters through conversations among key stakeholders. Decision filters are usually derived from goals and objectives.**

   Identify a few questions that encapsulate what you are trying to accomplish with your organization, product, project, release, or iteration. Use those decision filters to guide choices about what to do and how to approach it. Having useful decision filters therefore comes down to how you create the filters and how you use them to make decisions.

The decision filter technique can be used for a variety of purposes, often closely aligned with different levels of planning. Depending on the type of decision you're trying to guide, decision filters may be restatements of other key ideas such as objectives, conditions of satisfaction, or key success criteria. Regardless, decision filters are usually created the same way—through conversations.

Decision filter conversations usually include all of the people who provide the filters (the objectives, conditions of satisfaction, or key success criteria) and some of the people who have to enact the decisions. For more tactical decisions, the conversations will include more people who have to enact the decisions. These conversations can provide a great deal of background information for teams, but eventually people who weren't involved in these discussions will need to use the resulting decision filters. It is for those folks that the decision filters are really being created, to help guide their decisions on a day-to-day basis.

Decision filter conversations usually start with generating a large number of potential filters (divergence) and then converging on two or three.

2. **Communicate the decision filters to the teams responsible for realizing those goals and objectives.**

   How you communicate the decision filters is especially important if some or all of the people who need to use them were not included in the initial conversations. In that case, it is often helpful to include highlights of the creation conversations, to provide a bit of background for the team.

   The best way to see if the team understands the decision filters is to have them use the decision filters to make an actual decision and see if they apply them correctly. The team may not recognize missing information until they are using the decision filters for a specific purpose.

3. **Use the decision filters in those teams to determine what they will and will not deliver.**

   Decision filters are extremely helpful in backlog refinement and prioritization discussions. Once the team understands the decision filters, you need to make sure they are used consistently. I like to post decision filters (either physically on the wall or virtually on a team website) where the team can refer to them on a regular basis. When the team is struggling with a decision or when a discussion appears that seems to be going on a bit longer than it should, someone on the team can point to the decision filter on the wall and ask, "Is this helping us get to that?" I have used that technique for workshops, software development teams, and teams working on a transition, and in all cases I have found it to be a great way to refocus the team.

Caveats and Considerations

Strive for just a few decision filters; two or three is ideal. The more filters you have, the fewer things will satisfy all of the filters, and the greater the likelihood that they will be in conflict. The discussions you have to narrow down to these two or three key ideas can be very enlightening and can help a team establish a clear idea of what to deliver. It's easy to identify a long laundry list of things you want to work on, but narrowing the list down to those few critical factors really helps a team focus.

Avoid conflicting decision filters. This applies to goals and objectives as well. It may seem like common sense, but unless a team explicitly looks at their goals in entirety and establishes their goals as more than a check-the-box activity at the beginning of an initiative, it can be very easy for a project to have conflicting goals. This makes it difficult for a team to determine what to focus on, or it can lead to deliveries that end up conflicting with each other, resulting in a solution that does not appear to work.

It may be helpful to prioritize decision filters, especially when discussing them at the release level.

Decision filters need to be actionable, and they really need to be filters. If the filter is nebulous, such as "Make great software," it won't be very effective.

Additional Resources

Elssamadisy, Amr. "An Interview with the Authors of 'Stand Back and Deliver: Accelerating Business Agility.'" www.informit.com/articles/article.aspx?p=1393062.

McDonald, Kent. "Decision Filters." www.beyondrequirements.com/decisionfilters/.

Pixton, Pollyanna, Niel Nickolaisen, Todd Little, and Kent McDonald. *Stand Back and Deliver: Accelerating Business Agility*. Addison-Wesley, 2009.

Project Opportunity Assessment

What It Is

Marty Cagan in his book *Inspired* suggests a product opportunity assessment. Cagan's assessment consists of ten questions to ask when examining a product opportunity to elicit more information about it and determine whether it is worth pursuing. I've compiled a similar list of questions for people working in IT projects to use when initially looking at a project to determine if it is worth it. You can think of it as a project opportunity assessment.

The questions in the assessment are listed in Table 13.1.

Table 13.1 *Questions for Project Opportunity Assessment*

Question	Explanation
1. Exactly what problem will this solve?	This question may be difficult to answer, but it's very important to get it right so that you can ensure that you are attacking a clearly defined problem and don't just have a solution in search of a problem.
2. For whom do we solve that problem?	This question seeks to identify the key stakeholders and the people who will have a vested interest in the project.
3. What can be gained from solving this problem?	This question identifies the benefits to be gained from the project. Do not feel as if you need a highly precise answer at this point. An order-of-magnitude answer is usually good enough to determine whether the problem is worth solving.
4. How will we measure success?	This is a way of identifying measurable objectives relevant to the project.
5. What alternatives are out there now?	This is another way of asking what would happen if you don't solve this problem, as well as identifying different ways of solving it.
6. Do we have the right people to solve this problem?	This question seeks to identify whether you have the appropriate skill sets working on the team, and if not, whether you need to bring in help from inside or outside the organization.
7. Why now?	This question asks what time constraints, if any, exist for the project.
8. How will we encourage adoption?	This is to get you thinking about change management and implementation.
9. What factors are critical to success?	This singles out any specific requirements identified during the discussion or subsequent analysis. This question is not meant to identify the solution; rather, it highlights any dependencies or constraints that may exist.
10. Is this problem worth solving?	This question sums up the discussion. Based on what you've discussed up to this point, is this project worth it?

An Example

Table 13.2 shows a project opportunity assessment for the conference submission system (Chapter 7) when getting ready for Agile2013.

Table 13.2 *Project Opportunity Assessment for the Conference Submission System*

Question	Answer
1. Exactly what problem will this solve?	Need to accept session proposals, review proposals, provide feedback, and select sessions for Agile2013. The current submission system is based on an out-of-date platform and is difficult to maintain.
2. For whom do we solve that problem?	Submitters, program team
3. What can be gained from solving this problem?	Address several issues with the existing system and allow for ease of update going forward.
4. How will we measure success?	Do we get a good collection of sessions for the conference, and are submitters getting good feedback so that they can revise their submissions?
5. What alternatives are out there now?	• Revise the existing submission system. • Purchase a system.
6. Do we have the right people to solve this problem?	Yes
7. Why now?	Need to have the submission system available by December 1, 2012, to allow submitters sufficient time to submit their sessions.
8. How will we encourage adoption?	Notify people that in order to speak at the conference, they have to submit via the submission system.
9. What factors are critical to success?	• Automated testing • Ability to release in stages • Familiarity with the submission process
10. Is this problem worth solving?	Yes

When to Use It

These questions should be asked as early as possible in the project lifecycle, or even during initial consideration of a project—the earlier, the better. A project opportunity assessment often leads a team to question whether a project is worth doing at all, or only worth it in certain circumstances.

If the project is in progress and these questions have not been asked or answered, or if conditions have changed significantly, it is worth revisiting these questions.

Why Use It

A project opportunity assessment serves one of two possible purposes:

1. It can keep your organization from wasting time and money on satisfying poorly defined needs or problems that aren't worth addressing.

2. For those needs that are worth satisfying, it can focus the team and help them understand what will be required to succeed and how to define that success.

These questions structure initial discussions about the nature of a project and the value it delivers. The mere act of asking may identify the need for further research, or it may uncover undiscussed assumptions that point to the project not being worth it, or even feasible. The goal of the project opportunity assessment is to remind the team of important considerations when eliciting information that can be immediately helpful in evaluating a project without a great deal of effort. If a project has satisfactory answers to most or all of these questions, the team can then move on to more detailed analysis.

How to Use It

1. Gather the key stakeholders—the same ones who would discuss decision filters and the Purpose-Based Alignment Model if you were using those tools.

2. Discuss the ten questions, ensuring that you have a satisfactory answer for each question before moving to the next. In some cases, you may find that you do not know enough to answer the question in that discussion. You will have to use your judgment to determine whether it's appropriate to do some further research. In some cases, the fact that the group cannot agree on an answer may indicate that the need is not significant enough at this time to continue.

3. If you identified any additional research that's necessary, determine who will do that research (preferably volunteers) and when the group will reconvene to continue discussions.

Caveats and Considerations

This line of questioning focuses entirely on the need to satisfy (in the guise of a problem to be solved). The questions do not delve into possible solutions, because the initial focus of analysis should be on whether or not you understand the need and the impact of satisfying it.

These questions are intended to spark discussion and yet be answered fairly quickly. Do not continue with the project until you get these questions answered, but at the same time do not spend too much time and analysis trying to answer them. If you do some offline research, allow a week at most for that research so that project progress does not grind to a halt. If the project is truly not worth it, it's better to figure that out sooner rather than later.

This line of questions seems to mirror the six questions discussed in Chapter 12. However, the subject of the questions is different. The six questions focus on the organization as a whole. The project opportunity assessment focuses specifically on the problem a particular project is intended to solve.

Additional Resource

Cagan, Marty. *Inspired: How to Create Products Customers Love*. SVPG Press, 2008.

Problem Statement

What It Is

The problem statement is a structured set of statements that describe the purpose of an effort in terms of what problem it's trying to solve (see Table 13.3).

An Example

Since the most important part of this technique is the conversations that occur rather than the end product, I'd like to relay a story about a time when I used this technique with a team that was in the midst of an effort to revise their commission system. There were 11 people involved, including the sponsor, a couple of subject matter experts, and the majority of the delivery team. I had them do the problem statement exercise partly to build that shared understanding, but also to see where they were in relation to their understanding of the problem.

Table 13.3 *Components of the Problem Statement*

The problem of	[Describe the problem.]
Affects	[Who are the stakeholders affected by the problem?]
The impact of which is	[What is the impact of the problem?]
A successful solution would be	[List the critical benefits or key capabilities that the solution—however implemented—must have to be successful.]

When I had the group build their individual problem statements—for the same project, mind you—we ended up with 11 different perceptions of what the project was about, ranging from making some changes to the commission system to make it easier to maintain, to completely overhauling how the organization paid its agents. Needless to say, the team was a bit surprised about the differences in perspectives, especially considering that the project had been under way for a few months by that point. Everyone just assumed that they were "all on the same page" regarding what the project was all about until they did this exercise.

By working through each of the different portions of the problem statement, we were able to converge to a shared understanding of the purpose of the project. Later, the team members were able to use this as one way of deciding what they should and shouldn't focus on.

When to Use It

During kickoff activities, a problem statement activity is a good way to help a team build a shared understanding about the problem the project is trying to solve. You may use this technique to structure discussions around the first question from the project opportunity assessment.

If the project is already under way, you still may find it helpful to take a little time to create or revisit a problem statement, especially if you sense that the team does not have a shared understanding of what the project is really all about.

Why Use It

This technique provides a structure for conducting productive conversations. It describes things in term of a problem, but it provides some context around who is most concerned about the problem and why. It also focuses on characteristics of the solution without implying a solution by itself. That makes this a good technique to use when your team is dealing with a potential build/buy situation and needs a way to organize their thoughts on what they are looking for.

How to Use It

1. Get the sponsor, stakeholders, and delivery team together, and ask them to grab four sticky notes (or index cards) and a marker.

2. On each of the cards, each person should write his or her version of the four parts of the problem statement. For example, my cards for the conference submission system might look like those listed in Table 13.4.

Table 13.4 *Cards for the Conference Submission System*

Card 1	The problem of selecting conference sessions
Card 2	Affects presenters
Card 3	The impact of which is they frequently do not receive actionable feedback on their session proposals or know why they were/were not selected
Card 4	A successful solution would be open and transparent.

3. Once everyone has written their cards, ask participants to read their statements in order and place their cards on four parts of the wall (if you have self-sticking cards or sticky notes) or four parts of a table, each part corresponding to a part of the problem statement.

4. After everyone has read their statements, have the group work through each part of the problem statement and come up with a statement that they can all support.

Caveats and Considerations

This technique could easily become a check-the-box exercise, where people complete it for the sake of completing it, but I've found a way to make the problem statement an interactive exercise, which is good for sparking a great deal of conversation.

Chances are you will have as many different views of the problem as you do people involved in the exercise. By having them write their ideas on cards, you enable a large group to sort, combine, and move the various ideas to aid the discussion and converge on a problem statement. Again, you probably won't end up changing the real problem the effort is focused on (though you might), but you will certainly create a much better understanding of the problem you are trying to solve, assuming everyone in the group is involved in the discussion.

The best outcome of this exercise is not the problem statement specifically, but the conversations that occur as the group tries to converge on a single understanding of the project. Assumptions that people have in their heads but had never voiced come to the surface. The shared understanding consists of not only the resulting problem statement but also the information shared during the discussions.

Additional Resource

Gottesdiener, Ellen. *The Software Requirements Memory Jogger: A Pocket Guide to Help Software and Business Teams Develop and Manage Requirements.* Goal/QPC, 2005.

Chapter 14

Understanding the Solution(s)

Introduction

The title of this chapter implies that there may be multiple options to choose from for satisfying a given need. It is certainly worth considering in some situations, and teams ignore this possibility to their detriment. In other cases, however, there is a clear-cut way of satisfying a given need. The trick is figuring out when you need to create a list of options to pick from, and when you need to figure out all the things you need to do to deliver a clear solution.

Confused? How about a few examples?

You are on the board at a small private school and find that communications are choppy between the administration and faculty and the parents. In addition, you have received multiple complaints about the need to provide the same information during registration year after year.

One of the members of the board took it upon himself to research various options for student information systems and has brought a proposal to the board to consider allocating funds to purchase such a system. The board starts discussing all the features a student information system should have, but something just doesn't sit right with you. Does the school really need a student information system? What problem are we really trying to solve?

You let the conversation go on for a while, until you finally ask the question: "What problem are we trying to solve here, and how will we know whether we've solved it?" A hush descends over the room. A couple of the board members nod in agreement. The person who suggested allocating funds to buy a SIS scowls at the table in front of him (but it's really intended for you). Others look at the ceiling reflectively. Finally, the president of the board slowly starts nodding her head and says, "You're right. Let's back up and identify what we're trying to do, and then think about ways of getting there."

At this point you can suggest an approach such as impact mapping, which involves starting with a specific goal, then generating a list of actions by working through the people who can impact progress toward the objective, their behaviors, and what can be done to change those behaviors. This is an excellent situation in which to identify multiple options.

In another example, you are putting together a system to support the submission process for a conference. You know you need to replace the existing system, and it's really important to provide the appropriate functionality to support the session selection process. Impact mapping in this particular case is not very helpful; in fact, it can be a waste of time. You already know you need to build the system, and why. But you do need to understand what things you need to include in the new solution in order to meet the stated objectives. In this situation, a story map and some collaborative modeling can be very helpful in figuring out everything you need to deliver in order to provide a complete, workable solution.

The moral of the story is that while many of these techniques are helpful, they are not always appropriate. In some cases (probably more than you initially may realize), you want to explore options, not get so hung up on the currently popular approach. You have to really understand what organizational need you are trying to satisfy and identify all the possible options to satisfy that need.

On the other hand, you may know what the specific solution needs to look like—at least you may have a clear picture of why you are delivering that solution—and it's much more important to understand what you need to do to make the solution workable. In these cases, the project itself may have been launched as the result of an impact mapping exercise, but there is no value in trying to parse out the deliverable in terms of an impact map. It's the wrong tool for the job. These situations call for a way to organize your backlog to reflect the key things needed to provide a complete solution. Ways of organizing things graphically can help put in perspective what things are needed, and when they will be delivered.

Picking the right tool to do this is essential. You don't want to use an impact map to perform what amounts to a **functional decomposition**. You don't want options for different things you could do; you want to know what you *have* to do, and which things—still an aspect of the complete solution—might be optional.

This chapter introduces the various techniques you can use to identify possible solutions (impact mapping) or define and describe solutions (story mapping, collaborative modeling). This chapter also discusses three techniques for describing aspects of the solution: models, acceptance criteria, and examples.

You may have noticed that I don't spend a great deal of time on features or user stories in this chapter, or in fact in the entire book. I made this choice because there is already so much on user stories in the literature, and most of it tends to overemphasize their role. User stories were really intended to be placeholders and reminders to have further conversations about the solution. I have chosen to focus on the specifics of those conversations as characterized by models, acceptance criteria, and examples, rather than the reminders to have the conversations.

Impact Mapping

What It Is

Impact mapping combines mind mapping and strategic planning to help a team explore what behaviors they should try to influence in order to reach a particular objective. Teams use impact maps to discuss assumptions, align with organizational objectives, and develop greater focus in their projects by delivering only the things that lead directly to achieving organizational objectives. This also reduces extraneous activities.

Impact mapping structures conversations around four key questions:

- *Why* are we doing this? The answer to this question is the goal that the project is trying to accomplish as measured by an objective.

- *Who* can bring the organization closer to this objective, or conversely who may prevent us from reaching the objective? The answer to this question identifies the actors who can have some impact on the outcome.

- *How* should our actors' behavior change? The answers generate the impacts you're trying to create.

- *What* can the organization (specifically the delivery team) do to support the desired impacts? The answer to this question identifies the deliverables, which will typically be software features and organizational activities.

An Example

Figure 14.1 is an example impact map for Deep Thought Academy.

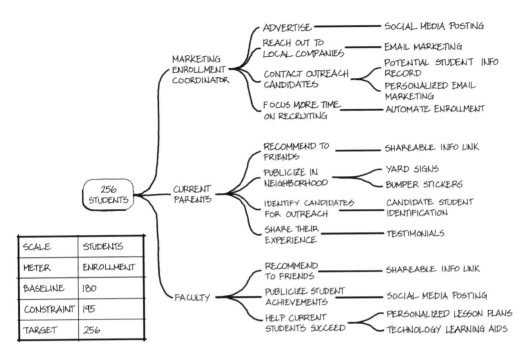

Figure 14.1 *Deep Thought Academy impact map*

When to Use It

Impact mapping does not work in every situation. If you used the Context Leadership Model (Chapter 12) to analyze your project, impact mapping would likely be a good technique to use in the colt and bull quadrants, especially if the uncertainty is from the business perspective.

Gojko Adzic, Ingrid Domingues, and Johan Berndtsson wrote an article on *InfoQ* titled "Getting the Most Out of Impact Mapping" (www.infoq.com/articles/most-impact-mapping) that describes four different contexts where impact maps can be useful. These contexts are based on two key factors: the consequences of being wrong (making the wrong decision) and the ability to make investments. (See Table 14.1.)

Most of the time when I have used impact mapping for IT projects, it has been in the iterate context. In these projects, we would create an impact map to identify potential deliverables, identify the deliverable we wanted to try first, deliver it, then check the resulting impact on behaviors, and more importantly on the objective, to see if the deliverable had the desired effect.

Table 14.1 *Contexts for Impact Mapping*

Context	Description
Iterate	Good ability to make investments and limited consequences of being wrong
	An example is an IT project making changes to an existing system where small changes can be deployed to users incrementally.
	In this context, your team can use impact maps to visualize assumptions, define desired business impacts, and explore user needs. Your team can use the immediate feedback from use of the solution to prove or disprove ideas quickly. You'll find yourself starting with an initial impact map, delivering an item from that map, then evolving the map based on the result, potentially delivering another deliverable from the map.
Align	Poor ability to make investments and limited consequences of being wrong.
	An example is an organization that has several decision makers competing for limited resources.
	In this context, you can use an impact map to drive stakeholder alignment and aid prioritization. You gather your stakeholders around an impact map to discuss the various deliverables that will help achieve a specific outcome and determine which ones will play the biggest part. In this case, multiple deliverables from the impact map can be delivered at the same time, and you aren't as concerned about the impact of any one particular deliverable. The impact map can be a big-picture view in these cases.
Experiment	Good ability to make investments and serious consequences of being wrong
	An example is an organization that has budget available, but its customers and users can't accept changes quickly, or the organization is working in a heavily regulated industry.
	In this context, you can use impact maps to discover opportunities, identify options, and compare solutions. You'll want to explore a variety of options through research with your users before deciding on your solution. Impact maps can help drive this experimentation and determine which solution is most closely aligned to the desired outcome.
Discover	Poor ability to make investments and serious consequences of being wrong
	An example is an organization that is looking to produce innovation products or has initiatives with huge financial risk, but a small budget or an onerous funding process.
	In this context, you can use impact maps to help guide your research efforts. The impact map helps you to visualize your assumptions and identify what research will best support your product development efforts. Your initial impact map will describe your initial hypothesis, and you will add further details as you conduct user studies and user testing.

The other context that occurs most frequently in IT projects is align, where you are trying to get multiple stakeholders to agree on priorities. Gojko described how he has handled that situation in a recent email exchange:

People pretty much know what they want (a transaction accounting system doesn't need a lot of discovery, the domain is pretty clear to everyone), but there are too many things on the list and stakeholders need to align to agree on the priorities that will actually give the organization something big rather than a stream of stories.

In cases such as that, I've used impact maps to paint the big picture and get the stakeholders and tech leaders to agree on the key priorities related to impacts, where the work is then divided [among] several teams. Multiple things can get delivered at the same time, and teams don't rely that much on measurement of impacts to decide what to do next (I still recommend measuring it to ensure that the thing was complete, but it's not the driving factor as in the iterate part of the quadrant, because there is more certainty on internal effects).

Why Use It

Impact mapping offers several advantages when used in the proper context:

- **It reduces waste.** Teams using impact mapping properly and in the proper context will deliver one deliverable at a time and measure the impact of that delivery on the objective. If they meet the objective, they can stop work on that project, satisfying their stakeholders' need with a minimum of new code.

- **It provides focus.** Deliverables are selected based on how they contribute to behaviors that will enable the organization to meet its objective.

- **It increases collaboration.** The discussions that occur while the impact map is created can be very helpful for surfacing assumptions and establishing a sequence for the actions to take in the project.

- **It verifies that the team is building the right thing.** Using impact mapping helps teams ensure that they are focusing on the right outcomes. Teams are also provided with a mechanism to discuss and test their assumptions.

How to Use It

1. Get the team and stakeholders together.

2. Identify the objective (why).

3. Think about people whose behavior can help the organization get closer to the goal, or people whose behavior will move the organization farther away from the goal (actors—who).

4. For all the actors you identified, think about what behaviors you want them to start, or change, to help your organization get closer to the objective, or behaviors that are preventing your organization from getting closer to those objectives (impacts).

5. For each behavior, identify possible things that the organization can deliver to help drive changes in those behaviors (deliverables).

6. Decide which deliverable to deliver first to gauge its impact on the targeted objective.

Caveats and Considerations

Although the second branch is described as exploring a "how" question, the "how" is focused on how you would like your actors' behavior to change, not how to deliver a particular piece of functionality. I find it better to refer to this as the impacts rather than "how," to reinforce the idea that it is focused on behavior.

The third branch, deliverables, is the first mention of IT. The goal is to focus on behavior change first and then explore ways we can support that behavior change.

Just because you identified a lot of different options does not mean you should enact all of them. You want to reach the stated objective, but do it with the least amount of work possible, so once your team has diverged on a list of options, they should then converge on what they believe to be the best first option.

If your project has multiple objectives, do an impact map for each objective.

Additional Resources

Adzic, Gojko. *Impact Mapping: Making a Big Impact with Software Products and Projects*. Provoking Thoughts, 2012.

Campbell-Pretty, Em. "Adventures in Scaling Agile." www.prettyagile.com/2014/02/how-i-fell-in-love-with-impact-mapping.html.

"Impact Mapping." http://impactmapping.org/.

Story Mapping

What It Is

A story map is a visual representation of a backlog that provides additional context regarding how backlog items are related to each other and when the team is planning to deliver them. This context is typically presented in terms of the personas that will use specific features, and the particular user stories that are associated with the features.

An Example

Figure 14.2 shows an example story map for the conference submission system.

When to Use It

Story maps as originally described by Jeff Patton are a very helpful elicitation technique when trying to understand a solution that has a great deal of user interaction. Creating the story map guides the team as they talk through the business process, identify the key activities (represented as features), and lay them out in a logical sequence.

There are many cases where the solution does not inherently support a single process or a logical step-by-step order is not so clear. In those cases, story maps can still be useful for visualizing the relationships between features and user stories and representing when specific user stories will be delivered for a given feature.

Why Use It

The unique visual structure of story maps helps the team determine if they have a complete, viable solution.

Story maps also help teams identify the appropriate contents of a given release. The release goal should be to deliver the minimum acceptable functionality while still providing a viable, valuable output with enough useful functionality for stakeholders to provide feedback about. Story maps help the team identify that minimum feature set.

Finally, story maps provide a useful graphical representation that shows which stories are planned for a given release and relates that in context to the features they support. It also encourages discussions about what aspects of a feature really need to be delivered. In many cases, a feature represents a broad area of functionality, and the user stories identified for that feature represent things that have to be done, things that are nice to have, and other things that could easily be considered bells and whistles. The story map generates conversations where the team determines the things that need to be delivered and skips the items that are nice to have. This delivers on the objectives of the solution without wasting time and effort on functionality that doesn't add to its effectiveness.

Story map (rotated). Personas and key activities:

Conference Chair
- Manage Tracks: Assign Roles; Create Track through admin pages; Delete Track through admin pages
- Moderate Content: Edit Keywords; Add new keyword; Delete a keyword; Delete Comment
- Manage Deadlines: Not Supported
- Build Program: Not Supported
- Manage Conference Theme: Manual CSS Changes
- Manage Conference Venue: Add room through admin page; Edit room through admin page; Delete room through admin page

Track Chair
- Manage Track: Assign reviewers (roles)
- Monitor Track: Show Review Activity

Track Reviewer
- Identify proposals to be reviewed: Identify new proposals; Notify of new proposals; Notify of track changes
- Review a proposal: Create a review; Delete my review; Edit my review; Notified of review reply; Reply to review response

Submitter
- Submit a session: Respond to review; Edit a session; Upload attachment; Delete a session; Specify co-presenter; View session reviews; Submit a session; Get notified of new review
- View my session: View session list; View session details
- Create/Manage my account

Attendee
- Provide feedback: Feedback Quick Link
- Plan my conference

Release 1 items (below the line):
- Conference Chair / Moderate Content: Expect presenters will use the admin page; If this functionality is needed we will use the admin page
- Conference Chair / Manage Deadlines: Lock down new submissions; Lock down submission editing
- Conference Chair / Build Program: Release to submitter for editing; Mark acceptance
- Track Chair / Manage Track: Mark recommendation; Edit track description; View Track Sessions

Release 2

Figure 14.2 Conference submission system story map

179

How to Use It

The Story Map as an Elicitation Tool

Gather together key stakeholders and team members. You want to strike a careful balance between having different perspectives in the group and having an unwieldy number of people. A general guideline is to follow the **two-pizza rule:** a good-size group is one you can feed with two large pizzas.

You're also going to want a large surface, either a wall or a table, where you can lay out the sticky notes or index cards you use for the map. Some groups have even resorted to using the floor.

Jeff Patton suggests the following steps for using a story map in an elicitation setting. This technique is especially helpful when eliciting information about a process.

1. **Write out your story one step at a time.** As a group, talk through the various things that happen in the process and write each thing down on a sticky note or index card. Each of these items is a user task, which in this context is a short verb phrase that describes something people do to reach a goal.

2. **Organize your story.** If you weren't already doing so when you identified the tasks, arrange them from left to right in the order they occur. This creates a narrative flow and implies the phrase "and then I . . ." between the tasks. If there are certain tasks that happen at the same time or in lieu of each other, place them vertically in a column.

3. **Explore alternative stories.** Once you have the tasks in a rough narrative flow, play "What About." Discuss alternative things that could happen at various points during the story. Write these thoughts on additional sticky notes or index cards and place them in the appropriate column.

4. **Distill your map to make a *backbone*.** Review all the tasks and where they combine into common groups, and use an easily distinguished note (for instance, a different color or shape) as a group title, or activity. The activity should also be written as a verb phrase that distills all the tasks underneath it. These activities should also form a narrative flow and provide the outline of a high-level story.

5. **Slice out tasks that help you reach a specific outcome.** Identify a specific outcome that you want to accomplish, and then identify the specific tasks that are absolutely essential to arriving at that outcome. Leave all the activities at the top of the story map, but move the tasks that don't

contribute to the particular outcome below the line for that outcome. This step allows you to focus on only the tasks and activities that are essential to accomplishing your desired outcome. Those outcomes can be thought of as a "happy path" through a process or a minimum viable product.

When you are ready to start delivering the solution represented by the map, you can think of each task as a user story. You especially benefit from the fact that the tasks are already written from a user perspective.

The Story Map as a Backlog Visualization Tool

Even if you are working on a solution that does not have a large amount of user interaction or does not clearly support a business process, the story map format can still help you understand the context of your backlog.

1. **Frame the problem.** Establish a shared understanding of what need the solution is intended to satisfy. The techniques described in Chapter 13 can be especially helpful here.

2. **Map the big picture.** Lay out the story map using features as the high-level items across the top of the map. If you have different types of users who can use specific types of features, it may be helpful to organize the features by user. If there are any obvious user stories that can be identified for those features, place them under the appropriate feature at this point.

3. **Explore.** Select the feature(s) you believe you will be delivering first and do a deep dive on them via conversation with the interested stakeholders. Sketch models to aid the conversation (you may find those sketches helpful later on when you start delivering those particular stories). As you have those discussions you may find that you will refine your map.

4. **Slice out a release strategy.** Look at the user stories identified for the features and determine the minimum user stories needed to deliver the desired goal. The idea is to identify the minimum output to deliver the maximum outcome. Organize these user stories into a set of releases by moving them vertically.

5. **Identify the items to start with.** Once you have identified a set of releases, you may find it helpful to identify the user stories you want to start with, as experiments where you are either trying to validate key assumptions or reduce risk. These stories become the topics of your first iteration.

Caveats and Considerations

It's very likely that you will identify and place more items on your story map than you actually deliver. This is appropriate and expected, as one of the reasons for a story map is to identify user stories that are needed and those that are extraneous in the broader context of what you are trying to accomplish.

If you have used the story map to elicit information about a process, it may be difficult to identify names for the activities, as the grouping may not be as natural as the individual tasks. When trying to name these activities, think about what your users/stakeholders would call them.

Do not try to use story maps in isolation from other techniques. They are ultimately an aid to collaboration and conversation, whether you are using them for elicitation purposes or to visualize the backlog.

Story maps can also be used to familiarize people with the process the solution is supporting. Members of the team can walk new folks through the process using the story map as a visual aid.

Additional Resources

Patton, Jeff. *User Story Mapping: Discover the Whole Story, Build the Right Product*. O'Reilly Media, 2014.

————. "User Story Mapping." www.agileproductdesign.com/presentations/user_story_mapping/.

Collaborative Modeling

What It Is

Collaborative modeling refers to the use of well-known requirements analysis and modeling techniques in a collaborative fashion to build and maintain a shared understanding of the problem space and the potential solution. The main premise is that requirements models, which have long been viewed as documentation techniques, can also be put to great use as elicitation and analysis techniques in a collaborative setting with the delivery team and stakeholders jointly discussing the problem and solution.

Modeling techniques that I find particularly helpful are listed in Table 14.2. Note that for consistency and familiarity I list each of these techniques based on the result they create, but I cannot stress enough that the artifacts are not

Table 14.2 *Collaborative Modeling Techniques*

Technique	Description
Data dictionary	Agree on entities and their attributes as well as the definitions and specific characteristics of both.
Context diagram	Understand the people, systems, or organizations impacted by a solution and the interfaces between those parties and the solution.
Logical data model	Relative to a possible solution, understand the data that stakeholders want to know and remember and how that data is organized.
State transition diagram	Understand the specific states a particular entity can be in and what causes the state to change.
Glossary	Agree on key terms and their definitions.
Organization chart	Understand the reporting relationships between people impacted by a solution.
Value stream map	Identify opportunities for improvement in the operations of an organization.
Functional decomposition	Understand complex processes, systems, functional areas, or deliverables by breaking them down into their simpler constituent parts.
Process flow	Understand the specifics of a particular process for the purpose of identifying changes to implement a solution.
Wireframe	Agree upon the nature of a user interface, including what information should be included.
Report mockup	Understand the information needs of stakeholders in order to help them answer questions or make decisions.

as important as the discussions held to create them. The artifacts can be helpful to document the discussions and any decisions made, but the discussions themselves are powerful ways to build shared understanding. The resulting artifacts go from being the sole means of communication to aids for the overall communication.

An Example

Figure 14.3 is a state transition diagram I put together for the submission system to represent a change for Agile2015.

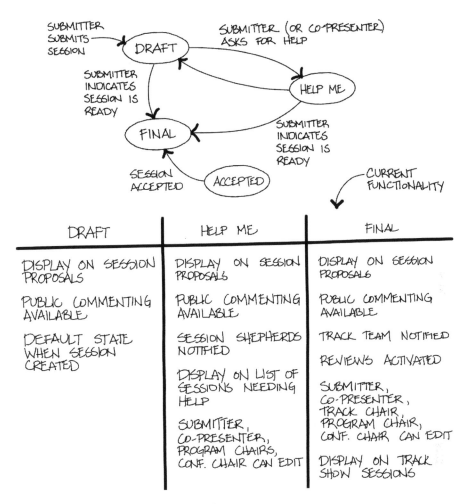

Figure 14.3 *Submission system state diagram*

When to Use It

Different collaborative modeling techniques are useful in different aspects of an IT project. The three aspects are listed here, followed by Table 14.3, which indicates which features apply when.

- **Define the problem space.** Your team can use collaborative modeling when it starts work on a new project and needs to understand the context in which a problem occurs (I often refer to this as the "problem space") and how potential solutions might impact the problem space.

- **Define a specific solution.** Your team can use collaborative modeling to define a specific solution and provide a foundation for the team to identify implementation options. When used for this purpose, the models help your team identify features and user stories based on a full understanding of the solution.

- **Describe specific aspects of the solution.** Your team can use collaborative modeling to further describe specific backlog items. The models you use for this aspect may be ones you initially created to define the solution, or your team may find it helpful to create more detailed models to get a better understanding about a particular aspect of the solution.

There are a variety of different modeling techniques that are all very useful in specific situations (see Table 14.4), but none of the techniques is applicable in all situations.

Table 14.3 *Applicable Collaborative Modeling Techniques*

Technique	Define the Problem Space	Define a Specific Solution	Describe Specific Aspects of the Solution
Data dictionary			X
Context diagram	X	X	X
Logical data model	X	X	X
State transition diagram			X
Glossary		X	X
Organization chart	X	X	X
Value stream map	X	X	
Functional decomposition	X	X	X
Process flow		X	X
Wireframe		X	X
Report mockup		X	X

Table 14.4 *Scenarios Where Collaborative Modeling Techniques Are Helpful*

When You Are in This Scenario . . .	These Techniques Can Be Helpful
Your solution has a lot of interfaces with other systems or organizations.	Context diagram
Your solution is fairly data intensive.	Context diagram Logical data model Data dictionary

Continues

Table 14.4 *Scenarios Where Collaborative Modeling Techniques Are Helpful (Continued)*

When You Are in This Scenario . . .	These Techniques Can Be Helpful
You are looking to identify improvements in business processes.	Value stream map
	Process flow
Your solution is aiming to support decision making or analytics.	Report mockup
	Data dictionary
	Logical data model
Your solution is fairly complicated.	Functional decomposition

Why Use It

Collaborative modeling provides a way for teams to build a shared understanding of the problem and solution options first, without having to go down the path of breaking the solution into implementation chunks (i.e., user stories). This approach addresses a couple of issues that occur when backlog creation relies on brainstorming alone.

Backlogs Don't Identify a Complete Solution

By discussing the solution via models first, the team can identify all the changes that need to occur to implement a viable solution because they have a picture to fall back on. Brainstorming alone does not provide that big picture as a way of validating that the team has identified what is needed.

Backlogs End Up Becoming a Wish List

When a team collaboratively models the solution and uses the model as a way of identifying the changes that need to happen, they can also use the model to help identify changes that aren't necessary. Building a backlog via brainstorming can often generate backlog items that are not absolutely essential to the desired solution. By having a model to reference that shows the specific changes that are necessary, the team can identify extraneous items that are not essential in order to solve the problem.

How to Use It

The general steps for collaborative modeling are quite simple:

1. Gather the right people together. The definition of "right" is based on the subject of the discussion and the intended outcomes.

2. Make sure the place where you gather is near a whiteboard and/or flip chart paper (preferably both) and that there are plenty of sticky notes and the right type of markers available.

3. Identify the reason for the discussion. Are you there to discuss the overall context of the solution, analyze a specific process, or agree on a particular user interface or report? Identify discussion acceptance criteria: in other words, how you will know the discussion was successful.

4. Make sure everyone has the same understanding of the current state. This is not as simple as asking if everyone is "on the same page." It's best to sketch out the current state quickly, or start with an existing representation of the current state, and explicitly ask if everyone is in agreement. If there is any disagreement, adjust the description of the current state until people indicate that it represents the true current situation.

5. Have the person with the best understanding of the desired change start describing the change by sketching on the whiteboard and talking through it at the same time. You may also find that it is helpful to have someone guide the discussion by asking questions of the stakeholder and sketching his or her interpretation of the answer on the whiteboard. The key is to talk and sketch things at the same time, to reinforce the conversation and lead to greater agreement.

6. End the discussion when everyone agrees that you have met the discussion acceptance criteria identified in step 3.

7. If anyone in the discussion thinks it would be helpful to keep the sketches that were made during the discussion, take pictures of them and save the pictures in a commonly agreed-upon repository for project documentation.

The specifics of these steps can vary depending on the reason for the discussion. Some of the main variations are described in Table 14.5.

Table 14.5 *Collaborative Modeling Variations*

Scenario	Right People	Suggested Acceptance Criteria
Define the problem space.	• Key stakeholders (those with decision-making authority and who are sponsoring the project) • Team	Clear shared understanding of scope from the perspective of which units in the organization are included, what objectives the project is trying to meet
Define a specific solution.	• Key subject matter experts • Stakeholders with decision-making authority • Team	Agreed-upon models of future state, backlog of items generated based on future state, or sufficient information to identify those backlog items at a later date
Describe specific aspects of the solution.	• Impacted stakeholders • Someone with testing perspective • Someone with development perspective	Models sufficient for describing the selected backlog items

Caveats and Considerations

The same models used to define a specific solution can also be used to further describe specific aspects of the solution. The models used to define a specific solution may be general in nature, and the discussions when describing specific aspects of the solution will describe parts of the models in further detail.

Collaborative modeling works best when the participants in the conversation are in the same room. If some members of your group work offsite, you can still do collaborative modeling with the aid of technology. Bring as many people together as you can in the same room, and then use a laptop or tablet camera to share the whiteboard with virtual team members. If all members of the team are distributed, use screen-sharing and handwriting apps to simulate an electronic whiteboard. The key in all cases is to supplement discussions with visuals.

Additional Resources

Agile Modeling. "Agile Models Distilled: Potential Artifacts for Agile Modeling." http://agilemodeling.com/artifacts/.

Agile Modeling. "Inclusive Modeling: User Centered Approaches for Agile Software Development." http://agilemodeling.com/essays/inclusiveModels.htm.

Acceptance Criteria

What It Is

Acceptance criteria are the conditions that a solution must satisfy to be accepted by a user, a customer, or, in the case of system-level functionality, the consuming system. They are also a set of statements, each with a clear pass/fail result, that specify both functional and nonfunctional requirements and are applicable at a variety of levels (feature and user stories).

Liz Keogh notes that acceptance criteria are useful for several things:

- Further defining the boundaries of a story
- Serving as the functional requirements for the story
- Serving as a set of rules that cover aspects of a system's behavior, and from which examples can be derived

Acceptance criteria point to things that need to be in place in order for the product owner or stakeholders to accept that the user story meets their needs.

As with all good functional requirements, the acceptance criteria should focus on business intent rather than detailing a solution, leaving those specifics for refinement during or right before delivery. Since we're not looking to declare a specific solution, acceptance criteria tend to be implementation agnostic—describing what the team wants to accomplish, not how they're looking to accomplish it. Those types of details can be left to models and examples, or to be figured out during actual delivery.

An Example

This example contains a set of acceptance criteria from the conference submission system, specifically the ability for a reviewer to provide a review of a session proposal.

```
As Reed the Reviewer
  I want to review a session
  So that I can provide feedback to a submitter.
```

Mind Map of Acceptance Criteria

Figure 14.4 is an example mind map of acceptance criteria for the conference submission system.

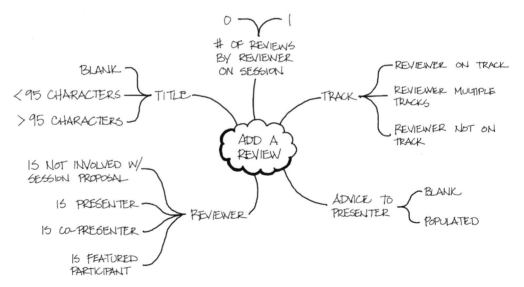

Figure 14.4 *Acceptance criteria mind map*

Potential Acceptance Criteria

- Reviewers must provide a title and description for the review.
- Reviewers may indicate whether they think the session should be included in the program.
- Reviewers may provide details of any conflicts of interest they have in reviewing the session.
- Reviewers may provide comments for the review committee.
- Submitters of the reviewed session can see only the title and description of the review.
- Submitters may see only reviews of sessions that they have submitted.
- Reviewers may review only sessions submitted to tracks on which they are reviewers.
- Reviewers may not review any session on which they are presenters or co-presenters.
- Reviewers may provide only one review for a session.
- The title of the review must contain 95 characters or less.

When to Use It

Acceptance criteria are used most frequently to provide further detail about features and user stories. Many teams find it helpful to identify some acceptance criteria fairly early, to assess the scope included in the story before they size it. Teams may then add acceptance criteria as they discuss the project further, understand the story better, and get closer to delivering the solution.

Why Use It

Defining acceptance criteria is a good way to start adding more detail to the skeleton of a story, and that's where I see most teams doing it. Acceptance criteria are helpful in describing the scope of a story even if (or perhaps especially when) you are using a model to further describe the story. The model may serve as a reference for multiple stories, so the acceptance criteria lend some perspective to specifically which aspects are being delivered with a given story.

How to Use It

1. Meet with the stakeholder(s) who is interested in the particular user story, someone with a development perspective, and someone with a testing

perspective near a whiteboard or flip chart paper. Many teams refer to this group as the **three amigos**.

2. Discuss the user story to determine what the stakeholder hopes to accomplish.

3. Start discussing various things that the team should verify in order to make sure that they deliver the user story correctly. Use a mind map to aid that conversation so the group can see what has been discussed and use that to inspire additional thoughts.

4. Note the acceptance criteria from the mind map and discuss whether all of the acceptance criteria should apply to that user story, or whether the number of acceptance criteria indicates that the user story should be split.

5. Note the related acceptance criteria in your backlog repository of choice.

Caveats and Considerations

Some teams like to preface everything with "Verify that . . ." to reinforce that in order to call a user story done they have to verify specific acceptance criteria, but that seems a bit repetitive and fairly clearly implied. Other teams like to state acceptance criteria in the first person, such as "I need to provide a title and description in order to submit a review." A derivation of that is describing acceptance criteria in terms of the subject of the user story, for example, "Reed needs to provide a title and description in order to submit a review." Either way probably works fine and becomes a matter of taste for the delivery team, but this is certainly something helpful for the team to discuss and agree on.

RuleSpeak, created by Ron Ross, is a "set of guidelines for expressing business rules in concise, business-friendly fashion" (www.rulespeak.com/en/). Since many acceptance criteria are a set of rules that cover aspects of a system's behavior, it may be helpful to apply the precise ideas behind RuleSpeak when describing acceptance criteria, especially if you are in an environment with people who get very specific about how things are written. My only caveat is that you don't want to get so hung up on getting the wording right that you spend more time on the form and lose site of the function. Again, the key is capturing information in a way that the members of the delivery team understand. Some precision is good. Excruciatingly exact precision at the expense of timeliness is not always so helpful. If the team chooses to use RuleSpeak in their acceptance criteria, the presence of a rule in the criteria indicates that enforcement of that rule is included in the delivery of that particular user story.

As with all the techniques described here, use your common sense to pick the pattern that works best. Don't try to force a particular piece of information into a structure that doesn't fit.

Some acceptance criteria items can also be conveyed by a model (such as the information included, and which pieces of information are required), but you may want to be explicit about how much you actually deliver with a given user story.

Also, since acceptance criteria are good for indicating the boundaries of user stories, you will often find that a long list of acceptance criteria is a good indication that the user story needs to be split into smaller stories.

Additional Resources

Keogh, Liz. "Acceptance Criteria vs. Scenarios." http://lizkeogh.com/2011/06/20/acceptance-criteria-vs-scenarios/.

Laing, Samantha, and Karen Greaves. *Growing Agile: A Coach's Guide to Agile Requirements*. https://leanpub.com/agilerequirements.

Mamoli, Sandy. "On Acceptance Criteria for User Stories." http://nomad8.com/acceptance_criteria/.

Ross, Ron. "RuleSpeak." www.rulespeak.com/en/.

Examples

What It Is

Examples are concrete descriptions of the expected behavior of an aspect of a solution using real-life data. Examples are useful for describing a solution and providing guidance on ways to validate it. The use of examples to describe a solution is also known as specification by example, behavior-driven development (BDD), or acceptance test driven development.

There are two common forms used to convey examples. Both forms arose around the needs of automated testing frameworks.

The first format was created to support Fit, the **Framework for Integrated Test**. The intent was to enable stakeholders to provide examples in tools familiar to them (such as a word processor), which developers could then hook up to "fixtures" to produce automated tests. The examples are formatted into tables (which resemble decision tables) in HTML files. Table 14.6 shows how this format works.

Note: Fit was used before the letters were assigned the meaning of Framework for Integrated Test. So while Fit is an acronym, it should not be capitalized.

The second format is often referred to as **Gherkin**, which is a business-readable, domain-specific language created to support the automated testing tool Cucumber. Gherkin is written as a set of statements, each one starting with a keyword.

Table 14.6 *Examples in a Decision Table*

Input1 Heading	Input2 Heading	Input3 Heading	Output1 Heading	Output2 Heading
Scenario 1 Input1 value	Scenario 1 Input2 value	Scenario 1 Input3 value	Scenario 1 Output1 value	Scenario 1 Output2 value
Scenario 2 . . .	Scenario 2 . . .	Scenario 2 . . .	Scenario 2 . . .	Scenario 2 . . .
Scenario 3 . . .	Scenario 3 . . .	Scenario 3 . . .	Scenario 3 . . .	Scenario 3 . . .
Scenario 4 . . .	Scenario 4 . . .	Scenario 4 . . .	Scenario 4 . . .	Scenario 4 . . .

```
Feature: A brief description of what is to be accomplished. Often refers to
a user story.

  Scenario: <A specific business situation>
    Given <precondition>
    And <precondition, if needed>
    And <precondition, if needed
    When <action>
    And <action>
    Then <testable outcome>
    And <testable outcome, if needed>

  Scenario: <Another specific business situation>
```

An Example

This example contains a set of examples from the conference submission system, specifically the ability for a reviewer to provide a review of a session proposal.

```
As Reed The Reviewer
  I want to review a session
  So That I can provide feedback to a submitter.
```

The Fit format is given in Table 14.7.

Table 14.7 *Examples for Conference Submission System*

Reed's Review Track	Presenter	Co-Presenter	Session Submitted to Track	Can Reed Add a Review?
Experience Report	Sam		Experience Report	Yes
Experience Report	Sam		Agile Boot Camp	No
Experience Report	Sam	Steve	Experience Report	Yes
Experience Report	Reed		Experience Report	No
Experience Report	Sam	Reed	Experience Report	No

```
In Gherkin:
  Feature: Add Review
  As a track reviewer
  I want to add reviews

  Background:
    Given I am logged in as "Reed"

  Scenario: Review a session
    Given a session exists on my review track
    When I add a review to that session
    Then the review should be added

  Scenario: Able to review draft sessions
    Given a draft session exists on my review track
    When I add a review to that session
    Then the review should be added

  Scenario: Unable to review for other tracks
    Given "Sam" has created a session on another track
    When I try to add a review to that session
    Then I should not be allowed

  Scenario: Unable to review my own session
    Given I have created a session on my track
    When I try to add a review to that session
    Then I should not be allowed

  Scenario: Unable to review sessions I'm a co-presenter on
    Given a session exists on my review track
    And I am the co-presenter on that session
    When I try to add a review to that session
    Then I should not be allowed

  Scenario: May only review a session once and must respond to existing review
    Given a session exists on my review track
    And I have already reviewed that session
    When I try to add a review to that session
    Then I should be taken to the "Existing Review" page
```

When to Use It

Examples are most frequently used to describe specific aspects of the solution, often as a way of providing further detail about the behavior of the solution in relation to a specific user story. Examples are very helpful when the team is automating their acceptance tests, but they can provide value even if the team is not automating their tests because it drives conversations around the solution's behavior in specific situations.

The different example formats tend to be better suited for different situations as well. The Fit format works best for business rules that have several inputs and/or outputs. Fit provides a way to lay out all the possible combinations of input variables and gives the team a chance to discuss what would happen in each case and, equally important, strike scenarios that won't happen in real life.

The Gherkin format is better suited to situations where someone is interacting with the solution. Examples in this form tend to describe the initial state of the solution followed by some action and the resulting state.

If your team is using a specific automated testing tool, that tool may dictate the example format you use. But if your team is using scenarios to help build a shared understanding of specific details, feel free to use both formats in whatever way seems most appropriate.

Examples are often used as ongoing documentation, providing a fairly accurate—and ideally easy-to-understand—reference of what rules the system enforces and expected interaction behavior that the solution exhibits. We make great use of acceptance criteria in the conference submission system as a starting point when someone reports a defect, or has a question about what the submission system does or should do. The examples represent the actual scenarios we accounted for because we associate automated acceptance tests with all of the code we write. When someone asks a question about the submission system, I first check the examples we have and find that when something doesn't seem to be working right, nine times out of ten it's because we didn't account for that particular situation.

Why Use It

Examples are helpful as a way of structuring the conversation about how a solution should behave in specific situations, remembering that discussion for future reference (i.e., documentation), and providing a way for the team to agree upon how to validate that whatever the team builds is working properly. It's very helpful to create examples as a group so that you can discuss and agree upon how the system should behave when certain scenarios are encountered. This may include discussing what type of messages the solution provides when a particular rule is violated, or actions that the solution does and does not allow.

How to Use It

1. Meet with your "three amigos": the stakeholder(s) interested in the particular user story, someone with a development perspective, and someone with a testing perspective. Meet near a whiteboard or flip chart paper. You may find that you discuss examples at the same time you are clarifying acceptance criteria.

2. Discuss the user story to determine what the stakeholder is hoping to accomplish.

3. If you created a mind map of your acceptance criteria, it may be helpful to refer to that when discussing examples.

4. For each particular interaction, or rule, talk about the various scenarios that could occur. These scenarios may include

   - Happy path
   - Negative path(s)
   - Alternative path(s)
   - Edge case(s)

5. For each scenario you identify, discuss whether that scenario will really occur. If it will not, disregard it. If it will, discuss the specifics, either the input and output values, or the precondition, action, and result, depending on which format you use.

6. Once you have identified all the scenarios that come to mind, discuss if the number of examples indicates the need to split the user story.

7. Note the examples in your repository of choice.

Caveats and Considerations

Acceptance criteria can provide the starting point for identifying examples. However, keep in mind that you do not need to create an example for all acceptance criteria. Examples are helpful for identifying clear ways to explain the acceptance criteria and conveniently lead to tests, but they are not essential for every specific item. Acceptance criteria, not examples, provide some clearer definition of the scope of a given user story, such as "How far does it go?" Examples provide deeper understanding of some aspects of that.

Create examples with real data you would expect to find in your solution.

Wait to figure the examples out until you are getting close to automating them. Examples may get into some specific implementation details and as a matter of course will tend to get identified closer to the delivery time frame, perhaps most effectively during three amigos discussions shortly prior to delivery.

Additional Resources

Adzic, Gojko. *Bridging the Communication Gap: Specification by Example and Agile Acceptance Testing*. Neuri Limited, 2009.

———. *Specification by Example: How Successful Teams Deliver the Right Software*. Manning Publications, 2011.

Fit "Customer Guide." http://fit.c2.com/wiki.cgi?CustomerGuide.

Gherkin description in Cucumber Wiki. https://github.com/cucumber/cucumber/wiki/Gherkin.

Keogh, Liz. Collection of BDD-related links. http://lizkeogh.com/behaviour-driven-development/.

———. *Behaviour-Driven Development: Using Examples in Conversation to Illustrate Behavior—A Work in Progress.* https://leanpub.com/bdd.

Chapter 15

Organizing and Persisting Solution Information

Introduction

In the previous chapter, I described techniques for understanding the solution that involved progressive elaboration—that is, defining a solution in broad brushstrokes, and then describing slices of it in greater detail. This approach certainly allows for a great deal of flexibility and allows learning to take place throughout, but it can be difficult for the team to have a good idea of where they are or what part of the solution they are working on. In addition, this gradual buildup of understanding and focus on documentation often leads to concern about not having any information about the solution available for use on future efforts.

This chapter describes some techniques to address those challenges.

The discovery board and definition of ready help teams with their discovery process, in other words, getting backlog items ready to deliver and building the shared understanding of each slice in due course. The discovery board provides a visual representation of where backlog items are in the discovery process, and the definition of ready provides a means of knowing when teams have enough information and keeps them from spending too much time on analysis.

The delivery board and definition of done do the same thing for work occurring in the delivery process, where parts of the solution are built and tested.

And finally, system documentation provides a way of persisting the relevant information for use by future projects impacting the same solution.

Discovery Board

What It Is

Discovery boards are ways for teams to visualize their backlog refinement process. The best discovery boards consist of a whiteboard or wall divided into columns that reflect the various steps a team takes to get product backlog items ready to be delivered (developed and tested) in an iteration. The backlog items are represented by sticky notes or cards that move across the board as the team builds a better understanding of the specifics of each story.

An Example

Figure 15.1 shows a sample discovery board, followed by a description of each column in Table 15.1.

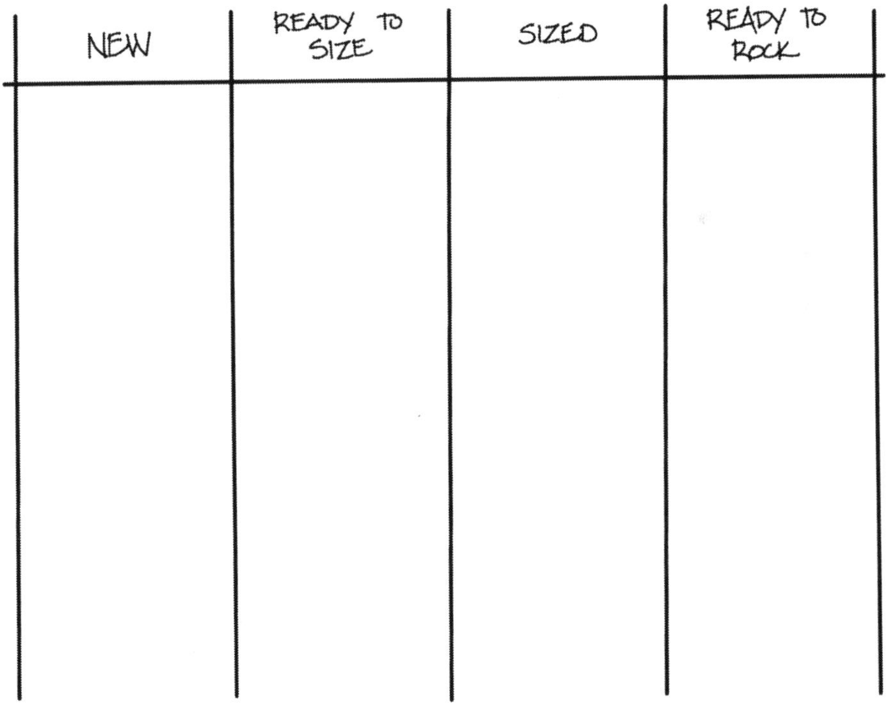

Figure 15.1 *Example discovery board*

Table 15.1 *Example Discovery Board Columns*

Column	Description	Policy (i.e., Entry Criteria)
New	Newly identified user stories and other backlog items. Also user stories that are undergoing further research, identified by a dot on the card. When the research is done, an *X* is marked through the dot.	User story
Ready to Size	User stories that are ready to be estimated. The team has identified a few clarifying acceptance criteria for the story. Serves as the agenda for the weekly sizing discussion.	User story Acceptance criteria
Sized	User stories that form the queue of stories that need examples, a wireframe, and the rest of the information needed to meet the definition of ready. User stories in this column are also potential candidates for three amigos sessions.	User story Acceptance criteria Size
Ready to Rock	User stories that are ready for delivery and can be considered for iteration planning.	User story Acceptance criteria Size Mockup Dependencies Stakeholder list Examples

When to Use It

Discovery boards are most useful in situations where a team is following an iterative approach, such as Scrum, and are working in a sufficiently complicated environment. In this situation, teams will find it helpful to perform analysis and dive into the details of user stories prior to the iteration in which the stories are delivered.

Why Use It

The discovery board brings visibility to the state of a team's backlog and shows how many backlog items are ready for the next iteration. The discovery board also provides team members with an idea of which product backlog items will be discussed during their estimating sessions and which stories will be fleshed out next. This helps teams hold much more effective iteration planning sessions.

The discovery board also provides a visual aid when talking to stakeholders about difficulties the team may be having with their backlog, such as too many backlog items coming in with insufficient information or not enough valuable stories to work on.

How to Use It

Creating the Discovery Board

1. Gather the team together and discuss whether it would be helpful to visualize the backlog refinement process. If so, continue.

2. Discuss the steps in the team's backlog refinement process. Determining which steps warrant a separate column is a little subjective, but there are some guidelines. If the different steps can be done by different people, or if discussions requiring some preparation occur at certain points, those may be good column candidates. Knowing whether every backlog item goes through the step can also guide the team.

3. Determine policies for each column. You can also think of these as entry criteria: What things need to be in place in order to have a backlog item in that column?

4. Determine if any buffer columns are needed between the process steps. These are especially helpful if the team finds value in knowing which backlog items are actively being worked on versus which ones are just waiting for the next process step.

5. Decide what information the team wants to display on the cards or sticky notes they use to track product backlog items, and create a card for each backlog item that is currently in process.

6. Place the in-process backlog items in the appropriate column.

7. Determine what tokens the team wants to use to stand in for things not indicated by the columns on the board, such as blocked backlog items or backlog items needing research.

Using the Discovery Board

Once the team has created their discovery board, they should use it as an ongoing reference point for the status of product backlog items in backlog refinement (the discovery process).

Depending on what columns are on the board, certain columns can be used as agendas for team events such as sizing discussions and can even provide an indication of whether a sizing discussion is needed at all (e.g., if there are no stories ready to be sized).

The discovery board can also serve as a to-do list for people who are focusing on the discovery process to determine which backlog items they need to get ready next. It also provides a clue to other team members that they need to help out to make sure the team has enough backlog items ready for the next iteration planning.

It is often helpful to have a member of the team accept the responsibility to focus on moving backlog items across the board and having the discussions with team members and stakeholders necessary to get the right backlog items (i.e., the ones that produce the most value when completed) ready for the next iteration.

Finally, it's very helpful to have the discovery board and the delivery board (discussed later in this chapter) next to each other so the team can do their daily coordination discussions (standups) at the boards. This focuses their discussions on items in play on either the discovery board or the delivery board instead of having people say what they did, what they are doing, and what obstacles are in their way.

Caveats and Considerations

Don't let the discovery board lead you to believe that all discovery happens while the team is getting backlog items ready. A great deal of discovery happens at this point, but some discovery will still happen as stories are developed and tested (when backlog items are tracked on the delivery board).

Each team's columns may be different. The format and layout of each board are based on how that team approaches backlog refinement.

Backlog items progress across the board from left to right. Within each column, the position of the backlog item represents its priority, with backlog items that should be dealt with first appearing at the top of that column.

The discovery board is roughly based on the idea of a Kanban board, where items continuously flow across the board as they are being readied for iteration planning, unlike a delivery board, which is effectively cleared off at the end of each iteration and reset.

In most of the cases where I have seen teams use discovery boards, they did not implement work in process (WIP) limits. That's not to say that at some point they wouldn't do so, especially if they found that work was not progressing through backlog refinement smoothly enough. But for those teams, using the target of having a sufficient number of backlog items ready for the next iteration planning seemed to be a sufficient regulator for items on the board.

The discovery board is most effective when it is an actual physical board where items are tracked by the team. People tend to be more likely to glance at the wall to get a quick check of status than to make an explicit effort to go to a tool and look at the status of items there. The physical board also aids with daily coordination discussions as people can physically move cards and point to them when they are discussing a particular item.

Physical boards are great for displaying status but are not as useful when the team is virtual, or the team needs to maintain detailed information about their product backlog items. An approach that works well for these teams is to have both the physical board and an electronic repository. The physical board is considered the source of record for status of the backlog item, and the electronic repository is the source of record for details about the product backlog item. If the board and the electronic repository differ, the board is trusted. Of course, when discrepancies are noted, the team should resync the two sources. Many agile tracking tools can graphically represent boards, and teams have found it helpful to replicate a view of both the discovery board and the delivery board for remote team members.

Additional Resources

Maassen, Olav, Chris Matts, and Chris Geary. *Commitment: Novel about Managing Project Risk*. Hathaway te Brake Publications, 2013.

McDonald, Kent J. "How Visualization Boards Can Benefit Your Team." Stickyminds.com. https://well.tc/5Rb.

Definition of Ready

What It Is

A definition of ready is an agreement on the set of conditions that need to be true in order to consider a backlog item ready to be included in an iteration for delivery.

An Example

The conditions that I see included most frequently in a definition of ready are

- Small enough user story
- Acceptance criteria
- Testable examples
- Mockups or appropriate model (where appropriate)
- Dependency list
- Impacted stakeholders

When to Use It

As with the discovery board, the definition of ready is most useful in situations where a team is following an iterative approach, such as Scrum, and are working in a sufficiently complicated environment. In this situation, teams will find it helpful to perform analysis and dive into the details of user stories prior to the iteration in which the stories are delivered.

Why Use It

It is helpful to have specific agreement on what should be known about a backlog item before it is included in an iteration. The definition of ready provides this agreement and also goes a long way toward defining what "just enough" analysis is. In effect, the team agrees to the specific level of information that they need to start testing and developing a story. If you have always wondered how to tell when you are "done" with analysis, a definition of ready may be just what you need.

A side benefit of having and using a definition of ready is that iteration planning tends to go a lot more smoothly. Because the necessary information for deciding whether or not to include a backlog item in the iteration is already well known, the team saves a great deal of analysis time during iteration planning.

How to Use It

1. Gather the team together at a whiteboard. Explain that the purpose of the discussion is to establish an agreement on what they need to know about backlog items before they consider them in iteration planning.

2. Have the team generate a list of all the things that would be nice to have identified about a particular backlog item prior to considering it in iteration planning.

3. Once the energy for adding new items seems to die down, go back and review the list. Ask the team to consider whether it's reasonable to expect to know all of the items they suggested for every backlog item.

4. Continue revising the list until the team feels comfortable with the resulting items, which will generally be fewer than on the first list. This list forms the team's definition of ready.

5. Use the definition of ready as an ongoing check to determine whether a backlog item is understood well enough to be considered for inclusion in an iteration.

Caveats and Considerations

The appropriate definition of ready is specific to a given team and is something the team determines as it is starting its work. This is a great discussion for the team to have as they prepare to start working together. As with many of the other techniques discussed in this book, the conversation about creating a definition of ready is invaluable, but the actual result of the discussion can be fairly helpful as well.

This discussion is particularly interesting with teams that are just starting to make the move to agile. This discussion is usually the first time team members begin to realize that they may not need to take analysis to the same extent they used to before adopting agile. Some may not grasp that point until they start trying to get backlog items ready using an extensive definition of ready.

The definition of ready usually rides on the assumption that the first thing that occurs in the iteration is developing code, be it test code or production code.

You may find that some conditions in your definition of ready are considered "when applicable," or you may have one or two conditions that a few team members pedantically insist on fulfilling as if their lives depended on these things happening on every story. If you have some of those items, leave them as part of your definition of ready for the time being and remind the team that the definition of ready is not set in concrete and is open to revision. This is not to say that the definition of ready can be ignored whenever it's convenient, but rather the team can intentionally discuss if their definition of ready is working for them during a retrospective and make revisions to it based on experience.

If a team is using a discovery board, the definition of ready serves as the policy for moving an item into the column designated "ready for iteration planning" ("Ready to Rock" in the example shown in the discovery board section).

Additional Resources

Agile Alliance. "Definition of Ready." http://guide.agilealliance.org/guide/definition-of-ready.html.

Linders, Ben. "Using a Definition of Ready." *InfoQ*. www.infoq.com/news/2014/06/using-definition-of-ready.

Delivery Board

What It Is

A delivery board is a way for a team to visualize their process for delivering functionality in a sprint. The best delivery boards consist of a whiteboard or wall divided into columns that reflect the various steps a team takes to develop and test backlog items in a sprint. The backlog items are represented by sticky notes or cards that move across the board as the team gets closer to having functionality to deliver.

An Example

Figure 15.2 shows an example delivery board; a description of each column appears in Table 15.2.

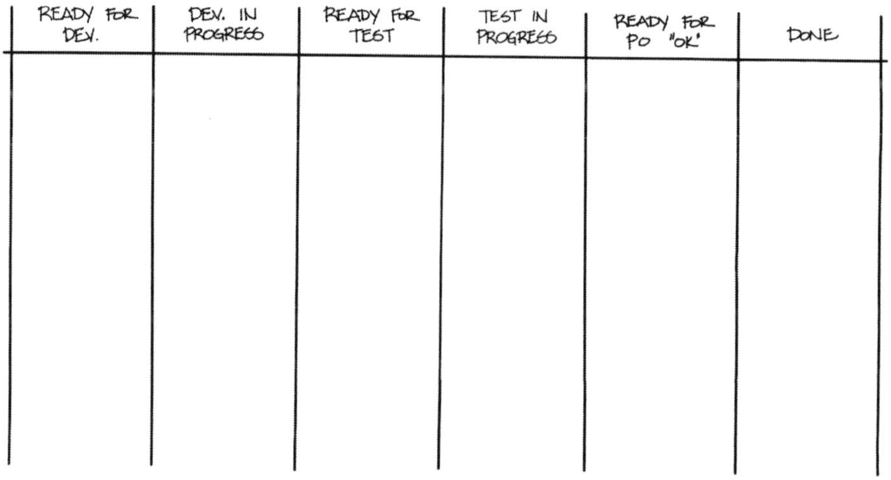

Figure 15.2 *Example delivery board*

Table 15.2 *Example Delivery Board Columns*

Column	Description	Policy (i.e., Entry Criteria)
Ready for Dev.	Queue column for backlog items that have been selected for the current iteration. This column is filled during iteration planning.	Backlog item is ready. Selected for delivery in the iteration
Dev. in Progress	Team is actively developing items in this column.	Team member(s) working on backlog item
Ready for Test	Queue column for those backlog items that are waiting to be tested.	Coded Unit tested Promoted to QA environment

Continues

Table 15.2 *Example Delivery Board Columns (Continued)*

Column	Description	Policy (i.e., Entry Criteria)
Test in Progress	Team is actively testing backlog items.	Coded Unit tested Promoted to QA environment Independent testing (by someone other than the person who developed) against acceptance criteria under way
Ready for PO OK	Queue column for view by product owner	Coded Unit tested Promoted to QA environment Independent testing completed—meets acceptance criteria Issues addressed
Done	Backlog item is ready to be deployed to production.	(Definition of done) Coded Unit tested Promoted to QA environment Independent testing completed—meets acceptance criteria Issues addressed Product owner OK

When to Use It

Delivery boards are most useful in situations where your team is following an approach with time-boxed sprints such as Scrum and finds it helpful to track the status of backlog items during an iteration. If your team is following a flow process, the discovery board and delivery board are often combined into a single board showing all the steps from new idea to done and deployed.

Why Use It

The delivery board brings visibility to the state of the backlog items in an iteration. It can eliminate the need for iteration-level burndown charts, as it graphically shows how quickly backlog items are (or are not) reaching "done" within the sprint.

The delivery board also provides a visual aid for updating those outside of the team on the progress of backlog items and can even help reset expectations regarding how much the team will accomplish in a given iteration.

How to Use It

Creating the Delivery Board

1. Gather the team and discuss whether it would be helpful to visualize the process for developing and testing backlog items. If the team finds this helpful, continue.

2. Discuss the steps in the team's development process. As with discovery boards, this determination can be a little subjective, but some of the same guidelines apply: Can the different steps be done by different people? Are there any discussions that occur at certain points that require some preparation? Does every backlog item go through the step?

3. Determine policies for each column. You can also think of these as entry criteria: What things need to be in place in order to have a backlog item in that column.

4. Determine if any buffers are needed between the process steps. These are especially helpful if the team finds value in knowing which backlog items are actively being worked on and which are just waiting.

5. Decide what information the team wants to display on the cards (sticky notes) they use to track product backlog items, and create a card for each backlog item that is currently in process.

6. Place each in-process backlog item in the appropriate column.

7. Determine what tokens the team wants to use to indicate things not included in the columns on the board. These may be things like blocked items or items needing research.

Using the Delivery Board

Once the team has created their discovery board, they should use it as an ongoing reference point for the status of backlog items in an iteration.

The delivery board can also serve as a to-do list for people who are focusing on the delivery process to determine which backlog items they need to work on next.

Finally, it's very helpful to have the delivery board and the discovery board (discussed earlier in this chapter) next to each other so that the team can do their daily coordination discussions (standups) at the boards and focus their discussions on items in play on these boards. This can be an alternative to having people say what they did, what they are doing, and what obstacles are in their way.

Caveats and Considerations

Each team's columns may be different. They are based on how that team approaches backlog refinement.

Backlog items progress across the board from left to right when process steps are represented as columns. Within each column, the position of the backlog item represents its priority, with backlog items that should be dealt with first appearing at the top of the column. If the priority of backlog items changes, their vertical position in a column changes as a result.

The delivery board is cleared off at the end of each iteration and reloaded as a part of iteration planning. That means that if there are backlog items still in progress at the end of an iteration, those items are pulled from the delivery board and put back into the backlog for consideration in future iterations. Those backlog items may get pulled into the next iteration, in which case they go back to the state they were in during the previous iteration, but this type of hangover from one iteration to the next should generally be avoided.

WIP limits tend to be more common in delivery boards than they are in discovery boards, often because teams need additional techniques to help them keep backlog items progressing through to done.

The delivery board is most effective when it is an actual physical board where items are tracked by the team. People tend to be more likely to glance at the wall to get a quick check of status than to make an explicit effort to go to a tool and look at the status of items there. The physical board also aids with daily coordination discussions, since people can physically move cards and point to them when they are discussing a particular item.

Physical boards are great for displaying status but are not as useful when the team is virtual, or the team needs to maintain detailed information about their product backlog items. An approach that works well is to use both a physical board and an electronic repository. The physical board is considered the source of record for backlog item status, and the electronic repository is the source of record for details about the product backlog item. If the board and the electronic repository differ, the board is trusted. Of course when discrepancies are noted, the team should sync the two sources. Many agile tracking tools can graphically represent boards, and teams have found it helpful to replicate a view of both the discovery board and the delivery board for remote team members.

Additional Resources

Maassen, Olav, Chris Matts, and Chris Geary. *Commitment: Novel about Managing Project Risk*. Hathaway te Brake Publications, 2013.

McDonald, Kent J. "How Visualization Boards Can Benefit Your Team." Stickyminds.com. https://well.tc/5Rb.

Definition of Done

What It Is

The definition of done is an agreement on the set of conditions that need to be true in order to consider a backlog item done and at a point where it can deliver value to stakeholders.

An Example

Typical items in a definition of done include

- Acceptance criteria are met
- Cleared by QA
- Accepted by product owner
- Accepted by sponsor
- Training script done
- Help documentation completed
- Code reviewed
- Integrated
- Compiled
- Usability testing completed
- Automated testing in place
- User documentation created
- Ops documentation created

When to Use It

The definition of done is most useful in situations where a team is following an iterative approach, such as Scrum, and needs an agreement as to what constitutes done for backlog items developed during an iteration. A concept similar to a definition of done is probably also used in flow-type approaches as the policies that exist to move a backlog item into the final step in the development process.

Why Use It

It is helpful to have specific agreements in place regarding what needs to happen with a backlog item in order to deliver it to stakeholders. The definition of done provides this agreement and specifically provides clarity on how much and what type of testing and documentation are done for any given backlog item.

A side benefit of having and using a definition of done is that wasteful, subjective discussions about whether a backlog item is truly done are eliminated. The team is clear about what they need to do in order to complete a backlog item. This understanding also aids estimating, as the team knows what needs to happen in order to deliver any given backlog item. This is especially helpful in regard to activities outside of coding that typically go along with delivering a backlog item such as testing and documentation.

How to Use It

1. Gather the team together at a whiteboard. Explain that the purpose of the discussion is to agree on what criteria must be met for a backlog item to be considered done.

2. Have the team generate a list of all the things that would be nice to do when delivering a backlog item.

3. Once the energy for adding new items seems to die down, go back and review the list. Ask the team to consider whether it's reasonable to expect all of the items they suggested for every backlog item.

4. Continue revising the list until the team feels comfortable with the resulting list, which will generally be shorter than the first one. This final list forms the team's definition of done.

5. On an ongoing basis, use the definition of done as a check to determine whether a backlog item can be delivered to stakeholders.

Caveats and Considerations

As with the definition of ready, the list of what should be in the definition of done is not intended to be exhaustive, nor is it intended to be a set of rigid rules where all the criteria absolutely have to be done for each item no matter what. The team discusses what must be true in order for them to consider a user story satisfied and establish that as their definition of done. The list is also not final, and the team may find occasion to review and revise it at a retrospective.

The definition of done should be used as a measuring stick to determine if the backlog item is ready to provide value to stakeholders, not whether the team has done enough to "get credit" for completing the backlog item.

The key points to discuss surrounding a definition of done are primarily what kind of testing the team is going to do story by story and, to a lesser extent, what documentation is needed story by story. The answers to those questions drive a lot of decisions about the team's process, and the testing question can generate a lot of concern within a team. Establishing a definition of done can address those concerns by establishing an initial set of tests, trying them out, and then seeing how things turn out. The team can then adjust their level of testing and revise their definition of done accordingly.

Some teams include deployment to production in their definition of done. Other teams that are not in a position to deploy to production at the end of each iteration may include deployment to a preproduction environment instead and have a separate set of release criteria that indicate what needs to be true before releasing code to production. These release criteria are often applied to the results of multiple iterations.

Additional Resources

Agile Alliance. "Definition of Done." http://guide.agilealliance.org/guide/definition-of-done.html.

Lacey, Mitch. "Definition of Done." www.mitchlacey.com/intro-to-agile/scrum/definition-of-done.

Scrum.org. "Definition of Done." www.scrum.org/Resources/Scrum-Glossary/Definition-of-Done.

System Documentation

What It Is

System documentation is information about an as-built solution and acts as a reference for future maintenance or update efforts. It is organized based on system functionality rather than when changes were made to the system, making it easier for people who maintain the solution to find the information they need quickly.

While the solution itself (and tests written against it) can provide a great deal of information, there will always be a need for additional sources of information, especially for aspects that are not readily apparent. This information can take many forms, but I usually like to have some combination of the following:

- Glossary: definitions for the commonly used terms in the domain in which the system operates
- Business rule catalog: descriptions of the rules, though without indicating how those rules are enforced (that information is typically noted in one of the other artifacts or represented by tests)

- Metadata: data about the data that the system collects, stores, and provides
- Process flows: descriptions of the business processes that the system supports
- User interfaces: descriptions of the operations behind the scenes or the enforcement of business rules related to the user interface
- Permissions: a description of which roles can perform which functions in the system

An Example

For the conference submission system we use GitHub for source control and for any documentation we need to communicate during the course of changes we are making. Each change is listed as an issue, and any specifics are described in the back-and-forth of the comments we use to clarify expectations.

We also keep the examples we write for each item. These examples are organized based on system features and serve as my first point of reference when we are investigating a case where the submission system does not seem to be working properly. Nine times out of ten, the defect ends up being a scenario that we did not account for during our development work, evidenced by the lack of an example.

To supplement the examples, and my bad memory, I've also created spreadsheets that reflect permissions, as well as notes about the specific notification messages that go out under certain circumstances. These tend to be the main pieces of information that are useful to store at a point of reference other than GitHub or the system itself.

When to Use It

System documentation is helpful anytime you have a solution that will be maintained and updated through its lifetime. In a broad sense, this applies to most systems built or implemented by an IT organization. System documentation is especially helpful when the system is maintained or updated by a different team from the one that originally built it and can even be useful for solutions that are built and maintained by the same team, especially if the solution is expected to have a long life (say, more than a year).

Why Use It

Creating documentation that describes the system is not essential for delivering value right now. It is, however, extremely helpful in the long run for those who are trying to maintain and update the system—helpful enough that you should do it, but not so tremendously valuable that you should spend an inordinate amount of time or effort on it. The same goes for documentation done during a project. In that case, the main purpose is to aid the building of shared understanding.

In both cases you are creating documentation with a purpose, and once you know that purpose it's usually a good idea to structure the documentation based on its purpose. In the case of system documentation, you want it to reflect the current state of the solution as built, and you want it organized in an intuitive way—most likely based on how the solution itself is organized.

How to Use It

1. Determine who will be the primary audience of the system documentation. Usually the audience is the people who will maintain the solution on an ongoing basis. This may or may not include the team currently working on the solution.

2. Treat those people as another group of stakeholders and find out what their needs are in conjunction with supporting the solution. Find out what information they need, what would be a good way of organizing it for them, and in what form they would like the information to be available (wiki, documents on a shared drive, three-ring binders, etc.).

3. Identify a plan for creating the system documentation that you are confident you will follow. Most teams create system documentation either by creating backlog items to create the system documentation or by including updated system documentation in their definition of done. Using the definition of done in this way usually increases the likelihood that the documentation will actually get created, since backlog items calling for the creation of system documentation may never get pulled into an iteration.

4. Establish an agreed-upon repository for system documentation that is accessible to the people who need it and is easily updatable. Your organization may already have standards in place for what this repository should look like.

5. Create it and keep it up-to-date.

Caveats and Considerations

The need for documentation comes from two places: customers ask for it (user guides, help, sometimes system documentation), or the team finds it helpful for doing their job (project documentation and system documentation).

It may be helpful at this point to differentiate project documentation from system documentation. I use the term *project documentation* to refer to any documents the team uses to help communicate or remember changes in a given project. This information is best organized based on the changes. The extent of the documentation is based on how well the team communicates via other means and the approach the team uses. My preference is for extremely light project documentation that includes the following:

- Backlog items: these are ways to keep track of the various things that the delivery team is trying to help their stakeholders accomplish—effectively a way to organize the various changes that the delivery team is looking to produce.

- Examples: structured information in the form of "Given—when—then" scenarios or decision tables that describe system behavior and the rules that are expected to be enforced when a user story is delivered.

- Models: wireframes, data models, or process flows that further describe the stories. Often the models are general in nature such that they help describe several stories, but sometimes they can be created specifically for a given story.

- Acceptance criteria: further descriptions of the stories that weren't covered by the examples or models.

Project documentation is temporary in nature; it is used to describe the specific changes that are needed during the effort and thus depends on a specific current and future state. I prefer to make project documentation as light as possible while still meeting the needs of the team. The definition of ready provides a definition of "just enough" for purposes of project documentation, then I create separate system documentation to act as a reference for future efforts. This software documentation contains information useful for maintaining a solution in an ongoing fashion and may contain some information originally created in project documentation.

Backlog items may be used as a source of release notes, and the examples, models, and acceptance criteria may provide a source for system documentation, but these things do not constitute the system documentation itself.

Many teams plan to use design documents and technical requirements as system documentation. If they do this, they certainly should update those documents to reflect what was actually built. But that doesn't change the fact that the documentation is organized based on when changes were made and thus may be hard to parse when working on the next effort.

There are mixed opinions on whether documentation is valuable or not. In some respects system documentation has gotten a bad reputation. In many approaches documentation was perceived as a measure of progress, and many delivery team members would view it as something they had to do—essentially a check on the list of required steps so they knew how the project was progressing. Agile approaches suggest that teams use a different measure of progress—working software or value delivered—relieving that burden from documentation.

Additional Resources

Ambler, Scott. "Best Practices for Agile/Lean Documentation." www.agilemodeling .com/essays/agileDocumentationBestPractices.htm (though I still insist there is no such thing as "best practices").

McDonald, Kent J. "Comprehensive Documentation Has Its Place." StickyMinds .com. https://well.tc/qxv.

Part IV

Resources

Glossary

Introduction

Following are definitions for key terms used in this book. Where the definition is pulled from a particular source, that source is listed under the definition. If I established the definition based on its usage in the book, no source is listed.

Definitions

Acceptance criteria
The conditions that a solution must satisfy to be accepted by a user, customer, or, in the case of system-level functionality, the consuming system. They are also a set of statements, each with a clear pass/fail result, that specify both functional and nonfunctional requirements and are applicable at a variety of levels (features and user stories).

Actionable metrics
Metrics that provide information that can help you make informed decisions and take corresponding actions.

Analysis
See Business analysis.
   Source: http://dictionary.reference.com/browse/analysis

Analyst
See Business analyst.

Anchoring effect
A cognitive bias that describes the common human tendency to rely too heavily on the first piece of information offered (the "anchor") when making decisions.
   Source: http://en.wikipedia.org/wiki/Anchoring

Appropriate practice
A practice that is effective within a given context. This term is intended to replace *best practice* in order to stress the context-specific nature of practices, meaning what works in one situation may not work in a different situation.

Arbitrary (decision mechanism)

A decision-making approach where the decision is made by some arbitrary means (such as Rock, Paper, Scissors).

Source: www.ebgconsulting.com/Pubs/Articles/DecideHowToDecide-Gottesdiener.pdf

Availability heuristic

A mental shortcut that relies on immediate examples that come to mind.

Source: http://psychology.about.com/od/aindex/g/availability-heuristic.htm

BABOK v3

Guide to the Business Analysis Body of Knowledge Version 3

Source: *Guide to the Business Analysis Body of Knowledge Version 3*

BACCM (Business Analysis Core Concept Model)

A conceptual framework for business analysts. It encompasses what business analysis is and what it means to those performing business analysis tasks regardless of perspective, industry, methodology, or level in the organization.

Source: BABOK v3

Backbone

A term used in user story mapping to refer to the basic flow of activities and the set of bigger activities that summarize that flow.

Bandwagon effect

The tendency to do (or believe) things because many other people do (or believe) the same. Related to groupthink.

Source: http://rationalwiki.org/wiki/List_of_cognitive_biases

Barely sufficient

A term originally coined by Alistair Cockburn in relation to software development methods. A method that is barely sufficient provides the least amount of prescription necessary for a team to be successful in a given context. Cockburn notes that barely sufficient is different for every team and may change from time to time for the same team.

Source: http://alistair.cockburn.us/Balancing+lightness+with+sufficiency

Break the Model

A technique used in Feature Injection (created by Chris Matts) where a model of a solution is repeatedly tested with new examples. If these examples (assumed to be valid) break the model, the model is adjusted to account for that example and all previous. This technique is a way to drive continuous learning in the nature of a solution.

Build-Measure-Learn loop

A core port of the Lean Startup methodology that is a loop process of turning ideas into products, measuring customers' reactions and behaviors against built products, and then learning whether to persevere or pivot the idea; this process repeats over and over again.

Source: http://en.wikipedia.org/wiki/Lean_startup#Build-Measure-Learn

Business analysis

The practice of enabling change in an enterprise by defining needs and recommending solutions that deliver value to stakeholders. Enables an enterprise to articulate needs and the rationale for change, and to design and describe solutions that can deliver value.

Source: BABOK v3

Business analyst

Any person who performs business analysis tasks, no matter his or her job title or organizational role.

Source: BABOK v3

Business case

A justification for a course of action based on the benefits to be realized by using the proposed solution, as compared to the cost, effort, and other considerations to acquire and live with that solution.

Source: BABOK v3

Business domain model

A model that logically represents an organization's key concepts and their relationships, often used to establish a shared understanding of what information is important to know about that organization.

Business value

The degree to which a product, activity, or project helps an organization meet one or more goals.

Business value model

A way of describing the value generated by a project in terms of the impact of a set of variables on selected objectives so that a project team regularly reevaluates expectations based on new information (i.e., changes in the variables) throughout the course of the project.

Change

A controlled transformation of organizational systems.

Source: BABOK v3

Clustering illusion

The cognitive bias of seeing a pattern in what is actually a random sequence of numbers or events.

Source: http://rationalwiki.org/wiki/Clustering_illusion

Cognitive bias

Describes the inherent thinking errors that humans make in processing information. These thinking errors prevent one from accurately understanding reality, even when confronted with all the needed data and evidence to form an accurate view.

Source: http://rationalwiki.org/wiki/List_of_cognitive_biases

Collaboration

Working together to achieve a common goal.

Collaborative modeling

The use of well-known requirements analysis and modeling techniques in a collaborative fashion to build and maintain a shared understanding of the problem space and the potential solution.

Commit to, Transform, or Kill

Decision choices about initiatives, IT projects, and solutions suggested by Johanna Rothman as a question that should be frequently asked about items in a portfolio.

Source: Rothman, *Manage Your Project Portfolio*

Commitment scale

A stakeholder analysis that gauges the current level of stakeholder commitment to a project as well as what level of commitment is needed to ensure the project's success.

Company building

The fourth step in the customer development framework that represents the point where company departments and operational processes are created to support scale.

Source: Cooper and Vlaskovits, *The Entrepreneur's Guide to Customer Development*

Company creation

The third step in the customer development framework that represents the point where the business is scalable through a repeatable sales and marketing roadmap.

> Source: Cooper and Vlaskovits, *The Entrepreneur's Guide to Customer Development*

Confirmation bias

The tendency for people to (consciously or subconsciously) seek out information that conforms to their preexisting viewpoints and subsequently ignore information that goes against them, both positive and negative. It is a type of cognitive bias and a form of selection bias toward confirmation of the hypothesis under study.

> Source: http://rationalwiki.org/wiki/Confirmation_bias

Consensus

A group decision-making process that seeks the consent of all participants. Consensus may be defined professionally as an acceptable resolution, one that can be supported, even if not the "favorite" of each individual.

> Source: http://en.wikipedia.org/wiki/Consensus_decision-making

Context

The circumstances that influence, are influenced by, and provide understanding of the change.

> Source: BABOK v3

Context diagram

An analysis technique that shows the system under consideration and the information/data flows between the system and parties and other systems impacted by the project.

Context Leadership Model

A model that classifies projects based on their uncertainty and complexity. The model can be used as a risk assessment and also provides guidance on the appropriate approach for a project.

Core concept

One of six ideas that are fundamental to the practice of business analysis: change, need, solution, context, stakeholder, and value. The Business Analysis Core Concept Model (BACCM) describes the relationships among these core concepts in a dynamic conceptual system. All the concepts are equal and necessary: there is no "prime" concept, and they are all defined by the other core concepts. Because of this, no one core concept can be fully understood until all six are understood.

Source: BABOK v3

Curse of knowledge, the

A cognitive bias that leads better-informed parties to find it extremely difficult to think about problems from the perspective of lesser-informed parties.

Source: http://en.wikipedia.org/wiki/Curse_of_knowledge

Customer

A stakeholder who uses or may use products or services produced by the enterprise and may have contractual or moral rights that the enterprise is obliged to meet.

Source: BABOK v3

Customer development

A four-step framework to discover and validate that you have identified the market for your product, built the right product features that solve customers' needs, tested the correct methods for acquiring and converting customers, and deployed the right resources to scale the business.

Source: Cooper and Vlaskovits, *The Entrepreneur's Guide to Customer Development*

Customer discovery

The first step in the customer development framework that focuses on validating that a product solves a problem for an identifiable group of users.

Source: Cooper and Vlaskovits, *The Entrepreneur's Guide to Customer Development*

Customer-problem-solution hypothesis

An element of customer development that refers to a hypothesis about the combination of an organization's customers, their problem, and a solution to solve that problem.

Source: Cooper and Vlaskovits, *The Entrepreneur's Guide to Customer Development*

Customer validation

The second step in the customer development framework that focuses on validating that the market is scalable and large enough that a viable business might be built.

Source: Cooper and Vlaskovits, *The Entrepreneur's Guide to Customer Development*

Data dictionary

An analysis technique that describes standard definitions of data elements, their meanings, and allowable values.

　　Source: BABOK v3

Decider

The person responsible for making a decision.

Decider decides with discussion

A decision-making pattern where the person responsible for making a decision discusses information about the decision prior to making a decision.

Decider decides without discussion

A decision-making pattern where the person responsible for making the decision makes that decision without consulting others.

Decision filter

A guiding objective phrased in the form of a question that is used to help clarify decision making. Useful for many different levels of decisions, including strategy, projects, features, meeting purpose, and so on. Example: Will this information help us improve projects through analysis?

Decision leader

A person responsible for making sure the right people make the decision with as much information as possible.

Definition of done

A technique in agile where the team agrees on, and prominently displays, a list of criteria that must be met before a user story is considered done.

　　Source: http://guide.agilealliance.org/guide/definition-of-done.html

Definition of ready

A technique in agile where the team agrees on, and prominently displays, a list of criteria that must be met before a user story is considered in sprint planning.

　　Source: http://guide.agilealliance.org/guide/definition-of-ready.html

Déformation professionnelle

The tendency to look at things from the point of view of one's own profession rather than from a broader perspective. It is often translated as "professional deformation" or "job conditioning." The implication is that professional training, and its related socialization, often results in a distortion of the way one views the world.

　　Source: http://en.wikipedia.org/wiki/D%C3%A9formation_professionnelle

Delivery

Work that transforms one or more allocated candidate solutions into a releasable portion or version of the product.

>   Source: Gottesdiener and Gorman, *Discover to Deliver*

Delivery board

A visualization board used by teams to track delivery work that occurs during a sprint.

Design

A usable representation of a solution.

>   Source: BABOK v3

Design thinking

A formal method for practical, creative resolution of problems and creation of solutions, with the intent of an improved future result. In this regard it is a form of solution-based or solution-focused thinking—starting with a goal (a better future situation) instead of solving a specific problem.

>   Source: http://en.wikipedia.org/wiki/Design_thinking

Differentiating activities

Activities of an organization that are both mission critical and market differentiating for that organization. Those activities associated with the sustainable competitive advantage of an organization.

Discovery

Work that explores, evaluates, and confirms product options for potential delivery.

>   Source: Gottesdiener and Gorman, *Discover to Deliver*

Discovery board

A visualization board used by teams to track the work that goes into getting backlog items ready for a sprint.

Domain

The body of knowledge that defines a set of common requirements, terminology, and functionality for any program or initiative solving a problem.

>   Source: BABOKv3

Elicitation

The iterative derivation and extraction of information from stakeholders or other sources.

>   Source: BABOKv3

Enterprise

A bounded, self-defining, self-governing entity that uses a set of related business functions to create, deliver, and capture value for its customers/clients and stakeholders.

Source: BABOKv3

Examples

An approach to defining the behavior of a system using realistic examples instead of abstract statements. Examples are often used to further describe user stories and are used as guidance for both development and testing.

Facilitate

To lead and encourage people through systematic efforts toward agreed-upon objectives in a manner that enhances involvement, collaboration, productivity, and synergy.

Source: BABOKv3

False consensus effect

A cognitive bias whereby people tend to overestimate the extent to which their beliefs or opinions are typical of those of others. There is a tendency for people to assume that their own opinions, beliefs, preferences, values, and habits are normal and that others also think the same way that they do.

Source: http://en.wikipedia.org/wiki/False-consensus_effect

Feature

A distinguishing characteristic of a solution that implements a cohesive set of requirements and delivers value for a set of stakeholders.

Source: BABOK v3

Feature Injection

An approach to analysis derived from the idea that as we pull business value from the system, we inject the features that represent the work the team does (outputs) to create that value (outcome).

Fist of five

A technique used by teams to poll team members and help achieve consensus. To use the technique, the facilitator states the decision the group is going to make and asks the team to show their level of support. Each team member shows his or her support based on the number of fingers held up:

1. I have major concerns.

2. I would like to discuss some minor issues.

3. I'm not in total agreement but I can support it.

4. I think it's a good idea and will work for it.

5. It's a great idea and would like to take the lead when we implement it.

Source: http://whatis.techtarget.com/definition/fist-to-five-fist-of-five

Fit
See Framework for Integrated Test.

Focusing effect
Prediction bias occurring when people place too much importance on one aspect of an event; causes errors in accurately predicting the utility of a future outcome.

Source: http://rationalwiki.org/wiki/List_of_cognitive_biases

Framework for Integrated Test
An open-source tool for automated customer tests. It integrates the work of customers, analysts, testers, and developers. Customers provide examples of how their software should work formatted in tables and saved as HTML. Those examples are connected to the software with programmer-written test fixtures and automatically checked for correctness.

Source: http://en.wikipedia.org/wiki/Framework_for_integrated_test

Framing effect
Drawing different conclusions from the same information depending on how that information is presented.

Source: http://rationalwiki.org/wiki/List_of_cognitive_biases

Frequency illusion
The phenomenon in which people who have just learned or noticed something start seeing it everywhere.

Source: http://rationalwiki.org/wiki/Frequency_illusion

Functional decomposition
An analysis technique that approaches the analysis of complex systems and concepts by considering them as a set of collaborating or related functions, effects, and components.

Source: BABOK v3

Functionality
How features are implemented in the product.

Get out of the building
An exhortation from Steve Blank that in order to truly understand your customers' needs you should observe them where they are.

Gherkin

A language used by the automated testing tool Cucumber. It is a business-readable, domain-specific language that lets you describe software's behavior without detailing how that behavior is implemented.

Source: https://github.com/cucumber/cucumber/wiki/Gherkin

Glossary

A list of terms with accompanying definitions relevant to a project, solution, or business domain.

Source: http://dictionary.reference.com/browse/glossary

Goal

An observable and measurable business outcome or result having one or more objectives to be achieved within a fixed time frame.

Source: BABOK v3

Group attribution error

A cognitive bias where it is assumed that individuals in the group agree with the decisions of the group. When people make decisions in groups, they often follow group rules and are influenced by the social dynamic within the group at the time, thus downplaying their own real preferences.

Source: http://changingminds.org/explanations/theories/group_attribution_error.htm

Groupthink

A cognitive bias that happens when a desire for conformity within a group transcends rational thought and issues of right and wrong. When this happens, individuals in a group fail to express their doubts about the group's dynamic, direction, or decisions because of a desire to maintain consensus or conformity.

Source: http://rationalwiki.org/wiki/Groupthink

Herd instinct

A common tendency to adopt the opinions and follow the behaviors of the majority to feel safer and to avoid conflict.

Source: http://rationalwiki.org/wiki/List_of_cognitive_biases

Impact mapping

A strategic planning technique that prevents organizations from getting lost while building products and delivering projects, by clearly communicating assumptions, helping teams align their activities with overall business objectives and make better roadmap decisions.

Source: http://impactmapping.org/about.php

Information radiator

The generic term for any of a number of handwritten, drawn, printed, or electronic displays which a team places in a highly visible location, so that all team members as well as passersby can see the latest information at a glance: progress of user stories and tasks, count of automated tests, velocity, incident reports, continuous integration status, and so on.

Source: http://guide.agilealliance.org/guide/information-radiator.html

Initiative

Specific projects, programs, or actions taken to solve business problems or achieve specific change objectives.

Source: BABOK v3

Inventory turn

The number of times that inventory cycles or turns over per year calculated by dividing annual cost of goods sold by the average inventory level. Also known as inventory turnover.

Source: www.supplychainmetric.com/inventoryturns.htm

Irrational escalation

The tendency to make irrational decisions based upon rational decisions in the past or to justify actions already taken.

Source: http://rationalwiki.org/wiki/List_of_cognitive_biases

IT

Information technology.

Iteration

In the context of an agile project, a time box during which development takes place, the duration of which

- May vary from project to project, usually between one and four weeks
- Is in most cases fixed for the duration of a given project

A key feature of agile approaches is the underlying assumption that a project consists exclusively of a sequence of iterations, possibly with the exception of a very brief "vision and planning" phase prior to development, and a similarly brief "closure" phase after it.

The fixed length of iterations gives teams a simple way to obtain, based on velocity and the amount of work remaining, a usually accurate (though not very precise) estimation of the project's remaining duration.

Source: http://guide.agilealliance.org/guide/iteration.html

IT project

Any project that results in solutions, often involving software, that support internal business processes, automate manual processes, or streamline current processes. Examples include building a system to support the session submission process for a conference, implementing a system to calculate and deliver commissions, reporting and data warehousing solutions, or implementing a solution to track student information at a nonprofit school.

Leading indicator

A metric in which changes of value predict a corresponding change in another value. Leading indicators can be used to get an early assessment of the impact of actions taken on an objective.

Logical data model

A visual representation of the data needed for a business area or an application software system used to explore the domain concepts, and their relationships, of a problem domain. This could be done for the scope of a single project or for an entire enterprise. Logical data models depict the logical entity types, typically referred to simply as entity types, the data attributes describing those entities, and the relationships between the entities.

Source: www.agiledata.org/essays/dataModeling101.html

Loss aversion

The loss of giving up an object is greater than the gains associated with acquiring it.

Source: http://rationalwiki.org/wiki/List_of_cognitive_biases

Majority vote

A decision mechanism where a decision is made based on a vote of all involved. The option receiving greater than 50% of the number of vote "wins."

Methodology

A structure that determines which business analysis tasks and techniques are used to solve a business problem.

Source: BABOK v3

Minimum marketable feature

A small, self-contained feature that can be developed quickly and delivers significant value to the user.

Source: Denne and Cleland-Huang, *Software by Numbers*

Minimum viable product

A concept from Lean Startup that describes the fastest way to get through the Build-Measure-Learn feedback loop with the minimum amount of effort.

Source: Ries, *The Lean Startup*

Mirror imaging

The assumption that people being studied think like the analyst.

Source: http://en.citizendium.org/wiki/Cognitive_traps_for_intelligence_analysis

MMF

See Minimum marketable feature.

Mom Test, the

A set of simple rules for crafting good questions about a product or solution that even your mom can't lie to you about.

Source: Fitzpatrick, *The Mom Test*

MVP

See Minimum viable product.

Need

A problem, opportunity, or constraint with potential value to a stakeholder.

Source: BABOK v3

Negotiation

A decision mechanism characterized by a bargaining (give-and-take) process between two or more parties (each with its own aims, needs, and viewpoints) seeking to discover a common ground and reach a decision.

Source: www.businessdictionary.com/definition/negotiation.html

Objective

A target or metric that a person or organization seeks to meet in order to progress toward a goal.

Source: BABOK v3

Observation selection bias

The effect of suddenly noticing things we didn't notice that much before—but we wrongly assume that the frequency has increased.

Source: http://io9.com/5974468/the-most-common-cognitive-biases-that-prevent-you-from-being-rational

Observer-expectancy effect

When a researcher expects a given result and therefore subconsciously manipulates an experiment or misinterprets data in order to find it.

Source: http://rationalwiki.org/wiki/List_of_cognitive_biases

One Metric That Matters (OMTM)

The one number you're completely focused on above everything else for your current stage.

Source: Croll and Yoskovitz, *Lean Analytics*

Organization

A collection of stakeholders acting in a coordinated manner and in service to a common goal. *Organization* usually refers to a legal entity. Organizations comprise organizational systems.

Organization chart

Visual representation of how a firm intends authority, responsibility, and information to flow within its formal structure. It usually depicts different management functions (accounting, finance, human resources, marketing, production, R&D, etc.) and their subdivisions as boxes linked with lines along which decision-making power travels downward and answerability travels upward.

Source: www.businessdictionary.com/definition/organization-chart.html

Outcome

The change in the organization and changes in the behavior of stakeholders as a result of an IT project.

Output

Anything that a team delivers as part of an IT project. This includes software, documentation, processes, and other things that tend to be measured in order to gauge how the project is going.

Parity activity

A type of activity as classified in the Purpose-Based Alignment Model that is mission critical for an organization but does not differentiate the organization from others in its markets. The appropriate way to handle these activities is to mimic, achieve and maintain parity, and simplify.

PDSA

See Plan-Do-Study-Act cycle.

Persona

A typical user of a solution. Personas are helpful for understanding the context in which user roles use the solution to help guide design decisions. Personas originated from Alan Cooper's work on user-centered design.

Pivot

A structured course correction designed to test a new fundamental hypothesis about the product, strategy, and engine of growth.

Source: Ries, *The Lean Startup*

Plan-Do-Study-Act cycle

The PDSA cycle is a systematic series of steps for gaining valuable learning and knowledge for the continual improvement of a product or process. Also known as the Deming Wheel, or Deming Cycle, the concept and application was first introduced to Dr. Deming by his mentor, Walter Shewhart of the famous Bell Laboratories in New York.

Source: www.deming.org/theman/theories/pdsacycle

Problem-solution fit

A condition in Lean Startup where you have identified that you have a problem that is worth solving. You can determine this by answering three questions:

1. Is it something customers want? (must-have)

2. Will they pay for it? If not, who will? (viable)

3. Can it be solved? (feasible)

Source: Maurya, *Running Lean*

Problem statement

A structured set of statements that describe the purpose of an effort in terms of what problem it is trying to solve:

The problem of . . .

Affects . . .

The impact of which is . . .

A successful solution would be . . .

Process flow (process modeling)

A standardized graphical model used to show how work is carried out and is a foundation for process analysis.

Source: BABOK v3

Product

Generally in the context of projects, results of a team's efforts and can refer to a commercial product that is sold to external customers, or a system used internally in the organization. In *Beyond Requirements*, *product* is intended to represent an outcome of a project that is intended for sale directly to entities outside of the organization producing it.

Program

A group of related projects managed in a coordinated way to obtain benefits and control not available from managing them individually.

> Source: Project Management Institute, *The Standard for Program Management, Second Edition*

Project

A temporary endeavor with a definite beginning and end undertaken to create a unique product, service, or result.

> Source: Project Management Institute, *A Guide to the Project Management Body of Knowledge, Fourth Edition*

Project documentation

Documentation that a team creates during the course of a project with the main purpose of building a shared understanding of the changes needed.

Project opportunity assessment

A set of ten questions to ask when examining a project opportunity to elicit more information about it and determine whether it is worth pursuing. Inspired by Marty Cagan's product opportunity assessment.

Purpose-Based Alignment Model

A model that classifies the activities of an organization based on whether they are market differentiating and mission critical. Categorizing projects in this manner allows you to determine your design approach for projects related to those activities, and to determine the strategic alignment of projects.

Real Options

A principle identified by Chris Matts that encourages deferring decisions to the last responsible moment.

> Source: www.infoq.com/articles/real-options-enhance-agility

Recency bias

The tendency to think that trends and patterns observed in the recent past will continue in the future.

> Source: skepdic.com/recencybias.html

Release

The deployable increment of a product that is the culmination of one or more iterations.

Release backlog

A subset of a product backlog that includes the product backlog items that a team is targeting for delivery in a given release.

Release planning

A collaborative discussion where a team or set of teams determines what features to deliver in an upcoming time period. Release planning usually covers a time period ranging from a few weeks to a few months.

Report mockup

A prototype of a desired report that is created during collaborative modeling in order to guide the discussion about the reporting needs of a stakeholder.

Requirement

A usable representation of a need.

> Source: BABOK v3

Response bias

The bias that results from problems in the measurement process. Some examples include leading questions (the wording of the question may be loaded in some way to unduly favor one response over another) and social desirability (people are reluctant to admit to unsavory attitudes or illegal activities in a survey).

> Source: http://stattrek.com/statistics/dictionary.aspx?definition=response+bias

Retrospective

The team meets regularly, usually adhering to the rhythm of its iterations, to explicitly reflect on the most significant events that have occurred since the previous such meeting and identify actions aimed at remediation or improvement.

> Source: http://guide.agilealliance.org/guide/heartbeatretro.html

Risk

An event that will cause a stakeholder to experience a loss if it occurs.

RuleSpeak

A set of guidelines for expressing business rules in concise, business-friendly fashion created by Ron Ross.

> Source: www.rulespeak.com/en/

Scope

The description and boundaries of a set of relevant activities and topics.

> Source: BABOK v3

Semmelweis reflex

A metaphor for the reflex-like tendency to reject new evidence or new knowledge because it contradicts established norms, beliefs, or paradigms. The name comes from the story of Ignaz Semmelweis, which some consider to be a myth: www.bestthinking.com/articles/science/biology_and_nature/bacteriology/expert-skeptics-suckered-again-incredibly-the-famous-semmelweis-story-is-another-supermyth.

   Source: http://en.wikipedia.org/wiki/Semmelweis_reflex

Service

The performance of any duties or work for a stakeholder, from the perspective of the stakeholder.

Six questions

A set of six questions used by Niel Nickolaisen to identify differentiating activities in an organization and to think about the implications of those differentiating activities.

SME

See Subject matter expert.

Solution

A specific way of satisfying one or more needs in a context.

   Source: BABOK v3

Sponsor

A stakeholder who authorizes or legitimizes an initiative or solution by providing financial resources and is ultimately responsible for the success of the initiative or solution.

Spontaneous agreement

This happens occasionally when there is a solution that is favored by everyone and 100% agreement seems to happen automatically. These types of decisions are usually made quickly. They are fairly rare and often occur in connection with more trivial or simple issues.

   Source: http://volunteermaine.org/blog/making-group-decisions-%E2%80%93-six-options

Stakeholder

A group or individual with a relationship to the change or the solution.

   Source: BABOK v3

Stakeholder analysis

A technique used to identify the key people who are impacted by and who impact a project and determine the best way to interact with them.

Stakeholder map

A two-by-two matrix that provides a means of classifying stakeholders into one of four quadrants based on their relative power and interest in the project. The quadrants provide guidance on how to interact with the stakeholders.

Startup

An organization dedicated to creating something new under conditions of extreme uncertainty.

Source: Ries, *The Lean Startup*

State transition diagram

A type of analysis technique used to describe the behavior of systems. State diagrams show the various states that an entire system or entity within that system can be in, and the events that cause a change of state.

Storyboard

A user experience technique that shows the flow through various user interface screens or pages that a user may experience when interacting with a system.

Story mapping

A recent practice intended to provide a more structured approach to release planning, consisting of ordering user stories along two independent dimensions. The "map" arranges user activities along the horizontal axis in rough order of priority (or "the order in which you would describe activities to explain the behavior of the system"). Down the vertical axis, it represents increasing sophistication of the implementation.

Given a story map so arranged, the first horizontal row represents a "walking skeleton," a bare-bones but usable version of the product. Working through successive rows fleshes out the product with additional functionality.

Source: http://guide.agilealliance.org/guide/storymap.html

Strategy

The framework by which companies understand what they are doing and what they want to do in order to build a sustainable competitive advantage over the long run.

Strategy analysis

A knowledge area in the *Business Analysis Body of Knowledge* that describes the business analysis work that must be performed to collaborate with stakeholders in order to identify a need of strategic or tactical importance (the business need), enable the enterprise to address that need, and align the resulting strategy for the change with higher- and lower-level strategies.

Source: BABOK v3

Subject matter expert

A stakeholder with specific expertise in an aspect of the problem domain or potential solution alternatives or components.

Survivorship bias

A form of selection bias focusing on what has survived to the present and ignoring what must have been lost.

Source: http://rationalwiki.org/wiki/List_of_cognitive_biases

System documentation

Information about an as-built solution which acts as a reference for future maintenance or update efforts. It is organized based on system functionality rather than when changes were made to the system, making it easier for people who maintain the solution to find the information they need quickly.

Team

A collection of individuals working together to achieve a common goal.

Texas sharpshooter fallacy

The fallacy of selecting or adjusting a hypothesis after the data is collected, making it impossible to test the hypothesis fairly.

Theme

An aggregation of user stories to show business value delivered and to help with prioritization as well as show planned product delivery at a high level.

Three amigos

A discussion where people from different perspectives (usually business, development, and testing) get together to discuss a user story and make sure the story is ready for consideration during sprint planning.

Triple constraints

Cost, time, and scope.

Two-pizza rule

The idea that the appropriate team size is one that can be fed by two large pizzas. Originally coined by Jeff Bezos of Amazon.

User analysis
An analysis technique that helps you understand who uses your solution, what they can do, and the environment in which they use it.

User modeling
An analysis technique that structures a conversation about the user roles involved with a solution and arrives as a consistent list that can be used to organize work and identify functionality gaps.

User role
A collection of defining attributes that characterize a population of users and their intended interactions with the system.
> Source: Cohn, *User Stories Applied*

User story
A description of a product feature used for planning and scoping purposes. User stories will be decomposed to a level that can be delivered in a single iteration and provide value.

Value
The importance of something to a stakeholder in a context.
> Source: BABOK v3

Value points
A technique in agile software development where features receive a number of points representing their relative value.

Value stream map
A lean management method for analyzing the current state and designing a future state for the series of events that take a product or service from its beginning through delivery to the customer.
> Source: http://en.wikipedia.org/wiki/Value_stream_mapping

Vanity metrics
Metrics that are easy to measure, easy to manipulate, and do not provide useful information for making decisions or taking actions.

Visualization board
A term coined by Chris Matts for a generic information radiator.

"Who cares" activities
Activities as classified in the Purpose-Based Alignment Model that are neither mission critical for an organization nor differentiating. The appropriate way to handle these activities is to minimize or eliminate them.

Wireframe

A visual representation of a Web page to show where each item should be placed.

Source: www.quickfocus.com/blog/difference-between-wireframe-prototype-mockup

Work group

A collection of individuals working on a project, but not aiding each other's efforts, and potentially striving toward different and conflicting goals.

References

Adzic, Gojko. *Bridging the Communication Gap: Specification by Example and Agile Acceptance Testing.* Neuri Limited, 2009.

————. *Impact Mapping: Making a Big Impact with Software Products and Projects.* Provoking Thoughts, 2012.

————. *Specification by Example: How Successful Teams Deliver the Right Software.* Manning Publications, 2011.

Adzic, Gojko, Ingrid Domingues, and Johan Berndtsson. "Getting the Most Out of Impact Mapping." *InfoQ.* www.infoq.com/articles/most-impact-mapping.

Agile Alliance. "Definition of Done." http://guide.agilealliance.org/guide/definition-of-done.html.

————. "Definition of Ready." http://guide.agilealliance.org/guide/definition-of-ready.html.

Agile Modeling. "Agile Models Distilled: Potential Artifacts for Agile Modeling." http://agilemodeling.com/artifacts/.

————. "Inclusive Modeling: User Centered Approaches for Agile Software Development." http://agilemodeling.com/essays/inclusiveModels.htm.

Ambler, Scott. "Best Practices for Agile/Lean Documentation." www.agilemodeling.com/essays/agileDocumentationBestPractices.htm.

————. "Personas: An Agile Introduction." www.agilemodeling.com/artifacts/personas.htm.

Ariely, Dan. *Predictably Irrational: The Hidden Forces That Shape Our Decisions.* Harper Perennial, 2010.

Blank, Steve. *Four Steps to the Epiphany.* K & S Ranch, 2013.

Cagan, Marty. *Inspired: How to Create Products Customers Love.* SVPG Press, 2008.

Campbell-Pretty, Em. "Adventures in Scaling Agile." www.prettyagile.com/2014/02/how-i-fell-in-love-with-impact-mapping.html.

Cohn, Mike. *User Stories Applied: For Agile Software Development.* Addison-Wesley, 2004.

Cooper, Alan. *The Inmates Are Running the Asylum: Why High-Tech Products Drive Us Crazy and How to Restore the Sanity.* Sams Publishing, 2004.

Cooper, Brant, and Patrick Vlaskovits. *The Entrepreneur's Guide to Customer Development: A "Cheat Sheet" to The Four Steps to the Epiphany.* Cooper-Vlaskovits, 2010.

Croll, Alistair, and Benjamin Yoskovitz. *Lean Analytics: Use Data to Build a Better Startup Faster.* O'Reilly Media, 2013.

Denne, Mark, and Jane Cleland-Huang. *Software by Numbers: Low Risk, High-Return Development.* Prentice Hall, 2004.

Elssamadisy, Amr. "An Interview with the Authors of 'Stand Back and Deliver: Accelerating Business Agility.'" www.informit.com/articles/article.aspx?p=1393062.

Fichtner, Abby. "Lean Startup: How Development Looks Different When You're Changing the World." www.slideshare.net/HackerChick/lean-startup-how-development-looks-different-when-youre-changing-the-world-agile-2011.

Fit "Customer Guide." http://fit.c2.com/wiki.cgi?CustomerGuide.

Fitzpatrick, Rob. *The Mom Test: How to Talk to Customers and Learn If Your Business Is a Good Idea When Everyone Is Lying to You.* CreateSpace Independent Publishing Platform, 2013.

Gamestorming. "Stakeholder Analysis." www.gamestorming.com/games-for-design/stakeholder-analysis/.

Gherkin description in Cucumber Wiki. https://github.com/cucumber/cucumber/wiki/Gherkin.

Gilb, Tom. *Competitive Engineering: A Handbook for Systems Engineering, Requirements Engineering, and Software Engineering Using Planguage.* Butterworth Heinemann, 2005.

Gottesdiener, Ellen. "Decide How to Decide." *Software Development Magazine 9, no. 1 (January 2001).* www.ebgconsulting.com/Pubs/Articles/DecideHowToDecide-Gottesdiener.pdf.

———. *The Software Requirements Memory Jogger: A Pocket Guide to Help Software and Business Teams Develop and Manage Requirements.* Goal/QPC, 2005.

Gottesdiener, Ellen, and Mary Gorman. *Discover to Deliver: Agile Product Planning and Analysis.* EBG Consulting, 2012.

Hubbard, Douglas. *How to Measure Anything: Finding the Value of "Intangibles" in Business.* Wiley, 2014.

"Impact Mapping." http://impactmapping.org/.

International Institute of Business Analysis (IIBA). *A Guide to the Business Analysis Body of Knowledge (BABOK Guide), Version 3.* IIBA, 2015.

Kahneman, Daniel. *Thinking, Fast and Slow.* Farrar, Straus and Giroux, 2013.

Keogh, Liz. "Acceptance Criteria vs. Scenarios." http://lizkeogh.com/2011/06/20/acceptance-criteria-vs-scenarios/.

———. *Behaviour-Driven Development: Using Examples in Conversation to Illustrate Behavior—A Work in Progress.* https://leanpub.com/bdd.

———. Collection of BDD-related links. http://lizkeogh.com/behaviour-driven-development/.

Lacey, Mitch. "Definition of Done." www.mitchlacey.com/intro-to-agile/scrum/definition-of-done.

Laing, Samantha, and Karen Greaves. Growing Agile: A Coach's Guide to Agile Requirements. 2014. https://leanpub.com/agilerequirements.

Linders, Ben. "Using a Definition of Ready." *InfoQ.* www.infoq.com/news/2014/06/using-definition-of-ready.

Little, Todd. "The ABCs of Software Requirements Prioritization." June 22, 2014. http://toddlittleweb.com/wordpress/2014/06/22/the-abcs-of-software-requirements-prioritization/.

Maassen, Olav, Chris Matts, and Chris Geary. *Commitment: Novel about Managing Project Risk.* Hathaway te Brake Publications, 2013.

Mamoli, Sandy. "On Acceptance Criteria for User Stories." http://nomad8.com/acceptance_criteria/.

"The Manifesto for Agile Software Development." http://agilemanifesto.org/.

Matts, Chris, and Andy Pols. "The Five Business Value Commandments." http://agileconsortium.pbworks.com/f/Cutter+Business+Value+Article.pdf.

Maurya, Ash. *Running Lean: Iterate from Plan A to a Plan That Works.* O'Reilly Media, 2012.

McDonald, Kent J. "Comprehensive Documentation Has Its Place." StickMinds.com. https://well.tc/qxv.

———. "Decision Filters." www.beyondrequirements.com/decisionfilters/.

———. "How Visualization Boards Can Benefit Your Team." Stickyminds.com. https://well.tc/5Rb.

MindTools. "Stakeholder Analysis." www.mindtools.com/pages/article/newPPM_07.htm.

Patton, Jeff. "Personas, Profiles, Actors, & Roles: Modeling Users to Target Successful Product Design," http://agileproductdesign.com/presentations/user_modeling/index.html.

———. *User Story Mapping: Discover the Whole Story, Build the Right Product.* O'Reilly Media, 2014.

———. "User Story Mapping." www.agileproductdesign.com/presentations/user_story_mapping/.

Pixton, Pollyanna, Paul Gibson, and Niel Nickolaisen. The Agile Culture: Leading through Trust and Ownership. Addison-Wesley, 2014.

Pixton, Pollyanna, Niel Nickolaisen, Todd Little, and Kent McDonald. *Stand Back and Deliver: Accelerating Business Agility.* Addison-Wesley, 2009.

"Principles behind the Agile Manifesto." http://agilemanifesto.org/principles.html.

Project Management Institute. *A Guide to the Project Management Body of Knowledge, Fourth Edition.* PMI, 2009.

———. *The Standard for Program Management, Second Edition.* PMI, 2011.

Rath & Strong Management Consultants. *Rath & Strong's Six Sigma Pocket Guide.* Rath & Strong, 2000.

Ries, Eric. *The Lean Startup: How Today's Entrepreneurs Use Continuous Innovation to Create Radically Successful Businesses.* Crown Business, 2011.

———. "Vanity Metrics vs. Actionable Metrics." www.fourhourworkweek.com/blog/2009/05/19/vanity-metrics-vs-actionable-metrics/.

Ross, Ron. "RuleSpeak." www.rulespeak.com/en/.

Rothman, Johanna. *Manage Your Project Portfolio: Increase Your Capacity and Finish More Projects.* Pragmatic Bookshelf, 2009.

Royce, Winston W. "Managing the Development of Large Software Systems." *Proceedings, IEEE Wescon.* August 1970, pp. 1–9. www.serena.com/docs/agile/papers/Managing-The-Development-of-Large-Software-Systems.pdf.

Scrum.org. "Definition of Done." www.scrum.org/Resources/Scrum-Glossary/Definition-of-Done.

Van Cauwenberghe, Pascal. "What Is Business Value Then?" http://blog.nayima.be/2010/01/02/what-is-business-value-then/.

Index

A

Acceptance criteria
    "On Acceptance Criteria for User
      Stories," 192
    "Acceptance Criteria *vs.* Scenarios,"
      192
    additional resources, 192
    appropriate use of, 190
    caveats and considerations, 191–192
    definition, 188–189, 221
    example, 189–190
    Growing Agile: A Coach's Guide to
      Agile Requirements, 192
    guidelines for expressing business
      rules. *See* RuleSpeak
    mind map of, 189
    potential criteria, 190
    process description, 190–191
    purpose of, 188, 190
    RuleSpeak, 191, 192
    in system documentation, 216
"On Acceptance Criteria for User
    Stories," 192
"Acceptance Criteria *vs.* Scenarios," 192
Acceptance test driven development. *See*
    Examples (Agile technique)
Actionable metrics
    appropriate use of, 36
    definition, 221
    purpose of, 34
Adaptation, characteristic of initiatives,
    11–12
"Adventures in Scaling Agile," 177
Adzic, Gojko
    examples (Agile technique), 62–63, 196
    focusing on the desired outcome, 4
    impact mapping, 174, 175–176, 177
    Specification by Example, 62
Agile Alliance, 213

The Agile Culture: Leading through
    Trust and Ownership, 150
Agile mindset. *See* Analysis, with an
    Agile mindset
"Agile Models Distilled: Potential
    Artifacts for Agile Modeling," 188
Agile Project Leadership Network
    (APLN), 12
Agreed upon, characteristic of objectives,
    18
Ambler, Scott, 140, 217
Analysis
    cognitive bias. *See* Cognitive bias,
      analysis
    of discovery and delivery, 20–23
    of needs and solutions, 15–19
    of outcomes and outputs, 19–20
    scope of, xv
Analysis, with an Agile mindset
    decision filters, identifying needs, 71
    delivery boards, 73
    diagram of, 70
    information radiators, 73
    needs, identifying, 71
    possible solutions, identifying, 71–72
    release backlog, 72–73
    release planning, 72–73
    story mapping, 72
    user stories, 72–73
    visualization boards, 73
Analyst. *See* Business analyst
Anchoring effect
    cognitive bias, 51
    definition, 221
APLN (Agile Project Leadership
    Network), 12
Appropriate practices
    vs. best practices, 9–10
    definition, 221

Arbitrary decision mechanism
    definition, 222
    description, 41
Ariely, Dan, 11, 48
Automated testing, 93
Availability heuristic
    definition, 222
    description, 51

B

BABOK v3, definition, 222
BACCM (Business Analysis Core
    Concept Model)
    core concepts, 16–17
    definition, 222
Backbone, definition, 222
Backlog items, in system documentation,
    216
Backlogs
    failure to identity complete solutions,
      186
    as wish lists, 186
Bandwagon effect. *See also* Groupthink
    definition, 222
    description, 49
Barely sufficient approach
    definition, 222
    description, 8–9
Baseline, attribute of objectives, 18
BDD (behavior-driven development). *See*
    Examples (Agile technique)
*Behavior-Driven Development: Using
    Examples in Conversation to
    Illustrate Behavior—A Work in
    Progress*, 197
Berndtsson, Johan, 174
Best practices, definition, 9. *See also*
    Appropriate practices
"Best Practices for Agile/Lean
    Documentation," 217
Bezos, Jeff, 241
Blank, Steve, 26, 230
Books and publications
    "On Acceptance Criteria for User
      Stories," 192
    "Acceptance Criteria *vs.* Scenarios,"
      192
    "Adventures in Scaling Agile," 177

*The Agile Culture: Leading through
    Trust and Ownership*, 150
"Agile Models Distilled: Potential
    Artifacts for Agile Modeling," 188
*Behavior-Driven Development: Using
    Examples in Conversation to
    Illustrate Behavior—A Work in
    Progress*, 197
"Best Practices for Agile/Lean
    Documentation," 217
*Bridging the Communication Gap:
    Specification by Example and Agile
    Acceptance Testing*, 196
Commitment, 46
*Commitment: Novel about Managing
    Project Risk*, 204
Competitive Engineering, 18
"Comprehensive Documentation Has
    Its Place," 217
"Customer Guide," 197
"Decision Filters," 163
"Definition of Done," 213
"Definition of Ready," 206
Discover to Deliver, 21
*The Entrepreneur's Guide to
    Customer Development*, 26
The Four Steps to the Epiphany, 26
"Getting the Most out of Impact
    Mapping," 174
*Growing Agile: A Coach's Guide to
    Agile Requirements*, 192
How to Measure Anything, 32
"How Visualization Boards Can
    Benefit Your Team," 204, 210
"Impact Mapping," 177
*Impact Mapping: Making a Big
    Impact with Software Products*,
    177
"Inclusive Modeling: User Centered
    Approaches for Agile Software
    Development," 188
*Inspired: How to Create Products
    Customers Love*, 163, 167
"An Interview with the Authors
    of 'Stand Back and Deliver:
    Accelerating Business Agility,'" 163
Lean Analytics, 32
Manage Your Project Portfolio, 69

"Personas, Profiles, Actors, & Roles: Modeling Users to Target Successful Product Design," 137, 140
Predictably Irrational, 48
Rath & Strong's Six Sigma Pocket Guide, 132
The Software Requirements Memory Jogger: A Pocket Guide to Help Software and Business Teams Develop and Manage Requirements, 169
Specification by Example: How Successful Teams Deliver the Right Software, 196
"Stakeholder Analysis," 129
Stand Back and Deliver: Accelerating Business Agility, 10, 147, 150, 157, 163
Thinking, Fast and Slow, 48
User Stories Applied: For Agile Software Development, 137
User Story Mapping: Discover the Whole Story, Build the Right Product, 182
"Using a Definition of Ready," 206
Box, George E. P., 61
Break the Model approach
    definition, 222
    Feature Injection, 62
Bridging the Communication Gap: Specification by Example and Agile Acceptance Testing, 196
Budgeting
    conference submission system case study, 90–91, 94
    vs. estimating, 94
Build-Measure-Learn loop
    definition, 223
    description, 30–31
    in the lean startup process, 29–31
    leap-of-faith assumptions, 31
Business analysis, definition, 223
Business Analysis Core Concept Model (BACCM)
    core concepts, 16–17
    definition, 222
Business analysts
    cognitive bias, 49–50
    definition, 223

Business case
    definition, 223
    presenting required information, 43
Business domain model, definition, 223
Business goals. *See* Goals
Business objectives. *See* Objectives
Business rule catalog, in system documentation, 213
Business rules, guidelines for expressing. *See* RuleSpeak
Business value
    case studies, 57–58
    definition, 56–57, 223
    Feature Injection, 56–57
    in Feature Injection, 56
Business value model
    definition, 223
    Feature Injection, 57–58

C

Cagan, Marty, 163, 167
Campbell-Pretty, Em, 177
Carlson, Brandon
    adding themes, 84–86
    budgeting Agile 2014, 90–92
    define-build-test, 81–84
    identifying solutions, 78–81
Case studies
    financial services company, 57
    Mercury space program, 47
    minimum viable products, 64–65
    new payroll system, 60
    nurse line service, 44
    organizing conferences, 58
Case studies, commission system
    change management, 99
    commercial off-the-shelf (COTS) systems, 99
    deliveries of value, 97–98
    identifying solutions, 96–97
    interdependencies, 99
    lessons learned, 98–99
    needs assessment, 96
    non-technical solutions, 98
    rounds of work, 97–98
Case studies, conference submission system
    acceptance criteria, 189–190
    adding themes, 84–90

Case studies, conference submission
    system (*continued*)
    automated testing, 93
    budgeting, 90–91
    budgeting *vs.* estimating, 94
    cards for, 169
    conveying requirements, 82
    define-build-test, 81–84
    deliveries of value, 79–92
    differentiating activities, 78
    distributed teams, 93–94
    documentation, 91–92
    examples (Agile technique), 193–194
    feature files (example), 83–84
    identifying solutions, 78
    key user roles and activities, 79
    lessons learned, 92–94
    letting approach dictate tools, 93
    needs assessment, 77–78
    project opportunity assessment, 165
    public commenting, 87–88
    reporting, 88
    story map, 79, 88–89
    story mapping, example, 179
    stubbed identity service, 82
    system documentation, example, 214
    team trust and transparency, effect on
        documentation, 92
    when even Scrum is overkill, 92
Case studies, data warehouse
    decision filters, 104
    deliveries of value, 103–109
    identifying solutions, 102–103
    lessons learned, 110
    needs assessment, 101–102
    performance metrics, 109
Case studies, student information system
    cost-benefit analysis, 119
    examples, 142, 144
    functional requirements, 117–118
    identifying solutions, 114–118
    lessons learned, 118–119
    needs assessment, 111–114
    Purpose-Based Alignment Model, 142,
        144
    RFPs, 114–118, 119
    six questions, 147–148
    solutions looking for problems, 119
Causal metrics, 35–36, 36

Cauwenberghe, Pascal Van, 58–59
Change
    in the BACCM, 16
    definition, 224
Change management, case study, 99
Cleland-Huang, Jane, 66
Clustering illusion
    cognitive bias, 51
    definition, 224
Cockburn, Alistair, 12, 222
Cognitive bias
    affecting analysts, 49–50
    affecting stakeholders, 49. *See
        also* Bandwagon effect; Curse
        of knowledge; Herd instinct;
        Response bias
    definition, 224
    overview, 48–50
    Predictably Irrational, 48
    Thinking, Fast and Slow, 48
Cognitive bias, analysis
    anchoring effect, 51
    availability heuristic, 51
    clustering illusion, 51
    déformation professionnelle, 51
    focusing effect, 51
    frequency illusion, 51
    observation selection bias, 51
    recency bias, 51
    Semmelweis reflex, 51
    sharpshooter fallacy, 51
    survivorship bias, 51
Cognitive bias, decision making
    false consensus effect, 52
    fist of five, 53
    group attribution error, 52
    irrational escalation, 52
    loss aversion, 53
    mitigating, 53
    sunk cost bias, 52–53
    throwing good money after bad, 52
Cognitive bias, elicitation
    affecting analysts, 49–50
    bandwagon effect, 49
    biases affecting stakeholders, 49
    confirmation bias, 50
    the curse of knowledge, 49
    framing effect, 50
    herd instinct, 49

mirror imaging, 50
mitigating, 49, 50
observer-expectancy effect, 50
response bias, 49
Cohn, Mike, 137
Collaboration
    characteristic of initiatives, 5–7
    vs. consensus, 6
    definition, 224
    examples, 6
    teams *vs.* workgroups, 6
Collaborative modeling
    additional resources, 188
    "Agile Models Distilled: Potential
        Artifacts for Agile Modeling," 188
    appropriate use of, 184–186
    caveats and considerations, 188
    context diagrams, 183
    data dictionaries, 183
    definition, 182–183, 224
    example, 183–184
    functional decomposition, 183
    glossaries, 183
    "Inclusive Modeling: User Centered
        Approaches for Agile Software
        Development," 188
    logical data models, 183
    organization charts, 183
    process description, 186–187
    process flow, 183
    purpose of, 186
    report mockups, 183
    state transition diagrams, 183, 184
    techniques, 183
    value stream maps, 183
    wireframes, 183
Commercial off-the-shelf (COTS)
    systems, case study, 99
Commission system. *See* Case studies,
    commission system
Commit to, transform, or kill, definition,
    224
Commitment, 46
*Commitment: Novel about Managing
    Project Risk*, 204
Commitment scale. *See also* Stakeholder
    engagement
    appropriate use of, 130
    caveats and considerations, 132

definition, 129, 224
example, 129–130
process description, 131–132
purpose of, 124, 130
*Rath & Strong's Six Sigma Pocket
    Guide*, 132
Commitments *vs.* options, 46–47. *See
    also* Real Options
Communicating a decision, 45–46
Company building, definition, 26, 224
Company creation, definition, 26, 225
Competitive Engineering, 18
Complexity attributes, Context
    Leadership Model, 151
Complexity risks, mitigating, 156
"Comprehensive Documentation Has Its
    Place," 217
Conference organizing, case study, 58
Conference submission system. *See* Case
    studies, conference submission
    system
Confirmation bias. *See also* Observer-
    expectancy effect
    definition, 225
    description, 50
Consensus, decision mechanism
    vs. collaboration, 6
    definition, 225
    description, 41
Constraint, attribute of objectives, 18
Context
    in the BACCM, 16
    characteristic of initiatives, 9–10
    definition, 225
Context diagrams
    collaborative modeling, 183
    definition, 225
Context Leadership Model. *See also*
    Purpose-Based Alignment Model;
    Six questions
    advantages of a two-by-two matrix, 9
    appropriate use of, 154
    caveats and considerations, 156–157
    complexity attributes, 151
    complexity risks, mitigating, 156
    definition, 150, 225
    example, 151–154
    process description, 154–157
    purpose of, 155

Context Leadership Model (*continued*)
  Stand Back and Deliver: Accelerating Business Agility, 157
  uncertainty attributes, 152
  uncertainty risks, mitigating, 156
Cooper, Alan, 138, 140
Cooper, Brant, 26
Core concept, definition, 225–226
Correlated metrics, 35–36, 36
COTS (commercial off-the-shelf) systems, case study, 99
Croll, Alistair, 32, 34, 37
The curse of knowledge
  cognitive bias, 49
  definition, 226
Customer, definition, 226
Customer development
  definition, 26, 226
  in IT projects, 26
  in the lean startup process, 25–29
Customer discovery
  definition, 26, 226
  in IT projects, 28
  process description, 27
"Customer Guide," 197
Customer validation, definition, 26, 226
Customer-problem-solution hypothesis, definition, 226

D

Dalton, Nigel, 43
Data dictionaries
  collaborative modeling, 183
  definition, 227
Data warehouse. *See* Case studies, data warehouse
Deadlines, determining, 47
Decider
  vs. decision leader, 40
  definition, 227
  determining, 39–41
Decider decides with discussion
  definition, 227
  description, 41
Decider decides without discussion
  definition, 227
  description, 42
Deciding wisely, characteristic of initiatives, 10–11

Decision filters
  additional resources, 163
  appropriate use of, 161
  case study, 104
  caveats and considerations, 163
  "Decision Filters," 163
  definition, 160, 227
  example, 160
  identifying needs, 71
  "An Interview with the Authors of 'Stand Back and Deliver: Accelerating Business Agility,'" 163
  process description, 161–162
  purpose of, 161
  role in delivering value, 4
  Stand Back and Deliver: Accelerating Business Agility, 163
"Decision Filters," 163
Decision leader
  vs. decider, 40
  definition, 227
Decision maker, determining, 39–41
Decision making. *See also* Cognitive bias
  building support, 45
  communicating the decision, 45–46
  determining a deadline, 47
  determining required information, 42
  determining the decision maker, 39–41
  enacting the decision, 46
  options *vs.* commitments, 46–47
  process structure, 39
  Real Options, 46–48
  timely decisions, 43–44
Decision mechanisms
  arbitrary, 41
  consensus, 41
  decider decides with discussion, 41
  decider decides without discussion, 42
  delegation, 41–42
  majority vote, 42
  negotiation, 42
  spontaneous agreement, 42. *See also* Groupthink
Deep Thought Academy. *See* Case studies, student information system
Define-build-test, case study, 81–84
Definition of done
  additional resources, 213
  appropriate use of, 211

definition, 211, 227
"Definition of Done," 213
example, 211
process description, 212
purpose of, 211–212
"Definition of Done," 213
Definition of ready
    additional resources, 206
    appropriate use of, 205
    caveats and considerations, 206
    definition, 204, 227
    "Definition of Ready," 206
    example, 204
    process description, 205
    purpose of, 205
    "Using a Definition of Ready," 206
"Definition of Ready," 206
Déformation professionnelle
    cognitive bias, 51
    definition, 227
Delegation decision mechanism, 41–42
Delivering value
    case studies, 79–92, 97–98, 103–109
    characteristic of initiatives, 4–5
    minimum viable product (MVP),
        63–64
Delivering value, Feature Injection. *See
    also* MMF (minimum marketable
    feature); MVP (minimum viable
    product)
    Break the Model approach, 62
    business value, 56–57
    business value model, 57–58
    examples, as specifications, 61–63
    identifying value, 56–59
    Increase Revenue, Avoid Costs,
        Improve Service (IRACIS), 56–57
    injecting the features, 59–61
    Key Example pattern, 62
    overview, 55–56
    role of value points, 59
    stakeholder expectations, 60–61
    story mapping, 60
Delivery
    analyzing, 20–23
    definition, 21, 228
Delivery boards. *See also* Discovery boards
    additional resources, 210
    analysis with an Agile mindset, 73

appropriate use of, 208
caveats and considerations, 210
*Commitment: Novel about Managing
    Project Risk*, 204
creating, 209
definition, 206–207, 228
example, 207–208
process description, 209
purpose of, 208
using, 209
Deming, W. Edwards, 30
Deming Cycle. *See* PDSA (Plan-Do-Study-
    Act) cycle
Deming Wheel. *See* PDSA (Plan-Do-Study-
    Act) cycle
Denne, Mark, 65–67
Denning, Steve, 57
Design
    definition, 228
    vs. requirements, 22–23
Design thinking
    definition, 228
    in the development process, 22–23
Differentiating activities
    case study, 78
    definition, 228
    identifying, 147
    in the Purpose-Based Alignment
        Model, 143, 146
Discover to Deliver, 21
Discovery
    analyzing, 20–23
    definition, 21, 228
Discovery boards. *See also* Delivery
    boards
    additional resources, 204
    appropriate use of, 201
    caveats and considerations, 203–204
    *Commitment: Novel about Managing
        Project Risk*, 204
    creating, 202
    definition, 200, 228
    example, 200–201
    "How Visualization Boards Can
        Benefit Your Team," 204, 210
    process description, 202–203
    purpose of, 201–202
    using, 202–203
Distributed teams, 93–94

Documentation. *See* System documentation
Domain, definition, 228
Domingues, Ingrid, 174
Done, definition of. *See* Definition of done

E

Elicitation
  cognitive bias. *See* Cognitive bias, elicitation
  definition, 228
Elssamadisy, Amr, 163
Email, conveying requirements with, 82
Enacting a decision, 46
Enterprise, definition, 229
The Entrepreneur's Guide to Customer Development, 26
Examples (Agile technique)
  additional resources, 196–197
  appropriate use of, 194–195
  Behavior-Driven Development: Using Examples in Conversation to Illustrate Behavior—A Work in Progress, 197
  Bridging the Communication Gap: Specification by Example and Agile Acceptance Testing, 196
  caveats and considerations, 196
  "Customer Guide," 197
  in a decision table, 193
  definition, 192–193, 229
  example, 193–194
  formats, 192
  Framework for Integrated Test (Fit) format, 192, 194–195
  Gherkin format, 192, 195, 197
  Key Example pattern, 62
  process description, 195–196
  purpose of, 195
  Specification by Example, 62
  Specification by Example: How Successful Teams Deliver the Right Software, 196
  as specifications, 61–63
  system documentation, 216
  in system documentation, 216
Examples (used in this book)
  acceptance criteria, 189–190
  collaboration, 6

collaborative modeling, 183–184
commitment scale, 129–130
Context Leadership Model, 151–154
decision filters, 160
definition of done, 211
definition of ready, 204
delivery boards, 207–208
discovery boards, 200–201
of the example Agile technique, 193–194
feature files, conference submission system case study, 83–84
impact mapping, 173–174
impact mapping, student information system case study, 173–174
metrics, 33
modeling user roles and descriptions, 135
personas, 138
problem statement, 167–168
project opportunity assessment, 164–165
Purpose-Based Alignment Model quadrants, 142, 144
six questions, 148
stakeholder maps, 125
story mapping, 178, 179
student information system case study, 142, 144
system documentation, 214
user modeling, 133–135
Exploratory metrics, 34–35, 36

F

Facilitate, definition, 229
False consensus effect
  in decision making, 52
  definition, 229
Feature, definition, 66, 229
Feature files (example), 83–84
Feature Injection
  Break the Model approach, 62
  business value, 56–57
  business value model, 57–58
  case study, 60
  definition, 229
  examples, as specifications, 61–63
  identifying value, 56–59
  Increase Revenue, Avoid Costs, Improve Service (IRACIS), 56–57

injecting the features, 59–61
Key Example pattern, 62
overview, 55–56
role of value points, 59
stakeholder expectations, 60–61
story mapping, 60
Fichtner, Abby, 25–26
Financial services company, case study, 57
Fist of five
   in decision making, 53
   definition, 229–230
Fit. *See* Framework for Integrated Test
Fitzpatrick, Rob, 28
Focusing effect
   definition, 230
   description, 51
The Four Steps to the Epiphany, 26
Framework for Integrated Test,
   definition, 230
Framework for Integrated Test (Fit)
   format
   appropriate use of, 194–195
   of examples (Agile technique), 192
Framing effect
   cognitive bias, 50
   definition, 230
Frequency illusion
   cognitive bias, 51
   definition, 230
Functional decomposition
   collaborative modeling, 183
   definition, 230
Functional requirements, case study,
   117–118, 119
Functionalist, definition, 230

G

Gamestorming, 129
Geary, Chris, 46, 204, 210
"Get out of the building" technique
   definition, 230
   description, 28
"Getting the Most out of Impact
   Mapping," 174
Gherkin format
   definition, 231
   examples (Agile technique), 192, 195
   online description of, 197
Gilb, Tom, 18

Glenn, John, 47
Glossaries, in collaborative modeling, 183
Glossaries, in system documentation
   definition, 213, 231
   for intermediate communication, 9
Glossary, of terms in this book, 221–243
Goals
   definition, 17, 231
   role in delivering value, 4
Good practices. *See* Appropriate practices
Gorman, Mary, 21
Gottesdiener, Ellen, 21, 169
Group attribution error
   in decision making, 52
   definition, 231
Groupthink. *See also* Spontaneous
      agreement
   bandwagon effect, 49
   definition, 231
   herd instinct, 49
*Growing Agile: A Coach's Guide to Agile
      Requirements*, 192
Guidelines for expressing business rules.
   See RuleSpeak

H

Herd instinct. *See also* Groupthink
   definition, 231
   in elicitation, 49
High influence/high interest stakeholders,
   128
High influence/low interest stakeholders,
   128
Holst, Darrin
   adding themes, 84–86
   budgeting Agile 2014, 90–92
   define-build-test, 81–84
   identifying solutions, 78–81
How to Measure Anything, 32
"How Visualization Boards Can Benefit
   Your Team," 204, 210
Hubbard, Douglas, 32

I

Impact mapping
   additional resources, 177
   "Adventures in Scaling Agile," 177
   align context, 175–176
   appropriate use of, 173–176

Impact mapping (*continued*)
  caveats and considerations, 177
  definition, 173, 231
  discover context, 175
  example, 173–174
  experiment context, 175
  "Getting the Most out of Impact
    Mapping," 174
  "Impact Mapping," 177
  *Impact Mapping: Making a Big Impact
    with Software Products*, 177
  iterate context, 175
  key questions, 173
  process description, 176–177
  purpose of, 176
  useful contexts, 174–175
"Impact Mapping," 177
*Impact Mapping: Making a Big Impact
  with Software Products*, 177
"Inclusive Modeling: User Centered
    Approaches for Agile Software
    Development," 188
Increase Revenue, Avoid Costs, Improve
    Service (IRACIS), 56–57
Information radiators, definition, 232.
    See also Delivery boards; Discovery
    boards
Initiatives
  definition, 232
  desirable characteristics of, 3
Injecting features. *See* Feature Injection
*Inspired: How to Create Products
  Customers Love*, 163, 167
Interdependencies, case study, 99
"An Interview with the Authors of 'Stand
    Back and Deliver: Accelerating
    Business Agility,'" 163
Inventory turn, definition, 232
INVEST (independent, negotiable,
    valuable, estimable, small,
    testable), 81
IRACIS (Increase Revenue, Avoid Costs,
    Improve Service), 56–57
Irrational escalation
  in decision making, 52
  definition, 232
IT (Information Technology), definition,
    232
IT project, definition, 233

Iteration
  characteristic of initiatives, 7–8
  definition, 232

K
Kahneman, Daniel, 11, 48
Keogh, Liz, 188, 192, 197
Key Example pattern, 62
Kraft, Chris, 47

L
Lacey, Mitch, 213
Lagging metrics, 35, 36
Laing, Samantha, 192
Leadership style, determining. *See*
    Context Leadership Model
Leading indicator, definition, 233
Leading metrics, 35, 36
Lean Analytics, 32
Lean startup
  Build-Measure-Learn loop, 29–31
  customer development, 25–29
  metrics, 31–38
Lean TECHniques, 78
Leap-of-faith assumptions, 31
Lessons learned, case studies
  commission system case study, 98–99
  conference submission system case
    study, 92–94
  data warehouse case study, 110
  student information system case study,
    118–119
Linders, Ben, 206
Little, Todd
  Context Leadership Model, 157
  decision filters, 163
  Purpose-Based Alignment Model, 147
  six questions, 150
  software prioritization, 91
Logical data models
  collaborative modeling, 183
  definition, 233
Loss aversion
  in decision making, 53
  definition, 233
Low influence/high interest stakeholders,
    128
Low influence/low interest stakeholders,
    128

M

Maassen, Olav, 46, 204, 210
Majority vote decision mechanism
 definition, 233
 description, 42
Mamoli, Sandy, 192
Manage Your Project Portfolio, 69
Marketable, definition, 66
Matts, Chris
 Break the Model approach, 62
 business value, 56
 business value model, 58
 Commitment, 46
 discovery boards, 204, 210
 Feature Injection, 55–56
 Real Options, 46, 237
 visualization board, 242
Maximizing work not done, 8–9
McDonald, Kent
 decision filters, 163
 discovery boards, 204, 210
 Purpose-Based Alignment Model, 147
 system documentation, 217
McMillan Insurance. *See* Case studies,
  commission system; Case studies,
  data warehouse
Measurable, characteristic of objectives,
 18
Mercury space program, case study, 47
Metadata, in system documentation, 214
Method, attribute of objectives, 18
Methodology, definition, 233
Metrics
 correlated *vs.* causal, 35–36, 36
 creating, 36–37
 desirable characteristics, 32–33
 example, 33
 exploratory *vs.* reporting, 34–35, 36
 leading *vs.* lagging, 35, 36
 in the lean startup process, 31–38
 One Metric That Matters (OMTM), 37
 qualitative *vs.* quantitative, 33, 36
 for specific situations, 36–37
 vanity *vs.* actionable, 33, 36
MindTools, 129
Minimum, definition, 66
Mirror imaging
 definition, 234
 in elicitation, 50

MMF (minimum marketable feature)
 definition, 233
 description, 65–67
 feature, definition, 66
 marketable, definition, 66
 minimum, definition, 66
 vs. minimum viable product, 66–67
Modeling
 BACCM (Business Analysis Core
  Concept Model), 16–17, 222
Models. *See also* Collaborative modeling;
  Context Leadership Model;
  Purpose-Based Alignment Model;
  User modeling
 BACCM (Business Analysis Core
  Concept Model), 16–17
 business domain model, 223
 business value model, 57–58, 223
 in system documentation, 216
 wrong *vs.* useful, 61
The Mom Test
 definition, 234
 description, 29
MVP (minimum viable product)
 case study, 64–65
 definition, 234
 description, 63
 vs. minimum marketable features,
  66–67
 purpose of, 64

N

Name, attribute of objectives, 18
Needs
 in the BACCM, 16
 definition, 234
 origins of, 19
 separating from solutions, 19
Needs assessment
 with an Agile mindset, 71
 case studies, 77–78, 96, 101–102,
  111–114
 case study, 77–78
 overview, 15–19
Needs assessment techniques. *See also*
  specific techniques
 decision filters, 160–163
 problem statement, 167–169
 project opportunity assessment, 163–167

Negotiation decision mechanism
    definition, 234
    description, 42
Nickolaisen, Niel
    Context Leadership Model, 157
    decision filters, 160, 163
    Purpose-Based Alignment Model, 142,
        147
    six questions, 150, 239
Non-technical solutions, case study, 98
Nurse line service, case study, 44

O

Objectives
    attributes for, 18
    characteristics of, 18
    definition, 17, 234
    role in delivering value, 4
Observation selection bias
    in analysis, 51
    definition, 234
Observer-expectancy effect. *See also*
        Confirmation bias
    definition, 234
    in elicitation, 50
OMTM (One Metric That Matters)
    definition, 235
    description, 37
Options *vs.* commitments, 46–47. *See
        also* Real Options
Organization (legal entity), definition, 235
Organization charts
    collaborative modeling, 183
    definition, 235
    determining a decision maker, 40–41
Outcomes
    analyzing, 19–20
    definition, 235
Outputs
    analyzing, 19–20
    definition, 235

P

Parity activities
    case study, 96
    definition, 235
    vs. purpose, 146
    Purpose-Based Alignment Model, 143,
        146

Partner activities, 143
Patton, Jeff
    personas, 139, 140
    story mapping, 178, 180–181, 182
    user modeling, 137
Payroll system, case study, 60
PDSA (Plan-Do-Study-Act) cycle
    definition, 236
    description, 30
Performance metrics, case study, 109
Permissions, in system documentation, 214
Personas
    additional resources, 140
    appropriate use of, 139
    caveats and considerations, 140
    definition, 138, 235
    example, 138
    *The Inmates Are Running the Asylum:
        Why High-Tech Products Drive
        Us Crazy and How to Restore the
        Sanity*, 140
    "Personas: An Agile Introduction,"
        140
    process description, 139–140
    purpose of, 124, 139
    useful characteristics, 139
"Personas, Profiles, Actors, & Roles:
        Modeling Users to Target
        Successful Product Design," 137,
        140
Pivot, definition, 236
Pixton, Pollyanna
    Context Leadership Model, 157
    decision filters, 163
    Purpose-Based Alignment Model, 147
    six questions, 150
Plan-Do-Study-Act (PDSA) cycle
    definition, 236
    description, 30
Pols, Andy, 58
Post-mortems. *See* Lessons learned
Predictably Irrational, 48
Problem statement
    appropriate use of, 168
    caveats and considerations, 169
    components of, 167
    definition, 167, 236
    example, 167–168
    process description, 168

purpose of, 168
The Software Requirements Memory Jogger: A Pocket Guide to Help Software and Business Teams Develop and Manage Requirements, 169
Problem-solution fit, definition, 236
Process flow
    collaborative modeling, 183
    definition, 236
    in system documentation, 214
Product, definition, 236
Program, definition, 237
Project documentation
    definition, 237
    description, 216–217
Project opportunity assessment
    appropriate use of, 165
    caveats and considerations, 166–167
    definition, 163, 237
    example, 164–165
    Inspired: How to Create Products Customers Love, 163, 167
    process description, 166
    purpose of, 166
    questions for, 164
Projects
    definition, 237
    stigma associated with, xvii
Public commenting, case study, 87–88
Pull systems, 56
Purpose *vs.* parity, 146
Purpose-Based Alignment Model. *See also* Context Leadership Model; Six questions
    advantages of a two-by-two matrix, 9
    appropriate use of, 145
    case studies, 96, 113, 119–120
    case study, 142, 144
    caveats and considerations, 146–147
    definition, 237
    description, 142–144
    process description, 145–146
    purpose *vs.* parity, 146
    Stand Back and Deliver: Accelerating Business Agility, 147
Purpose-Based Alignment Model, quadrants
    differentiating activities, 143, 146, 147
    examples, 142, 144

parity activities, 143, 146
partner activities, 143
"Who cares" activities, 144

Q

Qualitative metrics, 33, 36
Quantitative metrics, 33, 36

R

Rath & Strong Management Consultants, 132
Rath & Strong's Six Sigma Pocket Guide, 132
Ready, definition of. *See* Definition of ready
Real Options
    definition, 237
    description, 46–48
Realistic, characteristic of objectives, 18
Recency bias
    in analysis, 51
    definition, 237
Reflection, characteristic of initiatives, 11–12
Rehearsal. *See* Iteration
Release, definition, 237
Release backlog
    during analysis, 72–73
    definition, 238
Release planning
    during analysis, 72–73
    definition, 238
Report mockups
    collaborative modeling, 183
    definition, 238
Reporting, case study, 88
Reporting metrics, 34–35, 36
Requirements
    case study, 117–118, 119
    conveying, 82
    definition, 238
    vs. design, 22–23
    expressing, 89–90
    Growing Agile: A Coach's Guide to Agile Requirements, 192
    The Software Requirements Memory Jogger: A Pocket Guide to Help Software and Business Teams Develop and Manage Requirements, 169

Resources. *See* Books and publications
Response bias
    definition, 238
    effects on stakeholders, 49
Retrospectives
    characteristic of initiatives, 11–12
    definition, 238
    description, 11–12
    examples of. *See* Lessons learned, case
        studies
RFP (requests for proposal), case study,
    114–118, 119
Ries, Eric
    The Lean Startup, 25, 29
    leap-of-faith assumptions, 31
    on metrics, 36
    minimum viable product, 63–64
Risk, definition, 238
Risk management, 204
Ross, Ron
    acceptance criteria, 191, 192
    RuleSpeak, 191, 192, 238
Rothman, Johanna
    commit to, transform, or kill, 224
    Manage Your Project Portfolio, 69
    on portfolio projects, 69
Royce, Winston, 20–21
RuleSpeak
    acceptance criteria, 191, 192
    definition, 238

S
Scope
    definition, 238
    role in delivering value, 4
Scrum.org, 213
Semmelweis, Ignaz, 239
Semmelweis reflex
    in analysis, 51
    definition, 239
Service, definition, 239
Shared vision techniques. *See also specific*
        techniques
    decision filters, 160–163
    problem statement, 167–169
    project opportunity assessment, 163–167
Sharpshooter fallacy
    definition, 241
    description, 51

Shewhart, Walter, 30, 236
Simplification
    barely sufficient approach, 8–9
    characteristic of initiatives, 8–9
    maximizing work not done, 8–9
    perfect as the enemy of the good, 8–9
Six questions. *See also* Context
        Leadership Model; Purpose-Based
        Alignment Model
    The Agile Culture: Leading through
        Trust and Ownership, 150
    appropriate use of, 148
    case study, 148
    caveats and considerations, 149–150
    definition, 147–148, 239
    desired answers, 149
    example, 148
    process description, 149
    purpose of, 148–149
SMART (specific, measurable, agreed
        upon, realistic, time framed),
        17–18
SME (subject matter expert)
    definition, 241
    in the development process, 12
The Software Requirements Memory
        Jogger: A Pocket Guide to
        Help Software and Business
        Teams Develop and Manage
        Requirements, 169
Solution identification, case studies,
    78–81, 96–97, 114–118
Solution identification, refining. *See also*
        specific techniques
    definition of done, 211–213
    definition of ready, 204–206
    delivery boards, 206–210
    discovery boards, 200–204
    system documentation, 213–217
Solution identification techniques. *See*
        also specific techniques
    acceptance criteria, 188–192
    collaborative modeling, 182–188
    examples (Agile technique), 192–197
    impact mapping, 173–177
    story mapping, 177–182
Solutions
    analyzing, 15–19
    in the BACCM, 16

definition, 239
identifying (case study), 78
identifying, with an Agile mindset, 71–72
origins of, 19
separating from need, 19
Solutions looking for problems, 119
Specific, characteristic of objectives, 18
Specification by example. *See* Examples
  (Agile technique)
*Specification by Example: How
  Successful Teams Deliver the Right
  Software*, 196
Sponsors
  definition, 239
  as source of needs, 19
Spontaneous agreement decision
  mechanism
  definition, 239
  selecting a decision mechanism, 42
Stakeholder analysis
  definition, 240
  types of stakeholders, 123–124. *See
  also specific types*
"Stakeholder Analysis," 129
Stakeholder engagement. *See also*
  Commitment scale
  high influence/high interest, 128
  high influence/low interest, 128
  low influence/high interest, 128
  low influence/low interest, 128
Stakeholder expectations, Feature
  Injection, 60–61
Stakeholder maps
  with actions, 127–128
  additional resources, 129
  appropriate use of, 126
  caveats and considerations, 129
  definition, 240
  description, 124–125
  engagement levels, 127–128
  example, 125
  primary outcomes, 125
  process description, 126–128
  purpose of, 126
  "Stakeholder Analysis," 129
  uses for, 124
Stakeholders
  in the BACCM, 16
  building support for decision making, 45

definition, 239
"get out of the building," 28
talking to, 28
types of, 123. *See also specific types*
*Stand Back and Deliver: Accelerating
  Business Agility*, 10, 147, 150,
  157, 163
Startup, 240. *See also* Lean startup
State transition diagrams
  collaborative modeling, 183, 184
  definition, 240
Story mapping
  additional resources, 182
  during analysis, 72
  appropriate use of, 178
  as a backlog visualization tool, 181
  case study, 79, 88–89
  caveats and considerations, 182
  definition, 177, 240
  as an elicitation tool, 180–181
  example, 178, 179
  Feature Injection, 60
  process description, 180–181
  purpose of, 178
  *User Story Mapping: Discover the
    Whole Story, Build the Right
    Product*, 182
Storyboards, definition, 240
Strategy, definition, 240
Strategy analysis, definition, 240–241
Stubbed identity service, 82
Student information system. *See* Case
  studies, student information system
Subject matter expert (SME)
  definition, 241
  in the development process, 12
Sunk cost bias, 52–53
Survivorship bias
  in analysis, 51
  definition, 241
System documentation
  acceptance criteria, 216
  additional resources, 217
  appropriate use of, 214
  backlog items, 216
  "Best Practices for Agile/Lean
    Documentation," 217
  business rule catalog, 213
  caveats and considerations, 215–217

System documentation (*continued*)
"Comprehensive Documentation Has Its Place," 217
contents of, 213–214
contribution to the desired outcome, 5
definition, 213–214, 241
effects of teams, 91–92
example, 214
examples (Agile technique), 216
glossary, 213
metadata, 214
models, 216
permissions, 214
process description, 215
process flows, 214
project documentation, 216–217
purpose of, 214–215
user interfaces, 214

T

Target, attribute of objectives, 18
Teams
definition, 241
distributed, 93–94
organizational context. *See* Context Leadership Model; Purpose-Based Alignment Model; Six questions
trust and transparency, effect on documentation, 92
vs. workgroups, 6
Texas sharpshooter fallacy
definition, 241
description, 51
Themes
case study, 84–90
definition, 241
Thinking, Fast and Slow, 48
Three amigos, definition, 241
Throwing good money after bad, 52
Time framed, characteristic of objectives, 18
Timely decisions, 43–44
Tools, dictated by your approach, 93
Triple constraints
definition, 241
role in delivering value, 4
Tversky, Amos, 48
Two-pizza rule, 241

U

Uncertainty attributes, 152
Uncertainty risks, mitigating, 156
Units, attribute of objectives, 18
User analysis
definition, 242
description, 124
User interfaces, in system documentation, 214
User modeling
additional resources, 137
appropriate use of, 135
brainstorming users, 133–134
caveats and considerations, 137
definition, 133, 242
example, 133–135
organizing and consolidating users, 134
"Personas, Profiles, Actors, & Roles: Modeling Users to Target Successful Product Design," 137
process description, 135–137
purpose of, 124, 135–136
refining user roles, 135
user roles and descriptions, example, 135
User Stories Applied: For Agile Software Development, 137
User roles
case study, 79
definition, 242
user modeling, 133–135
User stories
during analysis, 72–73
definition, 242
User Stories Applied: For Agile Software Development, 137
User Story Mapping: Discover the Whole Story, Build the Right Product, 182. *See also* Story mapping
"Using a Definition of Ready," 206

V

Value
in the BACCM, 16
definition, 242
delivering. *See* Delivering value
identifying, case study, 57

Value points
    definition, 242
    in Feature Injection, 59
    identifying features, 59
Value stream maps
    collaborative modeling, 183
    definition, 242
Van Cauwenberghe, Pascal, 58–59
Vanity metrics
    appropriate use of, 36
    definition, 242
    description, 34–35
Vision, shared. *See* Shared vision techniques
Visualization boards
    during analysis, 73
    definition, 242
Vlaskovits, Patrick, 26

W

Waterfall planning technique, 20–21
"Who cares" activities
    definition, 242
    Purpose-Based Alignment Model, 144
Williams, Walter, 47–48
Wireframes
    collaborative modeling, 183
    definition, 243
Work groups
    definition, 243
    vs. teams, 6

Y

Yoskovitz, Benjamin, 32, 34, 37

.

Made in the USA
Las Vegas, NV
28 January 2021